HOW TO BE A
BILLIONAIRE

HOW TO BE A BILLIONAIRE

---

*Proven Strategies from
the Titans of Wealth*

Martin S. Fridson

John Wiley & Sons, Inc.
New York • Chichester • Weinheim • Brisbane • Singapore • Toronto

Library of Congress Cataloging-in-Publication Data:
Fridson, Martin S.
   How to be a billionaire : proven strategies from the titans of
wealth / Martin S. Fridson.
     p. cm.
   Published simultaneously in Canada.
   Includes bibliographical references.
   ISBN 0-471-33202-X (cloth : alk. paper)
    1. Billionaires—United States.   2. Rich people—United States.
I. Title.
HC102.5.A2F75   2000
332.024—dc21   99-38822

Printed in the United States of America.

10 9 8 7 6 5 4 3 2

To my children, Arielle and Daniel,
who are destined to dream great dreams
and pursue them unwaveringly

ACKNOWLEDGMENTS

I thank Myles Thompson of John Wiley & Sons, Inc., for having faith in my concept of a book about self-made billionaires. His associate, Mina Samuels, helped immeasurably in giving shape to that simple idea. Ann McCarthy and Jack Gaston provided valuable suggestions, as well. Dorothy Nelsen-Gille has earned my deepest gratitude through her tireless research. I am also indebted to Mary Daniello, the staff of Cape Cod Compositors, and two fellow writers who have inspired me over the years, Nick Taylor and Ron Bitto. Finally, let me express my appreciation for the moral support provided by my loving wife, Elaine Sisman, family members around the world, George Hirai, Ann Marie Mullan, and numerous other colleagues at Merrill Lynch & Co.

M. S. F.

CONTENTS

PART ONE

ACCEPTING THE CHALLENGE

1

DO YOU SINCERELY WANT TO BE SUPERRICH?

There is pain in getting, care in keeping,
and grief in losing riches.
— Thomas Draxe

Mapping the Territory

Congratulations!

Simply by opening up this copy of *How to Be a Billionaire,* you have taken an important step forward on the journey to extraordinary wealth. In fact, you are already far ahead of where the self-made billionaires stood when they began their careers. Unlike you, they had no road map. There was no manual that systematically and objectively analyzed the methods of the individuals who preceded them. As you will find when you read about their strategies, many of the greatest accumulators of wealth struggled for years before finding the paths that propelled them to the top of the heap in net worth. No one would seriously suggest that they could have gotten rich by reading alone, but the right sort of book could have saved them a great deal of wasted effort.

Most of the guides to self-enrichment that were available when today's billionaires began their careers were motivational books. This is not to say that they were without value. The self-help classics correctly emphasized that, just as in athletics or the arts, top-level achievement in the business world depended on exceptional internal motivation. A famous example of the genre, Napoleon Hill's *Think and Grow Rich*, offered role models such as Charles Dickens and Helen Keller, who overcame adversity to achieve greatness. Hill taught his readers how to envision themselves in possession of a vast fortune. Write a clear statement of the amount of money you hope to accumulate, he advised, as well as your time limit for acquiring it. Then read the statement aloud twice a day.[1] In general, the self-enrichment literature provided lots of inspiration, but little in the way of specific fortune-building techniques. One of the more practical books, *One Thousand Ways to Make $1,000*, was a childhood favorite of Warren Buffett's. It offered suggestions such as creating a business from selling homemade fudge.[2]

To identify the actual tactics employed by the self-made billionaires, today's titans of wealth would have had to compile bits of information from scores of books and articles. In other words, they would have had to undertake the laborious process that *How to Be a Billionaire* conveniently spares you. If the seekers of wealth had actually gone through the exercise, they would have learned that there was considerably more to the story than hard work and big dreams.

For example, a lot of tough negotiating underlies the great fortunes of the past. This simple fact would not be apparent from the autobiographies of the champion amassers of wealth. Typically, they have portrayed their success as a fair reward for a lifetime of bargaining in good faith. They never needed anything more than a handshake to seal a deal and, if their recollections are to be taken at face value, both sides generally profited. In the real world, many business transactions turn out to be rather one-sided.

Clearly, the less-informed parties who wind up on the short end are not the ones who subsequently write autobiographies recounting their ascent to billionaire status. For that matter, those who do publish their memoirs tend to downplay their interest in wealth altogether. As H. L. Mencken observed, the businessman is the only sort of person who, when he obtains the object of his labors, namely, making a lot of money, tries to make it appear that it was not the object of his labors.[3]

Billionaires' autobiographies have also misled their would-be successors on the relative importance of shrewd financial techniques. To most people, taking full advantage of the tax code or presenting a company to the stock market in the best possible light sounds less heroic than risking one's future on an unproven technology. The founders of the great fortunes understood the popular disdain for pencil pushers. Therefore, they did not emphasize tax and accounting intricacies in the stories they told of their rise to extraordinary wealth. Nevertheless, being financially astute is a must if you hope to become fabulously wealthy, and *How to Be a Billionaire* will teach you how.

This book is not a treasure trove of previously undisclosed facts about the lives of the billionaires. The surprises are the key aspects of the billionaires' careers that diverge from the images promoted in the financial media. For instance, journalists sell Warren Buffett short by portraying him merely as an investment wizard. In reality, he has done far more than make passive investments in underpriced companies and then wait patiently for the stock market to recognize the hidden value. Anyone who hopes to follow Buffett's model must be willing to take an active role, either as a corporate insider or by pushing companies from outside to exploit their assets more aggressively. It is also important to understand Buffett's reliance, throughout his career, on outright purchases of companies (especially insurance companies), as opposed to becoming a minority shareholder.

Plan of Attack

In setting out to write this book, I wanted to create a manual for future billionaires by analyzing the careers of past and present billionaires. I did not attempt to discuss *every* billionaire. *Forbes* lists 268 individuals with net worth of one billion dollars or more in the United States alone, as of 1999.

For readers interested in biographical sketches of the founders of great fortunes, books such as *The Wealthy 100*[4] provide a comprehensive treatment. In contrast, I have focused on a short list of individuals whose methods can be generalized into models for the billionaires of tomorrow. To round out the story in places, I have included pointers from a supporting cast of titans to whom I have not devoted full-blown profiles.

I have found that the best vehicle for communicating a broad concept is a highly specific case. For example, an abstract recommendation to keep abreast of changes in the competitive environment sounds like a mere platitude. The immense power of this simple idea becomes clearer when it is illustrated by the multibillion-dollar insight that led Sam Walton to switch to discount retailing, instead of concentrating his energies on maintaining his position as America's largest independent operator of five-and-ten-cent stores.

To comprehend how Wal-Mart's founder recognized his great opportunity, it is critical to understand the evolution of new retailing formats over the past several decades. Therefore, this profile has more industry-specific information than you will need, unless you intend to seek your fortune in the chain store business. Regardless of the industry you choose, however, it is vital to absorb the broader principle that Walton applied—namely, staying in front of the parade.

Keeping tabs on industry trends is especially important in the high-technology sector, where entire industries rise and fall within astonishingly short periods. I have deliberately omitted from this book the overnight billionaires churned up by the Internet boom. The long-run sustainability of their fortunes is too uncertain at this point. On the other hand, I have traced Bill Gates's path to billions in great depth. By its nature, computer software is an industry that must be examined in considerable detail in order to understand how one competitor achieved a commanding position in several segments. You do not need to master every technical point on the first read-through of the Gates profile, but it is worth returning to for closer scrutiny. After all, high-technology fields probably will generate a disproportionate share of tomorrow's billionaires. It is likely that at least a few of them will come from nontechnical backgrounds, as did Microsoft president Steve Ballmer.

The Road Ahead for Aspiring Billionaires

In the succeeding chapters of *How to Be a Billionaire*, I study the careers of all-time greats, living and dead, in the field of wealth accumulation. My object is not simply to tell their stories, but to isolate and highlight the methods underlying their extraordinary success. Each chapter is organized around a specific strategy or tactic that turns up repeatedly in reading about self-made billionaires. Extended profiles of 14 titans of wealth appear in chapters devoted to specific methods with which they are respectively associated. These individuals, along with other self-made billionaires whom I examine, generally appear in more than one chapter, because they have pragmatically combined several different methods of building fortunes.

Fundamental strategies constitute the bulk of this book. The study begins with the strategy "Take Monumental Risks," an essential ingredient in every self-made billionaire's success formula. Next, the analysis focuses, in sequence, on "Do Business in a New Way," "Dominate Your Market," "Consolidate an Industry," "Buy Low," "Thrive on Deals," "Outmanage the Competition," "Invest in Political Influence," and "Resist the Unions."

Key principles shared by the self-made billionaires are highlighted throughout. These include:

- Pursue the Money in Ideas
- Rules Are Breakable
- Copying Pays Better Than Innovating
- Keep on Growing
- Hold on to Your Equity
- Hard Work Is Essential
- Use Financial Leverage
- Keep the Back Door Open
- Make Mistakes, Then Learn from Them
- Frugality Pays
- Enjoy the Pursuit
- Develop a Thick Skin

A summary chapter, "Your Turn" (Chapter 12), pulls together the methods illustrated by specific examples throughout the book. It provides a clearer road map than the self-made billionaires had when they began their journeys to unfathomable wealth. Your task is to follow the map to the charmed circle of 10-figure net worth.

Overcome the Levelers

The power of the self-made billionaires' simple-sounding key principles will become clear as you read about specific ways in which they have been applied. You can assimilate the ideas most quickly by keeping in mind the one objective that ties them all together: *Overcome the levelers.* You must vanquish the mighty economic and social forces that conspire against your rise to massive wealth.

Originally, levelers were people, rather than the inanimate social and economic forces to which the term refers in this book. The Levelers formed a political faction during the English Civil War (1642–1648). They proposed to abolish the nobility's privileges and establish complete religious and political equality.

As their once-radical ideas won general acceptance, the Levelers of old faded from the scene. Today, the levelers against which you must struggle are the Menace of Competition and the Obstacle of Social Conventions. If you succumb to them, you will never rise above a comparatively modest level of wealth.

The Menace of Competition

The most insidious leveler of all is also the supreme virtue of the free enterprise system, namely, competition. As most politicians of both the left and right nowadays concede, competitive markets promote the general welfare. Wherever competition thrives, producers of goods and services vie to increase their profits by reducing their production costs. Reduced costs translate into lower prices to consumers and, ultimately, a higher standard of living as their incomes buy more goods and services.

Consumers' steadily rising standard of living, however, contrasts sharply with another by-product of vigorous competition: stagnation in producers' profit margins. In absolute terms, certainly, profits rise as the economy grows. But competition keeps a lid on *rates* of profit, measured as a percentage of sales or as return on capital.

When a company finds a new way to lower its costs, the resulting increase in its profit margin usually proves short-lived. Competitors quickly copy the cost-saving technique or devise equally effective economizing measures of their own. With all producers now earning high profits, it is inevitable that one competitor will cut its price to capture a bigger piece of the market. The others will be forced to match the price cut, lest they lose customers. Before long, profit margins will be back to where they were before the cost-saving innovation appeared. Consumers will continue to benefit from reduced prices, but the producers will be right where they started.

Students of economics will recognize this brief narrative as a description of *perfect competition*. As its name suggests, perfect competition is an idealized state that does not precisely match what is observed in the real world. Nevertheless, perfect competition is depressingly close to reality in most industries. Companies strive mightily, year after year, but never succeed in boosting their profit margins over any sustained period. Competition keeps driving profits toward the minimum rate required to induce investors to risk their capital in equity investments, rather than accept the lower but safer returns of high-quality bonds.

Over a long period of time, entrepreneurs trapped in this system may prosper through general growth in the economy, but they will not become fabulously wealthy. To pull out of the pack, they must earn much higher profits than the economy as a whole is generating. In short, if you hope to become a billionaire, you must overcome the scourge of competition, one way or another.

The most obvious antidote to competition is collusion. Suppose all producers make a solemn pact not to reduce prices as their costs go down. More important, assume they actually honor their solemn pact. By cooperating, they can retain the resulting increased margin between production cost and selling price, instead of passing it along to consumers.

Unfortunately, consumers have long since figured out this stratagem, known in legal parlance as conspiracy in restraint of trade. Unless you are willing to break the law and lucky enough to get away with it, collusion is not a real option. Besides, the preferred method of overcoming the leveling effect of competition has migrated over the years from collusion to monopolization and from monopolization to market dominance.

During the nineteenth century, oil refiner John D. Rockefeller Sr. experimented with collusion as a means of controlling output. He saw a collective benefit for refiners if they could coordinate their production to avoid the recurring episodes of oversupply that vigorous competition inevitably seemed to produce. Periodic gluts decimated everyone's profits, so Rockefeller reasoned that producers would act sensibly and embrace his scheme. In fact, though, they repeatedly broke ranks and exceeded their quotas.

Disgusted with the refiners' obstinate refusal to act in their own self-interest, Rockefeller devised a more efficient way to accomplish the objective he had failed to achieve through collusion. His new solution was to create a monopoly. By acquiring most of the oil refining capacity in the United States, the Standard Oil trust was able to manage supply to its benefit. Unlike monopolists in other industries of his era, Rockefeller did not exploit his position to extract artificially high prices from consumers. Instead, he managed prices with an eye toward reducing the gluts and shortages that formerly made the business so risky. He also kept prices low in order to discourage new competitors from entering the refining industry. In the neat, orderly world that resulted, Rockefeller earned excellent profits through the efficiencies of operating on a vast scale. He further leveraged his market power, and fattened his profit margins, by extracting preferential shipping rates from the railroads. This particular cost saving had to be obtained covertly, through secret rebates to Standard Oil.

For a time, it appeared that Rockefeller and his counterparts in industries such as steel and tobacco had licked the problem of competition. It turned out, however, that the levelers had not abandoned the battlefield. Ambitious politicians capitalized on popular resentment against the economic power that the trusts had amassed. Early in the twentieth century, the U.S. government largely undid the monopolists' work by stepping up enforcement of the antitrust laws. Most sectors of the economy were subjected once again to the rigors of genuine competition.

During the early years of the New Deal (1933–1935), major industries enjoyed a brief respite. In an effort to pull the country out of the Great Depression, President Franklin Roosevelt encouraged the formation of cartels to boost prices and raise corporate profits. The United States Supreme Court, however, eventually ruled the scheme illegal.

Today, there are essentially two strategies available to companies for overcoming the leveling effect of competition. One alternative is to fix prices and hope not to get apprehended by the Antitrust Division of the Justice Department. The other choice is to obtain unusual pricing power while still playing by the rules. This gambit in turn has several variants:

Lawful Sources of Pricing Power

1. Brand identity.
2. Patent protection.
3. Dominant market share.
4. Sustainable cost advantage.

The Obstacle of Social Conventions

Sam Walton's reputation for hard bargaining with vendors highlights a second leveler that aspiring billionaires must defeat. Society runs not only according to laws, but also according to certain conventions of behavior. Individuals who unfailingly abide by these informal rules are unlikely to amass billion-dollar fortunes. In Walton's case, the key to obtaining lower costs was a willingness to violate the retailing industry norm of cordial relations with vendors. Wal-Mart deviated even further from convention when it tried to go around manufacturers' representatives to deal directly with manufacturers.

Carl Icahn has reached the billionaires' ranks through hostile takeovers, a highly controversial activity. On the one hand, corporate raiders are popular among the shareholders who ride their coattails. Also in the raiders' cheering section are a number of laissez-faire economists who argue that by dislodging inefficient managers, the takeover artists benefit the general economy. At the same time, takeover artists arouse the ire of corporate managers who face ouster as control of their companies changes hands. One of Icahn's target companies filed litigation alleging that he was engaged in a "sophisticated scheme of corporate piracy."[5] Another denounced him as "one of the greediest men on earth."[6] Many editorial writers and screenwriters likewise portray corporate raiders in a highly unfavorable light.

Imperviousness to such criticism has been a key to Icahn's success. Although by some accounts he wants to be well-liked, making pals is hardly the central focus of his business activity. "If you want a friend on Wall Street," he advises, "get a dog."[7] Icahn revels in his role as a brutally tough negotiator, saying:

> At times I guess I would plead guilty to being a bully if you call a bully a guy who says, "Look, I have your stock and I'm going to do this, and I'm coming in, so why don't you sell me the company?"[8]

In a classic confrontation over Icahn's hostile bid for Phillips Petroleum, Morgan Stanley investment banker Joe Fogg declared the proposal preposterous. "What the hell do you know about the oil business?" he demanded to know. "You don't understand, Joe," Icahn calmly replied. "I'm not here for an interview."[9]

As an aspiring billionaire, you must reconcile yourself to the fact that winning a popularity contest and climbing to the upper echelons of the Forbes 400 are radically different undertakings. If Warren Buffett had set out to make some new friends, he would not have acquired the weekday-only *Buffalo Evening News* and launched a Sunday edition. That action broke up a comfortable modus vivendi with the *News*'s rival paper, the *Buffalo Courier-Express*. For many years, the *Courier-Express* had survived on the strength of its Sunday monopoly, while the *News* dominated the circulation battle during the balance of the week. The gentlemen's agreement shielded both papers from ruinous competition and prevented Buffalo from devolving into a one-newspaper town. On the other hand, the informal arrangement afforded Buffett the opportunity to enhance the value of his investment by converting the *News* into a seven-day-a-week paper. When the *Courier-Express* ceased publishing, leaving the *News* in a monopoly position, Buffett could have endeared himself to the paper's reporters and editors by including them in the *News*'s profit-sharing plan. Instead, he rebuffed their bid by saying that nothing anyone did in the newsroom could affect profits.[10] Notwithstanding his reputation for geniality, Buffett has stood resolute in the face of personal criticism when money was at stake.

Another surefire way to influence people without winning friends is to achieve a dominant market share. From 1902 to 1905, John D. Rockefeller Sr. had to endure a lengthy series of articles in *McClure's* magazine exposing and condemning every significant action undertaken by the Standard Oil Company since its founding. The author, Ida Tarbell, ventured that over the preceding 30 years, Rockefeller had never run a fair race with a competitor. His pious, churchgoing image, she charged, was nothing but a predatory businessman's hypocritical facade.[11] The index of Ron Chernow's 1998 Rockefeller biography, *Titan*, contains seven entries under the heading, "Rockefeller, John D., Sr.: death threats against."[12] Nine decades later, resentment of Microsoft's dominant market position has spawned web sites devoted exclusively to vilifying Bill Gates.

One way or another, if you succeed in amassing a billion-dollar fortune, you will also succeed in making some folks unhappy. If nothing else, you will upset the sort of people who cannot abide another person's success. You will certainly offend individuals who regard outstanding performance in the area of making money as inherently inferior to other accomplishments, such as taking first place in an athletic contest or getting elected to public office.

In a strictly logical sense, that view seems difficult to support. Business, sports, and politics are all intensely competitive fields. Making a billion dollars is not intrinsically less of an achievement than, say, a victory in a major tennis tournament or winning a race for the Senate. Nevertheless, there will always be people who flatter themselves by looking down on "mere" fortune builders.

Provided you have lived up to your own ethical standards, there is little to do but bear the critics' barbs with as much grace as possible. Do not waste energy on the leveling tones of latter-day socialists who consider it a crime to get rich. Ignore, as well, the envious types who call you greedy. As the saying goes, "It doesn't matter what people call you unless they call you pigeon pie and eat you up."[13]

The Paths Not Taken by Billionaires

Having mentally armed yourself against the levelers, you must now take care to avoid certain blind alleys of wealth accumulation. The experiences of past and present self-made billionaires not only reveal the most remunerative activities, but also, if studied properly, the activities that almost certainly will not produce billion-dollar fortunes. From a quick examination of the Forbes 400 list of America's richest people,[14] you can learn how individuals made the list and how they did not.

Forbes lists the primary source of wealth of its elite group, all of whom possess fortunes of $500 million or more. "Inheritance" appears frequently, along with a wide array of companies and industries. "Salary" does not appear at all. This is a not very subtle clue that owning a business is a more likely route to billions than being an employee. Also conspicuous by its absence from the list is "Playing the stock market."

Speculating in securities is a fascinating pastime, much like betting on horses or handicapping the Academy Awards. Passive investing has not landed a single individual on the current list of billionaires, however. If you entertain hopes of making the Forbes 400 list by shrewdly managing your personal portfolio, the record strongly suggests that you should abandon the notion and get onto a more productive track. Even if you match the record of the most successful money managers, beating the market averages by a few percentage points annually, you are not likely to parlay a modest stake into a billion dollars during your lifetime.

By way of illustration, the mean annual rate of return on the Standard & Poor's 500 Index over the period 1926–1998 was 13.2 percent. You will qualify for the portfolio managers' hall of fame if you succeed in beating the market over an extended period by three percentage points a year, net of commissions and taxes. At that rate of return (16.2 percent), if you begin with an investment of $100,000, you will have accumulated only $182 million after 50 years of patient labor. On the other hand, suppose that, like the vast majority of money managers, you do no better than match the market's performance over the long run. In that case, your accumulation after half a century will be a much more modest $49 million.

On the positive side, these figures demonstrate the phenomenal power of patiently compounding your returns over a lengthy period. Keeping in mind the principle that the first billion is the hardest, investing your fortune for the long run can enable you to pass on more money to your heirs or favorite philanthropies. The accumulation over five decades also shows, however, that if you hope to be a billionaire before you retire, speculating on stocks is the wrong vehicle.

At this point, you may be asking, "Can it really be true that nobody has made a billion dollars purely by playing the stock market?" After all, *Forbes* lists "Investments" as the primary source of wealth of seven of the wealthiest Americans in the billion-dollars-and-up category. A look at the profiles that *Forbes* also provides, however, makes it clear that these individuals did not make their fortunes primarily by spotting attractive stocks to put into their personal portfolios. Among the other activities that the "investment" specialists have engaged in over the years are:

- Starting a charter airline and selling it for a $104 million profit.
- Building the world's biggest hotel.
- Assembling a broadcasting empire and selling it for a $3.3 billion gain.
- Booting out management of Columbia/HCA following an investigation of alleged Medicare fraud.
- Expanding a single drugstore into a chain and selling it for $50 million.
- Engaging in hostile takeovers.
- Restoring a foundering bank to health and merging it to form NationsBank.

In short, *Forbes*'s definition of an investment, for purposes of compiling its wealthiest-Americans list, is not buying a stock and waiting for it to go up. Rather, the term means taking a substantial stake in a company and actively influencing its direction. Active influence may even include owning the business outright and running it. Indeed, John Kluge, one member of the billionaires' club whom *Forbes* characterizes as having made his fortune primarily in investments, told the magazine: "I'm an operator, not an investor."[15]

Even the man commonly (and with considerable justice) described as the world's greatest investor, Warren Buffett, ranks among the billionaires largely because of his corporate activism, rather than his passive investing. *Forbes* appropriately lists Buffett's primary source of wealth not as investments, but as the company he heads, Berkshire Hathaway. Contrary to a common misperception, Berkshire Hathaway is *not* for all intents and purposes a closed-end mutual fund managed by Buffett. While the Sage of Omaha takes no direct role in the management of Berkshire Hathaway's operating companies, he sets broad strategies and closely monitors each unit's managers.

Other billionaires who are identified with securities investing likewise made their money by means other than finding cheap stocks and waiting for the world to recognize their value. For example, Carl Icahn has not become fabulously wealthy by passively investing in companies he considers undervalued. His technique is far better described as "attempting to control the destinies of the companies in question."[16] That phrase appeared in a memorandum that Icahn and his associate, Alfred Kingsley, distributed in 1975 in connection with their first investment partnership. The specific tactics they envisioned represented a blueprint for their later coups:

Approaches to Profiting from a Corporate Control Battle (Carl Icahn—1975)

- Attempt to convince management to liquidate the company or sell it to a "white knight" (a friendly acquirer).
- Wage a proxy battle.
- Launch a tender offer.
- Sell back the acquired stock position to the company.

No one can realistically hope to replicate Icahn's phenomenal success by imitating only the first half of his method, namely, correctly identifying the companies that are trading below their potential value.

Similarly, picking good stocks alone has not been the road to fabulous wealth for George Soros or Julian Robertson, two other individuals for whom *Forbes* lists investments as the primary source of wealth. Highly talented investors to be sure, Soros and Robertson have surpassed the billion-dollar mark in net worth by founding hedge funds. These limited partnerships give the managers sizable overrides on the trading profits they produce for their investors. Losses are not shared in the same manner, although the popularity of the Soros and Robertson funds shows that investors are not dissatisfied with the arrangement. Finally, Ned Johnson and Abigail Johnson of Fidelity Investments and Fayez Sarofim derive their wealth largely from ownership of investment firms, rather than successful investments in their personal portfolios.

The Better Mousetrap Fallacy

A careful look at the sources of history's greatest fortunes not only exposes the futility of trying to speculate your way to billions, but also refutes a common misconception regarding the connection between original ideas and great wealth. It is true that new ideas have given birth to many immense fortunes, but the original thinkers have not generally been the ones who made the fortunes. A more dependable strategy is to learn how to make money from ideas, and then be prepared to capitalize on an original notion dreamed up by someone who is more skilled at that sort of thing.

If the foregoing seems lacking in idealism, consider the hard fact that *How to Be a Billionaire* is not a book about Gary Kildall. Neither does it dwell on "Crazy Ted" Judah, Edwin Drake, or Leonidas Merritt—all superb idea men. It is imperative to understand how it came to pass that this book *is* about Bill Gates, Leland Stanford, and John D. Rockefeller Sr., among others.

The dominant operating system for personal computers is DOS (disk operating system). The cornerstone of Microsoft's spectacular success, it is descended from a product developed by Gary Kildall, founder of Digital Research. In the 1970s, Kildall's CP/M (control program for microprocessors) was the premier operating system for microcomputers. In fact, when IBM decided to get into the personal computer business, Microsoft's Bill Gates advised the company to license CP/M. Kildall, however, held out for more than the flat $200,000 fee that IBM was willing to pay. Microsoft then stepped into the breach, snapping up the rights to a somewhat more advanced operating system developed on the foundation of CP/M. Gates licensed DOS to IBM for a paltry $50,000, shrewdly reckoning that he could generate far greater profits from licenses to other computer makers and software developers. Within a short time, Digital Research went into decline, finally getting folded into Novell in 1991. Three years later, Gary Kildall died at the age of 52 from head injuries sustained in a barroom brawl. Bill Gates went on to become the richest man in the world.[17]

The stories of other creative thinkers had less gruesome endings. All had similar plots, however. In each case, somebody amassed a fortune of $1 billion or more, but it was never the person who generated the original idea.

Theodore "Crazy Ted" Judah was an eccentric engineer who devised a plan to build a railroad across the treacherous Sierra Nevada mountain range. He obtained financial backing from four storekeepers with almost no experience in railroads, and in 1863 the Central Pacific began laying track eastward from Sacramento. Six years later, the Central Pacific joined the Union Pacific, which had been building westward from Omaha, to form the first transcontinental rail line. By then, however, Judah had been squeezed out of the venture. Unable to abide his backers' bribing of government officials, he died nearly penniless. Each of the merchants—Charles Crocker, Mark Hopkins, Collis Potter Huntington, and Leland Stanford—became billionaires, in today's dollars.[18]

Edwin Drake, a former railroad conductor, conceived the idea of adapting a drilling method used to create salt wells to extract oil in western Pennsylvania. A few years earlier, George Bissell had come up with the equally brilliant notion that the Pennsylvania rock oil could be refined into a higher-quality illuminant than the coal oil product then in use. Drake's 1859 breakthrough of producing commercial quantities of oil gave birth to the petroleum industry. It was John D. Rockefeller Sr., however, who figured out that the real money (at least in the industry's initial stage), was in refining, rather than production. Monopolistic control of the refining business enabled Rockefeller to amass, by one measure (percentage of gross national product), a fortune never equaled before or since. Among the charitable activities of one of Rockefeller's chief associates at Standard Oil Company, Henry H. Rogers, was assistance to Edwin Drake's impoverished widow.[19]

Finally, Leonidas Merritt and several of his relatives boldly conceived a plan to exploit the Mesabi Range, a vast iron ore vein in northern Minnesota. Borrowing aggressively, the backwoods operators acquired huge tracts of land and commenced construction of a rail line to transport the ore to Lake Superior. Then came the Panic of 1893. Iron prices plummeted and the financially overextended Merritts turned to John D. Rockefeller Sr. for a cash infusion. Rockefeller had no previous experience in the iron business, but he understood very well from his years in the oil business how to make profits on distressed properties. As iron prices continued to fall, the Merritts were eventually obliged to surrender complete ownership of the company to him. Rockefeller's fling with the iron ore business lasted much longer than he had expected, but he had the financial wherewithal to ride out the slump. One chunk of stock that he bought from the Merritts for $900,000 in 1894 was worth $9 million by 1901. For $525,000, Rockefeller settled the Merritts' legal claims that he had dealt unfairly with them.[20] Leonidas Merritt got another chance to tell his story when Congress investigated the affair in 1912, but apparently suffered a mental breakdown and was unable to provide a coherent account.[21]

The moral of these stories, and countless others like them, is very different from the lesson that Napoleon Hill drew from studying the careers of the wealthy. Hill advised the readers of *Think and Grow Rich* to emulate the dreamers, such as Thomas Edison, Wilbur and Orville Wright, and Guglielmo Marconi, who refused to give up on ideas that others considered crazy. In light of the contrasting experiences of Merritt and Rockefeller, however, Hill's stress on the importance of persistence was probably more on the mark than his extolling of originality.

Certainly, not every brilliant inventor winds up destitute. Edison, for example, was competent at translating ideas (including the incandescent lightbulb, the phonograph, and motion pictures) into money. At his death in 1931, his fortune was estimated at around $12 million. That was a substantial sum for the time, but only one-fifth as great as the fortune of Henry Phipps, who died one year earlier. Phipps, a partner in Andrew Carnegie's steel business, is not remembered for inventing anything.

It may be true that if you build a better mousetrap, the world will beat a path to your door.[22] The throng may consist, however, of financiers hoping to capture the profits of your invention for themselves. Looking at the bright side, you need not feel that a lack of original ideas precludes you from ever becoming a billionaire. Sam Walton, founder of Wal-Mart, prided himself on having appropriated nearly all of his good ideas from his competitors. More than any of the other retailing magnates, however, Walton thoroughly understood how to turn ideas into dollars.

The Right Stuff

How to Be a Billionaire focuses on identifying keys to the success of the wealthiest self-made individuals, rather than on uncovering tidbits to titillate, as celebrity biographies do. My objective is to separate the bona fide moneymaking ideas from the media fluff. In short, you should not read this book to learn about Howard Hughes's romantic liaisons and eccentricities, even though I have included a few colorful aspects of the self-made billionaires' lives.

Neither is this book an attempt to psychoanalyze the founders of great fortunes, however interesting a separate project that might be. My objective, after all, is to tell you how you can create your own great fortune. It would help you little to discover that your relationship with your parents or your childhood experiences failed to match some standard billionaire's profile. More to the point are the parts of the equation you can control—namely, the habits and strategies that you can borrow from others who have excelled in amassing wealth.

By the same token, when you undertake something as ambitious as creating a huge fortune, a bit of self-assessment is in order. Armed with the knowledge that self-made billionaires display a tendency toward certain character traits, you can strive to strengthen those traits in your own personality. Suppose, for example, you discover that you are substantially more risk-averse than the billionaires as a group. The defeatist's option is to ascribe differences in tolerance for risk entirely to genetics and upbringing, which implies that you have no hope of changing your attitude. The more productive course is to proceed on the assumption that your personality is at least partially malleable. By the same token, you can identify traits that are strong suits for you and that most self-made billionaires also display. While you work on correcting shortcomings that you perceive in your own makeup, you can meanwhile fashion a strategy that plays to your strengths. Given your particular personality and interests, certain billionaires profiled in subsequent chapters probably will serve you better as role models than others.

A Taste for Gambling

On the specific issue of risk, the billionaires' interest in card games, particularly poker, is striking. During his cotton-planting days, before entering the oil business, H. L. Hunt was compelled to support his family with his poker winnings after losing two consecutive crops to floods. As an undergraduate at Columbia University, John Kluge's obsession with the game attracted unwelcome attention from the administration. By graduation in 1937, Kluge had accumulated $7,000 in winnings, equivalent to $80,000 in 1999 purchasing power.

Bill Gates, too, devoted a great deal of his time at college to playing poker before dropping out of Harvard. Carl Icahn raised his first investment stake by clearing $4,000 playing poker during six months of active duty in the United States Army, a stint that followed his graduation from Princeton. Similarly, poker winnings helped to bankroll Kirk Kerkorian's launch of a charter airline that he ultimately parlayed into a billion-dollar fortune. Warren Buffett's fraternity brothers at the Wharton School of the University of Pennsylvania remember him chiefly for playing bridge. He became proficient enough to play on the Corporate America team, a group of chief executive officers that took on such opponents as a team composed of members of the British Parliament.

It requires no great conceptual powers to perceive the connection between prowess at the card table and success in financial dealings. Both situations involve uncertainties and place a premium on careful calculation of the odds. Outright recklessness will not defeat skilled opponents over many hands or over many deals. Neither, however, will victory come from interminable analysis, unaccompanied by a willingness to take a leap of faith.

From Brains to Billions

The self-made billionaires' demonstrated ability to gauge the odds gives lie to the belief in some quarters that the accumulation of wealth requires cunning but not intelligence. On the face of it, the Ivy League credentials of Buffett, Gates, Icahn, and Kluge, noted just above, suggest that some of the greatest fortune builders are in fact fairly cerebral. Laurence Tisch's stint at Harvard Law School, before dropping out to help in his family's business, offers similar evidence.

Lest anyone imagine that these individuals won admission to top schools on the strength of family connections and then earned gentlemen's Cs, there are plenty of other intellectual achievements to point to among the billionaires. Buffett earned the only A+ ever awarded by Benjamin Graham, the fabled father of securities analysis and his instructor at Columbia Business School. Bill Gates scored a perfect 800 on the mathematics portion of his Scholastic Aptitude Test and reportedly ranked among the top 10 high school math students in a nationwide competition. Philosophy major Carl Icahn took first place in the annual judging of Princeton senior theses. His topic was "The Problem of Formulating an Adequate Explication of the Empirical Criterion of Meaning." You may have to take his word for it, but the famed corporate raider claims, "In a funny way, studying twentieth-century philosophy trains your mind for takeovers."[23]

Certainly, a high level of academic achievement is not a prerequisite for making a billion dollars. Wayne Huizenga dropped out of college, Kirk Kerkorian quit school after eighth grade, and H. L. Hunt received only home schooling. All three entered distinctly proletarian occupations, ranging from garbage hauler to prizefighter to mule skinner. Their career paths by no means denoted lack of native intelligence, however. Hunt, for example, was a gifted child who learned to read at three and reputedly had a photographic memory. His formal education was limited not by his scholastic aptitude, but by the need to help out on his family's cattle farm. At the age of 19, he enrolled in Valparaiso University in Indiana, despite having completed only elementary school, but left after one year.

Horatio Alger, Revised

The career paths of Huizenga, Kerkorian, and Hunt shed light on another aspect of the self-made billionaires' profile. It would no doubt please boosters of the American free enterprise system if the three individuals' stints as common laborers reflected their rise from impoverished child-hoods. In reality, there are not many bona fide rags-to-riches stories among the self-made billionaires. Without denigrating their achievements in any way, it is fair to say that they came primarily from middle-class backgrounds, typically gaining familiarity with the business world from their fathers' experiences. Rather than pulling themselves up by their bootstraps from poverty, they extended the success of previous genera-tions. To some extent, perhaps, they were motivated by memories of busi-ness reverses that their fathers suffered.

Wayne Huizenga's grandfather emigrated to the United States from the Netherlands. He started life in the New World as a laborer but soon established his own waste hauling business. His son, Harry, became a home builder. Vagaries of the real estate market caused fluctuations in the family's circumstances, but the Huizengas were prosperous enough to send Wayne to a private school in Fort Lauderdale, Florida.

Kerkorian's father, an immigrant from Armenia, could barely read or write but he managed to borrow the capital to amalgamate several properties into a thousand-acre farm in California's San Joaquin Valley. He regarded himself as a gentleman farmer, was reckoned a millionaire in some quarters,[24] and owned an expensive Stutz Bearcat car. Hard times followed the 1921 recession. The Kerkorians forfeited their land and went to Los Angeles, where they moved frequently to stay a step ahead of the rent collector. Within two years, however, Ahron Kerkorian had restored his family's finances by becoming a produce dealer.

Hunt's father, a Confederate war veteran, started out with an 80-acre farm in Illinois, but expanded his business by acting as a middleman for other farmers. By branching out into agriculture futures in Chicago, he accumulated 500 acres and opened a bank. No economic necessity forced Hunt to leave home at 16 and work variously as a cowboy, as a lumberjack, and on a railroad gang. Rather, he preferred not to clerk in his father's bank. A few years later, a $5,000 inheritance from his father was sufficient, in a period of low land prices, for Hunt to establish himself as a cotton farmer.

The families of Warren Buffett, Ross Perot, Laurence Tisch, and Sam Walton all endured hardships during the Depression, but they were not among the one-third of the United States populace that Franklin Roosevelt described as ill-housed, ill-clad, and ill-nourished. Shortly after Warren Buffett was born, his father, Howard, lost his job as a securities salesman when the bank that employed him went under, taking his savings with it. Times got so tight that Buffett's mother gave up attending her church circle because she could not afford 29 cents to buy a pound of coffee. By the time Buffett entered school, however, his father had achieved reasonable success with the brokerage firm that he founded. Howard Buffett later served in the United States Congress, making his son anything but a marginal member of society who would have to compensate by getting rich. In a similar vein, Ross Perot's father did well enough in the cotton brokering and cattle trading businesses to enable the family to acquire a reputation for generosity to others hit hard by the economic troubles of the 1930s. A chain of clothing stores owned by Laurence Tisch's father ran into trouble but avoided bankruptcy. Al Tisch also owned a manufacturer of boys' clothing, which remained profitable despite the hard times. "There was never a period that I remember a hardship in the family," Laurence later recalled.[25] Sam Walton's father went bust in the insurance and mortgage business at the beginning of the Depression, but soon got a job handling repossessions for his half-brother's mortgage company. Walton reported that his father once swapped his wristwatch for a hog in order to put some meat on the table,[26] but the family avoided severe deprivations. The senior Walton eventually became a millionaire through his land holdings.

John Kluge, whose father died before the Depression, worked for a time on the assembly line at Ford Motor Company, then attended Columbia University on scholarship. Carl Icahn, born near the end of the Depression, enjoyed a middle-class upbringing in Queens, New York. His socialist-leaning father worked as a cantor and did not aspire to great wealth. Carl nevertheless acquired a yearning for the good life from an uncle who was a successful businessman. Bill Gates, who was born long after the Depression, grew up under fairly affluent circumstances as the son of a prominent Seattle lawyer. Richard Branson, too, is the son of a lawyer, as well as the grandson of a judge on the United Kingdom's High Court. He grew up in an affluent London suburb, although his mother, a former ballet instructor, glider pilot, and flight attendant, had to maintain a tight household budget to sustain the family's lifestyle. Phil Anschutz's father was an oil wildcatter, who borrowed aggressively and experienced wide swings in fortune as a result. J. Paul Getty's father, too, was an oil-man, successful enough to allow his son to grow up as something of a playboy.

In summary, the common thread of self-made billionaires' lives is not a desire to rise from poverty. For some of the great wealth gatherers, periods of family financial reversal may have created an intense desire for financial security. This is a thirst that no sum of money can completely extinguish.

Fathers and Sons

The more frequent, although not universal, theme in the self-made billionaires' early lives is a business-oriented father as a role model. Biographers particularly characterize Buffett and Perot as idolizing their fathers. Kerkorian has described his father as the toughest man he ever knew. He was "a big, rough man who didn't take anything from anybody," according to a childhood acquaintance of Kirk's.[27] A longtime employee of Sam Walton's father described him in similar, albeit cruder, terms.[28]

John D. Rockefeller Sr. was a conspicuous exception to the rule of a business-oriented father as role model. William Avery Rockefeller was a charlatan who peddled patent medicine and passed himself off as a doctor. He adopted various aliases, contracted a bigamous marriage, and generally became an embarrassment to his successful son. Even in this unusual case, however, the father managed to set a bit of a positive example, running a successful lumber business for a time and impressing John as a negotiator and manager of people.

The influence of the more conventional fathers probably played some part in the self-made billionaires' early enthusiasm for business enterprises. As youths, for example, Warren Buffett, Ross Perot, and Sam Walton all injected extraordinary energy into the commonplace parttime job of delivering newspapers. Buffett, for instance, put together a mammoth route of 500 customers. He also obtained a route covering the same territory for the *Washington Post*'s morning rival, the *Times-Herald*. If a customer canceled one paper in favor of the other, Buffett lost no business.

Where Are the Women?

Perhaps the importance of father-son relationships also explains, in part, the paucity of women among the self-made billionaires. In the 1998 Forbes 400 list, the women in the billion-dollars-and-up category are all associated with family fortunes. Male relatives founded all of the relevant businesses, except for the Hallmark Cards operation that vaulted the Hall family to the billion-dollar ranks.

To be sure, several of the billionaire women identified by *Forbes* have been actively involved in the businesses that produced their fortunes. They include Leona Helmsley (hotels), Abigail Johnson (Fidelity Investments), Martha Ingram (assorted distribution businesses), and Sydell Miller (hair products). Alice Walton played a role in several banks controlled by her family, although she had little involvement in the Wal-Mart retailing chain.

Early in 1999, moreover, Muriel Siebert's net worth edged above $1 billion when shares of Siebert Financial Corporation skyrocketed from $11 to $49.50. Investors bid up the price of Siebert Financial, the holding company for Siebert's brokerage house, during a boom in demand for shares of online trading companies. The sustainability of Siebert's billion-dollar fortune remains an open question. She owned 92 percent of the shares, meaning that the paper value of her holdings was determined by a small float of stock in a red-hot market for Internet-related equities.[29] A comparatively modest volume of selling could sharply reduce the aggregate value of all Siebert Financial shares.

While the longevity of her billionaire status remains to be seen, nobody can deny that Siebert has achieved remarkable things with the same sort of tenacity observed in other self-made billionaires. In 1967, she became the first woman to own a seat on the New York Stock Exchange, a feat that required considerable perseverance. She was turned down by nine of the first 10 men she asked to be her sponsor. Then, the exchange imposed a new requirement, demanding that she obtain a letter from a bank confirming that it would lend her $300,000 to buy a seat at the then near-record price of $445,000. The banks, on the other hand, declined to provide such a letter until the exchange agreed to admit her. Siebert eventually overcame this chicken-and-egg predicament, then went on to become the first woman to head a New York Stock Exchange member firm. She later served as superintendent of the New York State Banking Department before resuming operating control of Siebert Financial.[30]

With Muriel Siebert demonstrating that there is no inherent barrier to women surpassing the billion-dollar mark, it seems likely that others will replicate her success in the future. As career options for women have widened in general, successful businessmen and businesswomen have become role models for daughters who aspire to become billionaires. Perhaps even now the Girl Scouts are playing the critically important role for future billionaires that the Boy Scouts played in the lifelong success of Ross Perot, Sam Walton, and, to a lesser extent, Bill Gates. Perot made Eagle Scout in 16 months, a feat that typically takes three to five years and which fewer than 1 percent of Scouts achieve. Walton was the youngest Missourian up to his time to reach the Eagle ranking.

Enjoy the Pursuit

Whatever the mix of tomorrow's billionaires—by gender, by previous experience in newspaper deliveries and scouting, and so forth—one characteristic probably will remain a constant: joy in the pursuit of wealth.

Winning itself, rather than the prize, is the source of gratification that drives the great amassers of wealth to the extraordinarily select circle defined by a 10-figure net worth.

While it would be overstating the case to describe the self-made billionaires as indifferent to the things money can buy, many of them are notable for the simplicity of their lifestyles. Sam Walton and Warren Buffett declined to relocate to lavish estates as their wealth soared. Ross Perot and Phil Anschutz seem content to drive modestly priced cars and do not require the latest models. Others have shown less indifference to luxuries, yet have continued building their wealth beyond the level required to satisfy their material desires. Not content to rest on the laurels of the legendary success of Electronic Data Systems, Ross Perot started another company from scratch and reaped more than $2 billion when Perot Systems went public. Wayne Huizenga performed a comparable feat by heaping Blockbuster Entertainment's success on top of Waste Management's, then undertook to revolutionize the business of selling automobiles. Phil Anschutz, similarly, topped his previous achievements in the oil and railroad businesses when he entered an entirely new field to found Qwest Communications. By and large, the individuals who succeed in clearing a cool billion yearn to outdo themselves, rather than merely preserve what they have made.

Kirk Kerkorian once explained that when he started out in business, he aimed at accumulating $100,000. Later on, he figured he would have it made when he reached a million dollars. After he had passed the $100 million mark, he was asked what continued to motivate him. "Now it isn't the money," he explained, fresh from a successful tender offer for Metro-Goldwyn-Mayer stock.[31] Thirty years later, having exceeded the billion-dollar hurdle, the octogenarian Kerkorian was still doing deals. For him, the mere possession of wealth never replaced the thrill of the pursuit.

Be Prepared to Pay the Price

If you are ready to begin putting a plan for making a billion dollars into action, you are once again ahead of most self-made billionaires at similar stages of their quest for wealth. Few if any set out with the explicit objective of amassing a billion dollars of net worth, even though they all had some notion of becoming wealthy. In the early days of Microsoft, for example, Bill Gates vehemently disputed the possibility of a computer software company ever growing to the scale necessary to put its owners into that category.

Rest assured, the principles explained in the following pages will help you even if you have set your sights somewhat lower than the 10-figure level. Make no mistake about it, though: You will not reach even the hundred-million-dollar level without a clear focus and single-minded commitment. One of the greatest benefits of reading this book may be a fuller understanding of the wear and tear you and your family will sustain if you aim for the very top tier of the individual net worth rankings.

Wayne Huizenga devoted 20-hour days to his original waste-hauling business. In the course of consolidating scores of similar operations into Waste Management, he regularly went out of town from Sunday evening to Friday evening to negotiate acquisitions. Years later, he remarked with regret:

> I never saw my kids play Little League ball. The only play I ever saw was when our daughter Pam one time was in a play. I missed all that stuff with all the kids. That's not good and I wouldn't advise anyone to put that much into it.[32]

In fact, though, most of the billionaires did put that much into it, with other family members frequently bearing the brunt. John D. Rockefeller Sr., for example, worked on the morning and afternoon of his wedding day, rather than deviate from his routine. H. L. Hunt was so immersed in his work that until he entered the hospital two months before his death at 85, he continued to go to his office six days a week. In the final days, he went in by wheelchair.

To be sure, Phil Anschutz, Laurence Tisch, Ross Perot, and Sam Walton have proven that building a stupendous fortune is not incompatible with a long, stable marriage. Moreover, the high rate of divorce in society at large demonstrates that refraining from making a billion dollars is no guarantee of marital bliss. It is fair to say, however, that most families would be severely stressed by the single-minded devotion to business exhibited by most of the titans of wealth.

If you believe that you can manage the family strain, as well as the personal attacks that becoming a billionaire may entail, by all means proceed to Chapter 2. It addresses the question, "How Important Is Choosing an Industry?" Resolving the issues raised in the chapter is an important first step in charting your path toward the charmed circle of billionaires.

2

HOW IMPORTANT IS
CHOOSING AN INDUSTRY?

The strongest principle of growth lies in human choice.
—George Eliot

Choosing the single right industry to enter is not a prerequisite for be-coming fabulously rich. Among Americans with self-created fortunes of a billion dollars or more in 1998,[1] primary sources of wealth ranged from catheters, country clubs, hair products, and nondairy coffee creamers to potatoes, self-storage facilities, sunglasses, trading stamps, uniform rentals, and wedding invitations. Financiers Warren Buffett, Ronald Perelman, and Kirk Kerkorian reached the billionaire ranks without concentrating their investments in any particular industry. Joseph Jamail Jr. made the list through fees earned as a personal injury lawyer. ("There's no limit to how big a whore I can be," he explained.[2]) Real estate upheld its reputation as a prodigious wealth builder, with representation on the 1998 list by such luminaries as Donald Trump, Sam Zell, Mort Zuckerman, and Donald Bren, owner of Irvine Ranch in California.

Today's billionaires have sprung from many callings, yet an analysis of their industry backgrounds yields one clear theme. Among the five largest American fortunes listed in the Forbes 400, as of 1998, computer software accounts for three (#1 Bill Gates, #3 Paul Allen, and #5 Steve

Ballmer) and computers for another (#4 Michael Dell). Second-ranked Warren Buffett fits most comfortably into the finance category, while the remainder of the top 10 are all involved in media, telecommunications, semiconductors, or retailing. A group photograph of America's very wealthiest people, in short, is a portrait of a postindustrial economy.

Cutting-edge industries have been the wellspring of great fortunes for centuries. Figure 1 underscores the point with numbers. The table is derived from data in *The Wealthy 100*, a 1996 book that profiles the 100 richest Americans of all time. Everyone on the list would rank as a billionaire in contemporary terms.[3]

For generations born before 1800, the greatest opportunities arose in activities central to an economy driven by agriculture and commerce. Landowners, merchants, and shipping magnates predominated among the superrich. Industrialization changed all that. For those born between 1801 and 1850, becoming extraordinarily wealthy more often involved the era's dynamic growth industries, including mining and steel. Following the discovery of oil in Pennsylvania, astute entrepreneurs amassed immense wealth by supplying kerosene for illumination. Other great fortunes arose from the infrastructure (railroads and city transit) that facilitated industrialization and its by-product, urbanization. Creating these industries required vast sums of capital, which enabled bankers and financiers to amass great fortunes.

In later epochs, banking and finance remained cradles of the superaffluent. Another holdover, the oil business, was a springboard to the wealthiest-ever list for several individuals born between 1851 and 1900. During the years in which they amassed their wealth, though, gasoline replaced kerosene as the most important refined petroleum product. The advent of the automobile not only transformed the oil industry, but also created some of the leading fortunes of the day. Finally, as the preceding analysis of the Forbes 400 list also showed, industries characteristic of the postindustrial age accounted for the richest of the billionaires born after 1900. These included software, communications, and direct merchandising.

The best odds of becoming a billionaire, in summary, exist in industries that ride the key trends of economic development. This suggests that in newly industrializing countries, great opportunities may remain in infrastructure and basic industries. In the world's most developed economies, however, the cream of tomorrow's billionaires probably will emerge from communications, services, and technology.

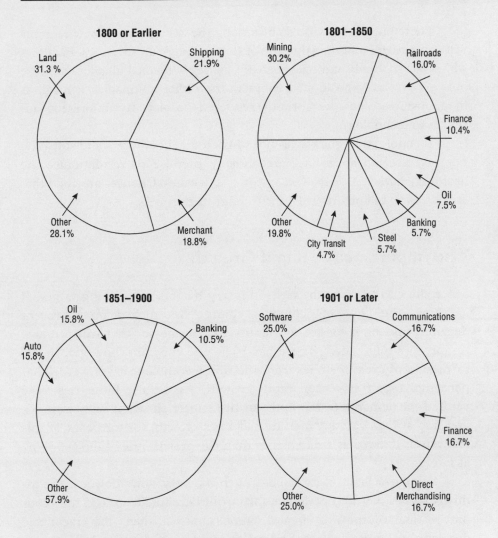

1800 or Earlier

Land 31.3%
Shipping 21.9%
Other 28.1%
Merchant 18.8%

1801–1850

Mining 30.2%
Railroads 16.0%
Finance 10.4%
Oil 7.5%
Banking 5.7%
Steel 5.7%
City Transit 4.7%
Other 19.8%

1851–1900

Oil 15.8%
Banking 10.5%
Auto 15.8%
Other 57.9%

1901 or Later

Software 25.0%
Communications 16.7%
Finance 16.7%
Direct Merchandising 16.7%
Other 25.0%

Note: For individuals classified in two industries, half a person is assigned to each. *Rounding may cause sums to differ from 100.0%.*

FIGURE 1   Primary Industry Affiliations of the 100 Wealthiest Americans by Year of Birth

Source: Michael Klepper and Robert Gunther, *The Wealthy 100: From Benjamin Franklin to Bill Gates—A Ranking of the Richest Americans, Past and Present* (Secaucus, NJ: Citadel Press, 1996).

These businesses will also be among the riskiest. Many new entrants will compete for a limited number of slots as long-run survivors. Fatalities will occur suddenly and unexpectedly, as newly formed alliances squeeze out less favorably positioned competitors. Other companies will fail as their business plans are abruptly rendered obsolete by unforeseen advances in technology.

Technology, by the way, is not restricted to computers and software. For instance, advances in biotechnology promise to revolutionize the health sciences and agriculture in coming decades. Chances are good that at least a few billionaires will be created in the process.

The Importance of Rapid Growth

Since the early 1800s, the right industry has been a moving target. If anything, the pace of economic change has picked up in recent decades, making it harder to identify the businesses that will produce tomorrow's billionaires. There has been one constant, however, in the formation of great fortunes from the nineteenth century onward. That perennial factor has been rapid growth. As a rule, industries have vaulted participants to the ranks of the superrich when sales were increasing at high rates. A high rate of sales growth, for purposes of this analysis, is defined as a rate higher than the growth rate of the economy at large.

Sooner or later, every rapid-growth industry slows down. If the industry's sales did not decelerate, they would eventually exceed the economy's total output, a logical impossibility. When the inevitable deceleration occurs, the baton passes to other businesses that begin growing at phenomenal rates and coining new billionaires.

To be sure, there are exceptions to the link between high-growth industries and the building of great fortunes. A few of them are discussed later in this chapter. Still, a study of large numbers of self-made billionaires leads to the conclusion that the slow-growth path is less traveled because it is more difficult.

A slow-growing industry tends to represent a settled, and therefore fairly predictable, environment. (Highly volatile, commodity-oriented industries represent an exception to this general rule.) Competitors within a highly predictable industry accept comparatively modest profits because the risk of loss is modest. The Menace of Competition, in short, levels out the field and leaves few prospects for the creation of massive new wealth.

Opportunities are more abundant in a rapidly growing industry, which is inherently somewhat chaotic and therefore fraught with risk. Investors are willing to commit capital to such an area only if the potential returns are high. The winners who emerge from this competitive free-for-all, while also holding on to their equity, become immensely wealthy.

Can a Slow-Growth Industry Produce a High-Growth Company?

Naturally, there is a catch to the idea of generating rapid earnings growth by choosing a high-growth industry: The industry's expected high growth may not materialize. Demand for the product or service may not come about as expected. In that event, you might lose a substantial investment in the form of time devoted to learning the business. Why not, as an alternative, reduce your risk by entering an established industry and create a company that grows more rapidly than its peers? This is an especially tempting option if you are talented in selling and in motivating a sales force.

To an extent, it is true, growth rates vary among companies because some are better than others at selling their wares. The importance of sales to a successful business has spawned a large industry devoted to training and motivating salespeople. Countless books, seminars, and videocassettes exhort sales professionals to qualify their prospects, identify customers' needs, maintain a positive mental attitude, and close, close, close. This "human capital" investment is expensive, but it can yield an excellent payback. Up to a point, an energetic and enthusiastic sales force can indeed enable a company to grow faster than its peers.

Only up to a point, however. A company in an industry that is growing at a mere 2 or 3 percent a year will find it extremely difficult to grow at 10 or 15 percent while also making decent profits. Even with the help of winning smiles, well-shined shoes, and a burning desire to succeed, the sales force must offer customers a solid reason to do business with them. If the reason is a low price, the company's profits will come under pressure. Modest profits, in turn, will make it tough to build a billion-dollar net worth.

Disadvantages of Mature Industries

Granted, there are situations in which a company can boost its profits by selling more units at a smaller markup. Typically, however, the company's competitors have the same opportunity. Soon, they will try to win back their customers by cutting their own prices. Before long, a full-scale price war will level down the entire industry to a new low in profitability. Trying to amass a billion-dollar fortune under such conditions is like trying to somersault up a steep incline. It can be done, but it is definitely doing it the hard way.

Generally speaking, industries achieve their highest growth rates in their early stages. It is not hard to see why. The sales volume of a brand-new product, at its point of introduction, is zero. Potential sales, however, can number tens or hundreds of millions of units. In the case of a consumer product, for example, the potential may amount to one unit per household throughout the developed world. Starting from a sales volume of zero units per year, the newly created industry must grow at a staggering rate to satisfy demand.

Eventually, though, the product achieves saturation, defined in this example as the point at which every household owns one. Sales do not halt when saturation occurs. Each household must buy another unit when its first one either wears out or becomes obsolete because of improvements to the original model. These replacement sales, however, merely maintain volume at the annual level attained at the time of saturation. Further growth occurs only through the formation of new households. In essence, growth in the once-hot business slows to the level of population growth. By definition, the industry has matured.

"Dog-eat-dog competition" is an apt description of the conditions in most mature industries. In a familiar pattern, producers try to boost their growth above the replacement-sales level by cutting prices. "Profitless growth" is the best they can hope to achieve by such tactics.

Another strategy for grabbing market share is to preempt competitors' capacity additions. Suppose, for example, that unit sales volume is projected to grow at 2 percent a year. At that rate, all existing factories will be running flat out in another two years, necessitating the construction of additional facilities. Assume further that building a new factory will require two years and, in order to be cost-efficient, must be capable of producing the equivalent of 10 percent of the industry's present annual volume.

Company XYZ is the first to announce plans to build a new plant and reckons that ought to settle the matter. After all, with the industry growing at only 2 percent a year, the 10 percent expansion of productive capability will create excess capacity during the first few years after the plant comes onstream. That is, the industry's ability to supply its customers will exceed customers' demand, causing prices to come under pressure. Surely, thinks the management of Company XYZ, no competitor will exacerbate that problem by deciding to build its own new plant. Such a move would boost industry capacity by 20 percent. Prices would drop severely, causing misery for all producers, including the company that adds capacity on top of Company XYZ's.

Not infrequently, however, a competitor does precisely what Company XYZ fears. It declares its intention to build a new plant, hoping that Company XYZ's management will back down to avoid a price war. The result of this giant game of chicken is often that both plants get built and prices plummet. Worse still, the drama gets played out every time population-driven growth causes demand to begin to catch up with industry capacity. The hoped-for better tomorrow of fat profit margins and industry prosperity never arrives.

There are simple, logical solutions to the problems of competition in a mature industry. Instead of fighting one another tooth and nail, all producers could agree not to sell below a price that covers their costs, plus a satisfactory profit margin. Alternatively, they could coordinate their expansion plans to prevent excess capacity from ever becoming a severe problem. Unfortunately, these strategies are illegal under the antitrust laws. They have immense appeal all the same, as a result of which participants in mature industries sometimes spend more time fending off price-fixing charges than multiplying their personal net worth.

> *All things considered, mature industries do not represent the path of least resistance toward a billion-dollar fortune.*

No Easy Pickings

Even in a rapidly growing industry, making a cool billion is by no means inevitable. For an individual with the requisite motivation and determination, however, the odds are much better than in a mature business. Again, the reasons have to do with supply and demand, which in turn influence pricing and profits.

Typically, when a new product first comes to market, manufacturers do not immediately build sufficient capacity to satisfy all potential demand. Aside from the physical constraints of constructing factories, it would be extremely risky to build far in advance of demand. A staggering percentage of promising new products fail and it is far better to wind up with a little useless factory space than to wind up with a lot. Accordingly, when a new product does succeed, demand is likely to outstrip capacity for the first few years. Under such conditions, management's most pressing task is not to increase sales by taking market share away from competitors. In the near term, the biggest challenge is simply to fulfill existing orders. Producers do not have to worry about ferocious price competition eating into profit margins.

Even though profit pressures are likely to be greater in mature industries, readers certainly should not conclude that young industries offer easy pickings. Once capacity begins to catch up with demand, competition can become very intense, even if it takes a form different from the price wars that plague mature businesses. Instead of being condemned to grind out mediocre profits decade after decade, producers of a new product face a high risk of getting knocked out of the business altogether.

Typically, young industries have many competing producers, each accounting for a small share of total output. Exactly the opposite conditions generally prevail in a mature industry, with a small number of producers accounting for the lion's share of total output. Between these two stages of growth comes a shakeout, in which many competitors leave the field by going bankrupt, switching to other lines of business, or being acquired by one of the survivors.

Generally, the survivors are the producers that capture substantial market share early in the game. These are the companies that achieve maximum economies of scale. This means, in brief, that they can spread their fixed costs of production over a larger number of units than their competitors, thereby achieving the lowest cost per unit.[4] Over time, the companies that gain an edge in sales volume outlast producers that fail to achieve comparably low costs per unit.

Economies of scale and unit costs, it is true, have their greatest analytical value in traditional manufacturing businesses. In other industries, low unit costs are not necessarily the chief benefit of gaining market share during the rapid-growth phase. Instead, the objective may be to establish an industry standard. For example, a key to Bill Gates's early success was establishing Microsoft's operating system as the one that designers of software applications chose to support. At a certain point, Microsoft attained an overwhelming advantage because computer users could run many more programs on DOS than on other systems.

Whether the goal is achieving low unit costs or creating an industry standard, however, the survivors are generally the companies that focus early on building market share. This strategy may require keeping prices low during the shakeout phase, which in turn means sacrificing profits in the short run. Over the long haul, however, the entrepreneur who pulls away from the pack in a young industry has a genuine shot at a billion-dollar net worth. In a mature industry, by contrast, a number of highly capable and fiercely competitive business executives may slug it out for decades without *collectively* amassing a billion dollars of net worth.

High Growth Produces High Stock Value

The difference between low growth and high growth really begins to affect net worth when a company goes public, that is, when it begins to raise money in the stock market. In the world of quoted shares, all companies are decidedly not created equal. Two corporations may have similar levels of sales and earnings today, yet receive radically different values in the stock market. The underlying reason is that investors strive to base their valuations on the future, rather than on the present. What matters most is not current-year sales and profits, but a consensus expectation regarding the level of future sales and profits.

Whether a company has glamorous or dull prospects, the aggregate value of its outstanding shares (total market capitalization) generally can be expressed as a multiple of its current annual profits.[5] Suppose, for example, that a company earned $50 million in the latest year and has 25 million shares outstanding. If the stock currently trades at $40 a share, its total market capitalization is 25 million times $40, or $1 billion. The ratio between the company's total market capitalization and profits, or *price-earnings multiple*, is $1 billion divided by $50 million, which equals 20.

This arithmetic has an important bearing on aspiring billionaires' industry choice because price-earnings multiples vary greatly. Suppose there is a second company, also with $50 million in profits and 25 million outstanding shares, but which commands a price-earnings multiple of 50. Each share represents a claim on profits of $50 million / 25 million = $2. The market values each share at $50 \times \$2 = \$100$. Total market capitalization comes to 25 million $\times \$100 = \$2.5$ billion.

As subsequent chapters will demonstrate, holding on to a major portion of a company's ownership, or equity, is a key objective for aspiring billionaires. The benefits of succeeding increase sharply when the company trades at a high price-earnings multiple. A 40 percent stake in the second company, which has a total market capitalization of $2.5 billion, qualifies its founder as a billionaire. By contrast, a 40 percent interest in the first company gives its founder a net worth of only $400 million. That is not a bad position to be in, but the exercise teaches an important lesson:

> *Good old-fashioned hard work and risk taking pay much better in industries that carry high price-earnings multiples.*

The underlying reason for wide disparities in price-earnings multiples is a fundamental relationship in financial theory:

> *The more rapidly a company's profits are expected to grow, the more valuable is a dollar of those earnings today.*

Table 1 illustrates why this relationship exists. In the current year, profits (alternatively referred to as earnings, income, or bottom line)[6] of both So-So Corp. and High Flier, Inc., are $10 million. Over the next decade, however, So-So's earnings are expected to grow at a rate of just 10 percent a year, while High Flier's are expected to grow at 20 percent a year. If the projections prove accurate, then in 10 years, So-So's annual profits of $25.9 million will pale next to High Flier's $61.9 million.

Assume that after 10 years of rapid growth, High Flier's earnings growth will decelerate sharply to the same 10 percent annual rate as So-So's.[7] At that point, investors will view both corporations as businesses with modest growth prospects and apply the same price-earnings multiple to their respective earnings. Suppose that multiple happens to be 15. So-So's total market capitalization will be $25.9 million × 15 = $388.5 million, while High Flier's will be $61.9 million × 15 = $928.5 million.

TABLE 1   IMPACT OF EARNINGS GROWTH RATE ON VALUATION

	So-So Corp.	**High Flier, Inc.**
Today		
Earnings in current year	$10 million	$10 million
Expected annual growth rate	10%	20%
Shares outstanding	13 million	13 million
Ten Years from Now*		
Earnings	$25.9 million	$61.9 million
Price-earnings multiple	15 times	15 times
Total market capitalization	$388.5 million	$928.5 million

*Projected.

Bringing the analysis back to the present, let us assume that the multiple for companies with expected earnings growth of 10 percent is 13. (This happens to be below the 10-years-hence multiple of 15, reflecting the fact that price-earnings multiples vary over time.) Based on current-year earnings of $10 million, So-So's current total market capitalization is $130 million.

Now comes the payoff: The market *must* award High Flier's $10 million of earnings a higher price-earnings multiple than it assigns to So-So's $10 million bottom line. Granted, it seems unfair. So-So's founder has worked just as hard as High Flier's. Both entrepreneurs retain 25 percent interests in their respective companies. High Flier's founder nevertheless winds up getting paid a lot better. The arithmetic makes this result unavoidable.

For both companies, today's price per share is $10 (market capitalization of $130 million / 13 million shares outstanding = $10). Given the stated assumptions, one So-So share a decade hence will be worth $29.88 ($388.5 million / 13 million = $29.88). Today's So-So shareholders, in other words, will not quite triple their investment over 10 years. Each share of High Flier, on the other hand, will soar to $71.42 ($928.5 million / 13 million = $71.42). That represents more than a 600 percent increase over 10 years, versus a little less than 200 percent for owners of So-So stock. If the two stocks are selling at the same price today, every So-So shareholder with a lick of common sense will sell out immediately and invest the proceeds in High Flier stock.

In fact, if such a bargain existed for even a brief period, money would come gushing out of numerous stocks with comparatively modest appreciation potential like So-So's and flood into High Flier shares. The heavy buying would drive up the price of High Flier stock dramatically.

How high would the price go? This exercise simplifies real-world conditions somewhat, but High Flier's shares essentially ought to trade at a level that will produce the same 10-year percentage increase in value that is available on stocks such as So-So. Dividing So-So's future total market capitalization ($388.5 million) by its present total market capitalization ($130 million) produces a ratio of 2.988. Dividing High Flier's future total market capitalization ($928.5 million) by the same 2.988 indicates that the company's present total market capitalization should be $310.7 million. The appropriate price-earnings multiple for High Flier is therefore $310.7 million / $10 million = 31. In summary, High Flier's expected high growth rate causes the market to value its stock at 31 times earnings versus just 13 times for slower-growing So-So.

Variations and Exceptions

At this point, you may be concluding that you have already taken a fatally wrong turn in your life. If you are involved in a mature industry, either as an employee or as an entrepreneur, you may feel doomed to miss out on the premium valuations accorded to young, rapidly growing enterprises. To make matters worse, highly sophisticated technologies account for much of high growth in a contemporary, postindustrial economy. Are there no billion-dollar opportunities for the unfortunates who were *not* stigmatized as computer nerds back in high school?

In reality, there is no reason to despair. If history is any guide, the high-tech entrepreneur track will be only one of several that transport individuals to the upper echelons of the Forbes 400 in the future. A number of alternative strategies exist for aspiring billionaires who fear that they are not in the right place at the right time.

To begin with, techies have not been the only ones to get rich from high technology. As a case in point, John Arrillaga and Richard Peery rose to the billionaire ranks through their real estate holdings in Silicon Valley, California's high-tech heartland. Steve Ballmer, who placed fifth in the 1998 *Forbes* rankings with an estimated $12 billion net worth, was the first nonprogrammer hired by Microsoft. The move represented a career change for Ballmer, who brought recruiting and sales skills from his prior experience in consumer goods at Procter & Gamble. Other multibillionaires first built fortunes in lower-technology businesses, then successfully transferred their investment and managerial know-how to cutting-edge industries. Phil Anschutz, for example, hit it big in fiber optics after earlier success in oil and railroads.

Shrewd deal making was a key to Anschutz's attaining billionaire status before entering the sort of young, high-growth industry from which the superrich more commonly spring. It is noteworthy that he initially capitalized on his negotiating skills in oil exploration, an industry already a century old when he entered it. Venerable though it is, the business of drilling for oil and natural gas does not fit the mold of a mature industry locked in a competitive stalemate that mitigates against the sudden creation of vast new wealth. Wildcatting, which entails exploration outside proven oil-producing fields, remains extremely risky despite advances in seismic technology. Frequently, the fruit of a large drilling outlay is a dry hole containing no economically recoverable reserves. The price of oil must offset this huge risk of loss by providing a big payoff on successful wells. Otherwise, exploration would cease and supply would fall below demand as known reserves were pumped to the surface and consumed. In light of these economics, the requirements for success in oil and gas exploration have not changed dramatically since the early-twentieth-century exploits of H. L. Hunt and J. Paul Getty. Skill at negotiating to acquire the most promising drilling sites (or prospects), combined with exceptionally high risk tolerance, can still transform a small operator into a billionaire. Real estate, with its similarly high risk and emphasis on deal making, is another source of new fortunes that lies outside the category of young industries.

Phil Anschutz's migration to fiber optics, a dynamic growth area of his era, has many historical parallels. John D. Rockefeller Sr. began his career as a commission agent dealing in produce, with no particular expertise in the oil business. Breaking in was comparatively easy, however. The petroleum industry had just been born with Edwin Drake's 1859 discovery and (no less important) successful extraction of oil in Titusville, Pennsylvania. Rockefeller's home base, Cleveland, was well situated to become a refining center. It was as an investor in a start-up refinery that he began his ascent to monopolistic power through the Standard Oil Company. More recently, Sam Walton started the Wal-Mart discount chain after first achieving success as a more traditional operator of five-and-ten-cent (or variety) stores. His example may be a good one to emulate, based on his ranking for a time as the wealthiest of the United States's billionaires.

Another success story that goes against the grain of young, high-growth industries is Wayne Huizenga's reaping of riches from waste hauling. The business was hardly new but it was ripe for consolidation. This is one of the processes by which the number of competitors in an industry tends to decline over time, as discussed earlier. Waste Management, run by Huizenga and Dean Buntrock, acquired scores of local mom-and-pop operators. Increasing the scale produced operating efficiencies and improved managerial methods. In addition, and not incidentally, Waste Management told its story very effectively to stock market investors. Huizenga later applied what he had learned about growth through acquisition to a high-growth business, the Blockbuster chain of video rental stores.

Warren Buffett represents the premier role model for would-be billionaires who wonder whether they can achieve their dreams outside of glamorous, high-technology businesses. Perennially near the top of the richest Americans list, along with his friend Bill Gates, Buffett has consciously avoided investing in technology stocks on the grounds that he has no expertise in the area.

Buffett has acquired a reputation for spotting cheap assets in frequently mundane-sounding businesses. A study of his career in Chapter 7 shows, however, that he has not prospered by buying companies that were deservedly low-priced. One of Buffett's least successful investments was a textile company, Berkshire Hathaway, that ultimately contributed little but its name to his vast industrial empire. The manufacturer of suit liners (not of Hathaway brand shirts, as is sometimes supposed) was a dying company and, as it turned out, no bargain. From that experience and countless other observations, Buffett has concluded that a bad business usually will prevail over a good management.

While he has not concentrated his investments in young industries with huge growth potential, Buffett has sought other attractive characteristics, such as a strong franchise and monopoly-like pricing power. The big gains in his portfolio have not arisen from the price-earnings multiple magic of growth industries, illustrated in Table 1. Instead, they have generally resulted from improved earnings, often brought about through Buffett's own intervention. In building his personal net worth, he has leveraged the impact of his capital gains by investing through insurance companies.

Aside from the strategies already described, billionaires past and present have employed several secondary techniques to improve upon the odds dictated by their choice of industry. In many cases, they have overcome the leveling effects of competition by applying superior management skills or investing in political influence. Finally, a recurring theme in the stories behind many great fortunes is successful resistance to unionization. None of the individuals discussed in the following chapters amassed wealth purely by defeating organized labor. Many, however, placed great importance on avoiding the partial loss of control associated with a successful union organizing effort.

Certain Methods Apply Regardless of Industry Choice

As you read this book you will notice a number of recurring themes. Certain methods pop up repeatedly in a study of the great fortune builders. Any idea that has reaped huge rewards for many different titans of wealth is likely to be particularly worth assimilating. *How to Be a Billionaire* distills the great mass of material describing the world-class fortune builders and highlights the essential attitudes and habits that crop up again and again.

One fact that emerges from this comparative study of champion wealth amassers is that they have employed several distinct business strategies. For example, Ross Perot, Sam Walton, and Richard Branson built brand-new businesses from the ground up, whereas Wayne Huizenga made his fortune through consolidating small mom-and-pop operations into vast enterprises. In contrast to John D. Rockefeller Sr. and Bill Gates, these four aimed for strong, rather than dominant, positions in their markets. Several fundamental business strategies emerge from studying the founders of great fortunes:

- Take Extraordinary Risks
- Do Business in a New Way
- Dominate Your Market
- Consolidate an Industry
- Buy Low
- Thrive on Deals
- Outmanage the Competition

If present-day billionaires had meticulously studied self-enrichment books and financial titans' biographies of the past, they could have identified each of these concepts. By limiting themselves to those two types of sources, however, they would have overlooked some valuable elements of the story. The missing pieces were two additional strategies more controversial than taking risk or developing innovative business plans:

- Invest in Political Influence
- Resist the Unions

Understandably, the great wealth amassers of the past did not draw attention to their reliance on political influence or their strategies for discouraging unionization. The writers of inspirational books, eager to maintain an upbeat tone, likewise skated over such practices. Consequently, accounts of the tough side of labor and government relations appeared mainly in the writings of muckrakers (investigative reporters, in contemporary parlance). That genre was not customarily featured in the business or self-help sections of the bookstore.

The final component of this book's plan of attack is the identification of certain attitudes and modes of behavior that the champion accumulators of wealth share, regardless of differences in their basic business strategies. Beneath the widely diverse personalities of the individuals profiled in *How to Be a Billionaire* are surprising similarities in their habits. Already enumerated in Chapter 1, these key principles bear repeating here:

- Pursue the Money in Ideas
- Rules Are Breakable
- Copying Pays Better Than Innovating
- Keep on Growing
- Hold on to Your Equity
- Hard Work Is Essential
- Use Financial Leverage
- Keep the Back Door Open
- Make Mistakes, Then Learn from Them
- Frugality Pays
- Enjoy the Pursuit
- Develop a Thick Skin

Watch for practical examples of these key principles in action as you proceed to Part Two ("Fundamental Strategies") of *How to Be a Billionaire*. As you do so, you will come to understand how the great accumulators of wealth have integrated their thoughts and actions into successful plans of action. You will then be prepared to obtain maximum benefit from Part Three ("Putting It All Together"). This, the final section, consists of a single chapter: "Your Turn."

PART TWO

FUNDAMENTAL STRATEGIES

3

TAKE MONUMENTAL RISKS

Fortune assists the brave.
—Terence

Correlation of risk and reward is one of the most fundamental precepts of finance. The greater the danger of loss in an investment, the greater is the potential gain. On this principle, corporate bonds provide higher yields than government bonds, as compensation for their larger risk of default. Stocks, in turn, are riskier than bonds and therefore provide still higher potential returns, in the form of dividends plus long-run price appreciation. There is an even greater chance of a large loss in investments such as commodity futures and venture capital, which offer commensurately bigger potential gains.

Each of these disparate assets has its devotees because individuals vary widely in their tolerance for risk. In selecting their investments, risk takers of varying levels sort themselves out. The process resembles a large poker game in which the most aggressive players repeatedly raise the ante. One by one, the more conservative players drop out, leaving only a few high-stakes gamblers at the table. A similar thinning out of the crowd occurs with each step along the investment risk-reward spectrum. For example, some individuals who feel comfortable with the risk of blue chip stocks have no appetite for shares of small technology companies, which may either hit it big or go bust.

Even at the fairly high level of risk represented by speculative stocks,

51

however, the players number in the millions. This is hardly surprising, because few buyers of even the most volatile stocks ever place themselves in serious financial jeopardy. Considered in its full context, the downside for most investors is minor.

By way of illustration, consider a man who has a secure job paying $75,000 a year and a stock portfolio worth $100,000. Suppose that in response to a hot tip, he invests $10,000 in a stock, hoping to double or triple his money. If, contrary to his expectations, the company goes bankrupt and he loses his entire investment, his family will not go hungry. Not only does he continue to draw his paycheck, but he can retrieve part of the loss through an income tax deduction. Furthermore, he probably has some winners in his portfolio to make up for the highflier that crashed.

Precisely because so many people are able to take this kind of risk, the rewards are not astronomical. To attract buyers, speculative stocks must offer greater upside than blue chips, but not the kind of upside that propels individuals to the Forbes 400 list. The result, as noted in Chapter 1, is that no one has amassed a 10-figure net worth purely through passive investment in the stock market.

Self-made billionaires take risks of a completely different order of magnitude. While amassing a fortune in highway construction, Dennis Washington repeatedly pledged his home as security with the bonding company underwriting his current project. He insists, moreover, that his willingness to gamble in that way was not a matter of supreme confidence in his own ability to calculate the odds. "What makes a superstar is luck," says Washington.[1]

Steve Ballmer has similarly demonstrated the difference between billionaire-style risk taking and owning a diversified stock portfolio. In March 1989, Microsoft received an unfavorable ruling in its ongoing litigation with Apple Computer. The software company's stock plummeted as investors fretted that Microsoft would be blocked from using certain Macintosh-like features in future versions of its Windows operating system. Sales chief Ballmer, who correctly foresaw that Apple would not ultimately prevail, shelled out $46 million to add to his existing large holdings of Microsoft stock. Three years later, he followed Bill Gates and Paul Allen into the billionaire ranks. By then, the Microsoft shares that Ballmer had purchased for $46 million at a low point in the company's fortunes were worth more than $350 million. Ballmer prospered by putting all of his eggs in one basket, doubling down on a company that already represented the bulk of his net worth.

Among the self-made billionaires, attitudes toward risk vary considerably. Kirk Kerkorian plainly thrives on it, as evidenced by his past renown as a high roller at Las Vegas craps tables. Others take less intrinsic pleasure in risk, but acknowledge it as a prerequisite for acquiring great wealth.

Sam Walton, for example, maintained an exceptionally strong balance sheet at Wal-Mart to avoid the risks inherent in deep indebtedness. This conservatism was probably reinforced by the memory of the many farmers whose mortgages his father had foreclosed on during the Depression. Before Wal-Mart went public to increase its access to capital, however, Walton rapidly expanded his retailing empire by incurring huge personal debts. Later on, he bet heavily on technologies such as bar coding and a private satellite communications network, not knowing whether they would prove viable in general merchandise retailing.

Like Wal-Mart under Sam Walton, Standard Oil under John D. Rockefeller Sr. followed extremely conservative financial policies. Moreover, Rockefeller's basic strategy was to reduce the inherent risks of the oil industry by creating a monopoly. Nevertheless, he was willing to take a chance when circumstances warranted. When he committed Standard Oil to huge acquisitions of leases in Ohio, it was not yet clear that the region's sulfur-laden crude could be refined into usable kerosene. Similarly, Rockefeller invested in the Mesabi Range before engineers solved the problem of smelting the region's powdery iron ore.

To be sure, self-made billionaires have sometimes hedged their bets, a principle described by Kirk Kerkorian in the phrase "keeping the back door open." For example, Ross Perot worked as a consultant to generate personal income during the start-up phase of Electronic Data Systems. The comparatively low capital requirements of the computer services business enabled him to launch the venture without digging too deeply into the savings he had accumulated as a successful computer salesperson.

If EDS had flopped, Perot would not have been ruined, by any means. On the other hand, he clearly cut the umbilical cord by leaving IBM. Not every self-made billionaire has been a financial daredevil, but all have dared to reject the safe-but-sure path. H. L. Hunt and John Kluge exemplify the use of monumental risk taking as a road to extraordinary riches.

The Billionaire How-To

Fundamental Strategies

- Take Monumental Risks
- Thrive on Deals

Key Principles

- Keep on Growing
- Keep the Back Door Open
- Use Financial Leverage

H. L. Hunt

A man who has $200,000 is about as well off, for all practical purposes, as I am.[2]

In 1957, 68-year-old widower Haroldson Lafayette Hunt married for the second time (not counting a bigamous relationship he had entered into three decades earlier).[3] Under the influence of his new wife, a former Baptist choir singer, Hunt gave up smoking and drinking. He also began exercising regularly, took up yoga, and became a health food devotee. The most startling transformation of all, however, was the billionaire oilman's renunciation of gambling.

Until his conversion to the straight and narrow, H. L. Hunt was one of America's biggest bettors on football and horse racing. Often, he had half a million dollars or more riding on a single day's sporting events. At one time, he even employed personal handicappers.[4] While Hunt unquestionably had the nerve to take monumental risks, however, he also utilized several other classic billionaires' methods.

～

Among the forms of gambling Hunt enjoyed, it was cards, rather than sports betting, that figured most prominently in his phenomenal financial success. Legend has it that he won his first oil well in a game of five-card stud poker. Hunt always insisted, however, that his empire began with some shrewd trading of leases.

In fact, Hunt's technique in his early days in El Dorado, Arkansas, was the antithesis of gambling. He first asked a farmer to name a price for the drilling rights on his land. Then, Hunt hurried to town and offered the rights to an oil driller at a higher price. Once he had both sides of the trade in place, he would buy and sell nearly simultaneously, pocketing a profit without risking a nickel.

Within six months, Hunt had cleared enough profit to lease half an acre of his own. He struck oil on his first try and in just two years had 44 wells producing in El Dorado and the nearby town of Smackover. All the while, the rising wildcatter continued playing poker, reportedly using the winnings to pay his drilling crew's wages. By 1924, Hunt was able to cash in a half-interest in 40 of his wells for a $600,000 note.[5]

Hunt's big strike in El Dorado was a remarkable accomplishment for a man who began in the oil business in 1921 with no experience and only a $50 borrowed grubstake. In succeeding decades, H. L. Hunt expanded his operations throughout the United States and Canada, then to Libya, where his company brought in one of the biggest finds of all time. The high-stakes player liked to boast that during World War II, the Hunt Oil Company and its affiliates provided the Allies more oil than Germany's total supply, including the portion it obtained from Romania.

In 1948, *Life* proclaimed Hunt the wealthiest American. A few years later, billionaire-watchers began debating whether Hunt or his fellow oil operator, J. Paul Getty, was the richest man in the world. Said Getty, "In terms of extraordinary, independent wealth, there is only one man—H. L. Hunt."[6]

Living on the Edge

Countless other wildcatters sought their fortunes in the regional oil boom launched by the South Texas Spindletop discovery in 1901. (Six wells in that field had the capacity, at the time, to produce as much oil as the rest of the world combined.) A newcomer stood at a distinct disadvantage to experienced operators with established, bankable records for finding oil. Competition for choice drilling prospects was intense. What special qualities enabled H. L. Hunt to rise to the top of the heap?

A strong predilection for gambling unquestionably helped. Once, by Hunt's account, he parlayed $100 into $10,200 in a single day, while pitted against some of America's most famous poker players. His advantage, he later explained, lay in knowing more about them than they knew about him.[7] Be that as it may, Hunt obviously felt comfortable with risks that would have overwhelmed most mortals.

The willingness to take a flier emerged early in "Junie" (short for "Junior") Hunt's case. At 16, he rejected the security of a clerk's position in his father's Illinois bank. For six years he roamed the country, employed mainly as a manual laborer. On one occasion, evidently not satisfied with the risks of a poker game with some fellow railroad workers, he traveled about six miles to play *cancoon* at a camp of Mexican laborers. As Hunt told the story, he was less familiar with the game, played with a Spanish deck of 40 cards, than with poker. He nevertheless managed to win $4,000, a sum that apparently represented every bit of cash in the camp. Collecting his winnings, Hunt hightailed it to his own camp, cutting through the woods. Perhaps not unreasonably, he feared that if he followed the railroad tracks to rejoin his crew, the cleaned-out workers would overtake him in a handcar and retrieve their losses by force.[8]

When his father died in 1911, Hunt seemed to subdue his compulsion to live on the edge. With an inheritance of about $6,000, he bought a 960-acre Arkansas cotton plantation. Hunt's plans to settle down as a farmer, however, were foiled when the Mississippi River flooded in both 1916 and 1917, destroying his crop. Now faced with supporting a wife and two children, he once again turned to poker. By day, he won as much as possible in the small town of Lake Village. By night, he played for higher stakes in the larger town of Greenville. Periodically, Hunt traveled downriver to New Orleans to enter the genuinely big-money games.

Meanwhile, the struggling cotton planter took up a second form of gambling, namely, speculating in farmland and futures. Riding a boom that was fueled by rising cotton prices, he ran his land holdings up to 15,000 acres. In 1920, however, Hunt's luck ran out when he bet on a drop in cotton prices by selling short. When prices continued to rise instead, margin calls exhausted his cash, relieving him of a small fortune. To add insult to injury, cotton prices then collapsed, vindicating his judgment even as it devastated the value of his land.

It was then that H. L. Hunt conceived the notion of entering the oil business. A more cautious soul might have raised cash for the new venture by selling his cotton acreage. Hunt, in contrast, reckoned that land values would rebound once the post–World War I agricultural recession ended. Accordingly, he borrowed $50 and lit out for El Dorado.

Following his early, rapid success as an oil driller, detailed earlier, the restless Hunt once again set off in an entirely new direction in 1925. He exchanged his $600,000 note for a discounted sum of cash and headed to Florida to capitalize on an incipient land boom. With his lawful family safely ensconced in Arkansas, Hunt married again. Shuttling back and forth between the two broods, each ignorant of the other's existence, he fathered seven children in the space of eight years. All the while, he kept a hand in the oil business, expanding his operations into Oklahoma and Louisiana. Then, in 1930, Hunt cut the deal that propelled him to the ranks of the superrich.

The Rusk County, Texas, discovery was a classic case of a man with a good idea meeting another man who better knew how to make money on it. Columbus Marion "Dad" Joiner had been drilling for oil since 1897, without ever hitting it big. At the age of 70, he appeared to be at the end of the line after striking 17 consecutive dry holes.

By luck, a widow named Daisy Bradford permitted Joiner to drill for free on her land. The nearly down-and-out wildcatter clung to the slim hope that he would find oil there, based on a glowing report by a patent medicine salesman with no formal training in geology. According to "Doctor" A. D. Lloyd, all major oil trends in the United States intersected in East Texas, forming an "apex of the apex" unique in all the world. (Lloyd, incidentally, had changed his name from Joseph Idelbert Dunham, apparently to escape the wrath of his six different wives.[9] It was fitting that a serial bigamist played a pivotal role in the fortunes of H. L. Hunt.)

Lloyd's analysis may have seemed a thin reed, but the poverty-stricken farmers of Rusk County were just as desperate to strike oil as "Dad" Joiner was. Thanks to their subscriptions to $25 certificates, vaguely entitling them to shares of any profit that the venture might produce, Joiner raised enough cash to acquire a rudimentary rig. On the strength of handshakes and sketchy documentation, the old-timer also leased substantial acreage surrounding Daisy Bradford's property.

Despite a series of calamities, Joiner finally made the big strike he had pursued for 30 years. Unfortunately, Daisy Bradford #3 behaved differently from any well that the established operators had previously encountered. It produced a small amount of oil, then dried up until the following day. The major oil companies consequently showed no interest in developing the prospect. At the same time, Joiner's creditors were eager to get their cash back. To top it all off, Joiner's questionable titles posed a threat of costly litigation.

At this perilous pass, H. L. Hunt entered the scene, having heard from a friend that Joiner needed capital to complete his well. Sizing up the prospect, Hunt concluded that it was situated on the edge of a major field. The geological and legal risks were formidable, besides which the Depression had decimated oil prices. Nevertheless, Hunt offered to buy Joiner out for a combination of $50,000 in cash, $45,000 in notes, and a guarantee of $1.3 million from proceeds of future production—if any. By offering to pay on the come, Hunt introduced the production payment to the oil business. The technique eventually became a standard feature of energy financing, but only after surviving extensive legal challenges.

According to Hunt, the genial Joiner responded to his offer to purchase Daisy Bradford #3 by warning him, "Boy, you would be buying a pig in a poke!"[10] Hunt nevertheless accepted the gamble and it paid off in spades. The site proved to be the biggest discovery in the world up to that time, tapping a lake of oil 43 miles long and up to 9 miles in width. For his efforts, Hunt gained a share of the profits that totaled, by conservative estimate, $100 million.[11]

Without a doubt, H. L. Hunt's fortune was built on the foundation of a high tolerance for risk. At the same time, he shaded the odds in his favor whenever possible. In old age, Hunt explained that he had been successful in poker partly because he possessed a photographic memory. Besides recalling the cards that had been played, he could anticipate roughly where they would turn up in the next hand, thanks to players who shuffled only desultorily before dealing.[12] It was also rumored that in his Rusk County negotiations, Hunt somehow gained information about the field's immense value, which he prevented "Dad" Joiner from obtaining. By some accounts, he essentially locked the veteran driller in a hotel room and supplied him with women and liquor until a favorable deal emerged.[13] There seems to be little dispute, at any rate, that Joiner "was an amiable man with a poor head for figures and a weakness for the bottle."[14]

A more profound case of shading the odds involved Hunt's lobbying for the oil depletion allowance. Hunt was an early advocate of the tax preference, which contributed generously to the wealth of oil patch operators. A fuller description is found in Chapter 10 ("Invest in Political Influence").

John Kluge

He took a small idea and turned it into something grand.
—Patricia Kluge[15]

H. L. Hunt was by no means the only billionaire to bankroll his early successes with poker winnings. John Kluge (pronounced "klōōgy") played the game avidly while attending Columbia University on a scholarship during the Depression. His penchant for the game attracted the notice of the dean, as well as a stern warning. "You'll never catch me gambling again," promised the young man. "But," Kluge wryly recalled, decades later, "I never said I wouldn't play."

For the remainder of his college days, Kluge played poker with a book close at hand. If the dean came knocking at his dormitory door during a late-night game, he would hastily fold his hand and pretend to be studying. Once, during a game of five-card stud, the future wealthiest American had two fives showing and a third in the hole. The other players had nothing, but before Kluge could finish the hand and claim the pot, a knock on the door was heard. Quickly jettisoning the cards and grabbing his book, Kluge admitted the visitor, who, as it turned out, was not the dean. Instead, it was a fellow student with a headache, seeking some aspirin. "He might have gotten rid of the headache, but I immediately got one," Kluge lamented.[16]

The lessons Kluge absorbed at the poker table, and in escaping detection, undoubtedly made him more money in later years than anything he learned in the classroom. Columbia offered a fine education, including a course taught by Warren Buffett's mentor, Benjamin Graham. Proven methods for becoming a billionaire were not in the curriculum, but Kluge discovered them nevertheless and soon began applying them.

To its immense benefit, Columbia failed to cure Kluge of the gambling bug. Over the years, he has donated more than $100 million to the school. After serving in U.S. Army Intelligence during World War II, Kluge began acquiring radio stations while also working in a wholesale food brokerage. Regarding one of his early deals, he recalled:

I borrowed $5,000 from the bank and only used $1,000 of it, and
then sold the business for $500,000. I told the bank what happened
and they said to me, "That's some leverage!" And I responded with,
"What's leverage?" Years later, I was sorry I had asked.[17]

The deal that caused Kluge to joke about ruing his discovery of
leverage was his 1984 buyout of Metromedia. Dissatisfied with the stock
market's valuation of the broadcasting empire he had created over the
preceding quarter century, and of which he owned 25 percent, he decided
to take it private. Kluge defied financial handicappers by borrowing $1.2
billion for the transaction. It was the largest communications industry
leveraged buyout (LBO) ever attempted up to that time and, in the view
of many experts, one of the riskiest.

Under the terms of his LBO loans, Kluge was required to break up
Metromedia and sell off the pieces to liquidate the debt in short order. It
quickly became apparent, however, that it would not be feasible to peddle
the assets quickly at premium prices. The problem was partly that potential acquirers were constrained by Federal Communications Commission
(FCC) limits on the number of stations they could own. Faced with possible default on his loans, Kluge turned to the investment bank Drexel
Burnham Lambert for a new financing package that granted him additional time to complete the asset sales.

Over the next two years, with the help of a surge in prices for broadcasting properties,[18] Kluge unloaded seven television stations and 11 radio stations. Onto the block as well went an outdoor advertising business,
the Harlem Globetrotters, the Ice Capades, and Kluge's cellular telephone and paging operations. In the end, the consummate high roller
managed not only to pay off the huge debt burden, but to net an estimated $1.6 billion. Before long, Kluge was plowing his profits back into
telecommunications and assorted other ventures that vaulted him to the
top of *Forbes*'s list of richest Americans by 1989.[19]

Naturally, Kluge did not entirely cast his fate to the winds during
the Metromedia buyout. In an astute financial move, he laid off a substantial part of the risk on bondholders. At the time, the market for high
yield bonds (sometimes pejoratively labeled "junk bonds") was undergo-
ing explosive growth. Small investors were pouring vast sums of cash into
mutual funds specializing in these risky but high return securities. As a result, Wall Street began finding it difficult to satisfy the demand with clas-

sic high yield issuers, that is, debt-heavy companies in mature businesses that tended to throw off lots of cash. Leveraged buyouts started to fill the gap, even though such transactions had previously relied on the private "mezzanine" market—an arena in which lenders received "equity sweeteners," such as warrants, to compensate for the substantial risk of failure in a venture with extraordinarily high levels of debt. In the high yield market, no such sweeteners were offered, meaning that lenders shouldered a large share of the risk without participating in the potential gains. Metromedia was not the first leveraged buyout to tap the high yield market, but it represented a watershed by virtue of its size.

Besides employing financial savvy, Kluge benefited from an element essential to taking gigantic risks, namely, luck. *U.S. News & World Report* flatly stated that if interest rates had risen or if the prices of broadcasting properties had not risen, the Metromedia buyout would have bankrupted Kluge. One card in his hand that kept him flush was his cellular telephone and paging business, which he managed to sell for $1.3 billion. Just four years earlier, Kluge had bought the properties for only $300 million. He made that investment, by his own account, "without thinking it clearly through."

Based on experiences such as these, Kluge makes no bones about the benefits of a lucky break: "The greatest factor in my life—and I know entrepreneurial people don't want to express it, they think it diminishes them—but luck plays a large part."[20] He recalls that it was only through a chance encounter with an acquaintance that he learned of the opportunity to acquire the remnants of the old Du Mont television network in 1959. That transaction launched the development of Metromedia into America's largest group of independent (non-network-affiliated) television and radio stations.

To be sure, luck comes in two varieties—good and bad. Kluge has had his share of the latter. Among the ventures he tried after completing the Metromedia sale were the Orion Pictures motion picture studio and the Ponderosa and Bonanza steak house chains. Neither time did he hit the jackpot. The restaurant experience led him to wisecrack, "If things get worse, we've always got a place to eat."[21] Kluge also came up snake eyes on a $32 million investment in the Fugazy Express limousine-franchising operation, which went bankrupt.[22] Asked to sum up the comparative contributions of luck and calculated risk to his success, Kluge replied, "If I told you it was all luck, I wouldn't be truthful. But if I told you it was all strategy, it would be a downright lie."[23]

Naturally, fortune is friendliest to those with a knack for calculating the odds. As Damon Runyon observed, "The race isn't always to the swift, nor the battle to the strong, but that's the way to bet." Even as devoted a gambler as John Kluge has occasionally chosen to take some money off the table. For example, he cashed in his cellular telephone chips in 1989, despite perceiving further upside in the business. "Sometimes I might not maximize an investment," he explained. "But I don't deal in 100 percent. I deal in 80 percent to 85 percent."[24] (For the record, Kluge did take back some stock in the sale, in order to keep a stake in the cellular business.) Notwithstanding his reputation as an outright plunger, Kluge has said, "I think the ability to gauge risks is crucial. I never ordinarily take on things that I can't see some end to, where you pile risks on risks."[25]

4

DO BUSINESS
IN A NEW WAY

———

*I do not create. God creates. I assemble, and I will steal from anywhere
to do it.*

—George Balanchine

Innovation in business has two highly appealing characteristics for aspiring billionaires. First, it offers a way to achieve the high growth rates that lead to high price-earnings multiples. Second, it does not require an especially original mind.

Ross Perot is given credit for inventing the computer services industry, but IBM was in the business in a modest way before he founded Electronic Data Systems. Perot's great insight was to recognize services as a sensational growth opportunity, rather than just an adjunct to the sale of computer mainframes. After failing to bring IBM management around to his point of view, he went into business for himself. Perot, in short, did not have to create an entirely new concept to become a billionaire. Knowing how to turn an idea into dollars was sufficient.

Similarly, Sam Walton did not invent discount merchandising. Michael Cullen introduced the formula of low overhead, low margins, and high volume to the food retailing business in 1930, when he opened his first supermarket in Jamaica, New York. Martin Chase adapted the discounting concept to apparel merchandising by cofounding the Ann & Hope

63

store in Cumberland, Rhode Island, in 1953. By the time Walton got into the game in 1962, discounting was already a $2-billion-a-year industry.

How to Be a Billionaire is not a book about Michael Cullen or Martin Chase, however. Sam Walton is one of its main characters because his Wal-Mart chain executed the discounting idea far more effectively than its competitors. The key to Walton's superb execution, by his own admission, was supreme devotion to copying the methods of other successful discounters.

If innovation enables you to create immense equity value and requires no originality, what is the catch? The biggest drawback is the backlash inevitably triggered by change. Upsetting the status quo is a sure way to draw fire from the sort of people who invariably liked things better the way they used to be. They begin with the sound proposition that not every change represents progress, but carry the notion much too far.

Perot's critics castigated him as a Medicare billionaire, a capitalist who got rich by servicing the welfare state. Without computerization, however, health care administration would have been considerably less efficient. To be sure, other companies would have computerized the process eventually if Perot had not been in the right place at the right time. The fact remains, however, that his business efforts did more to eliminate public sector waste than the politicians who won cheap applause by railing against bloated government bureaucracy. Catching flack was just part of the cost of shaking up the established order.

It was Walton, though, who wrote the book on ticking people off with innovation. Leading the attack, not surprisingly, were small-town retailers who could not compete with Wal-Mart's low prices. Long-established storekeepers closed their doors when Wal-Mart arrived, causing critics to bemoan the vanishing character of America's small towns.

Walton was more impressed by the fact that shoppers flocked to his stores. Evidently, they liked Wal-Mart's low prices more than they disliked its cultural and esthetic ramifications, which were subjective matters in any case. By all indications, Walton sincerely believed he was doing good by helping consumers stretch their incomes. They vindicated his belief by making Wal-Mart America's largest retailer.

In the course of becoming billionaires, Ross Perot and Sam Walton were supported by an unwavering assurance that they were on the right path. Their personal lives, too, were marked by strong convictions. Religious devotion and family bonds were values they prized.

THE BILLIONAIRE HOW-TO

Fundamental Strategies

- Do Business in a New Way
- Outmanage the Competition
- Thrive on Deals
- Take Monumental Risks

Key Principles

- Frugality Pays
- Hold on to Your Equity
- Make Mistakes, Then Learn from Them
- Enjoy the Pursuit
- Copying Pays Better Than Innovating
- Keep on Growing
- Use Financial Leverage
- Hard Work Is Essential
- Develop a Thick Skin

These specific traits are not essential for the accumulation of great wealth. Warren Buffett, a skeptic regarding organized religion, and J. Paul Getty, who was as noted for his extramarital liaisons as his several marriages, displayed no less determination than Perot and Walton in building their fortunes. The real point for aspiring billionaires is that innovation, the route chosen by Perot and Walton, requires exceptional resistance to the levelers. If you sincerely want to be superrich, you cannot let yourself be deterred by the unavoidable fact that change upsets people.

Ross Perot

Eagles don't flock. You have to find them one at a time.[1]

Ross Perot is an extraordinary figure, even in a peer group composed of the remarkable and, in some cases, outlandish characters who have made a billion dollars or more. Perot has distinguished himself as an entrepreneur, a philanthropist, a corporate gadfly, and a political crusader. In 1986, Prince Charles, heir to the British throne, flew to Dallas to present Perot with the Winston Churchill Foundation leadership award. Prime Minister Margaret Thatcher of Great Britain and the American statesman Averell Harriman were the only two previous recipients. With less fanfare, Perot has also proven himself a shrewd practitioner of Texas-style horse-trading.

Since 1969, when he organized an effort to try to free American prisoners of war in North Vietnam, Perot has rarely been out of the public eye. A best-selling book (*On Wings of Eagles*, by Ken Follett), as well as a television miniseries, described his 1979 formation of a commando unit to rescue two employees held for ransom in a Teheran prison by the Iranian government. In 1980, Perot chaired a Texas task force that led to the passage of tougher penalties for drug abuse. Three years later, he headed a statewide drive for educational reform. Braving the wrath of rabid high school football fans, Perot pushed through a clause banishing students from the gridiron if they failed their academic courses. (The joy of this legislative victory was tempered by accusations of grandstanding, as well as a perception in the Lone Star State, according to humorist Molly Ivins, that he had gone "seven bubbles off plumb, crazy as a peach-orchard boar.")[2]

In 1992, Perot ran for President of the United States as an independent, despite his long-standing protests that he had too little patience with red tape to make a good politician. "Nothing, nothing, nothing" could induce him to run for public office, he had said, explaining that he could achieve more outside the governmental sphere. He added that his abrasiveness would wear thin if he were to be elected.[3] Even so, voter preference surveys in the spring put his support at 34 percent, enough to win in a close three-way race. Perot slipped in the polls as the electorate became more familiar with his quirky personality, but he finished with 19 percent of the popular vote. That represented the strongest showing by an independent or third-party candidate since Theodore Roosevelt's Bull Moose campaign of 1912. Undeterred by his loss, Perot again threw his hat into the ring in 1996. By that time, he had spent an estimated $80 million of his own fortune in pursuit of the White House.[4]

Perot's philanthropic activities have been no less audacious than his decision to seek the presidency in his first campaign for public office. He paid $1.5 million for one of the four copies of the Magna Carta, which he loaned to the National Archives to be displayed along with the U.S. Constitution and Bill of Rights. When a number of veterans expressed dissatisfaction with the official Vietnam Memorial in Washington, D.C., Perot underwrote the cost of erecting a more heroic sculpture 120 feet away.

Neither Perot's political ventures nor his charitable undertakings, however, could quite overshadow his stellar achievements in the business world. He ranked behind only Sam Walton in the 1985 *Forbes* tabulation of richest Americans. (The governor of Texas demanded to know why Perot could not reach the top spot, joking that his second-place finish was an embarrassment to the state.)[5]

A pioneer in computer services, Perot built Electronic Data Systems (EDS) from scratch to nearly $2 billion in stock market capitalization in less than a decade. Before age 40, he amassed a personal net worth of $1.5 billion. Through selling EDS to General Motors in 1984 for a combination of cash and stock, he became the automaker's largest shareholder, as well as a director. In characteristic fashion, Perot also became a thorn in the side of GM's management, which then bought his stock at a $350 million premium to the market to induce him to go away. Leave he did, but as soon as his noncompete agreement expired he founded Perot Systems and went head-to-head against EDS. Despite giving away vast sums to educational causes and sitting out the 1990s equity bull market with a big concentration in bonds, Perot had an estimated net worth of $3.7 billion in 1998.[6]

An Early Introduction to Trading

The Perot saga began in 1930 in Texarkana, a town split down the middle by the Texas-Arkansas border. It was a colorful place, habituated by outlaws who might need to escape across the state line in a hurry. Among Perot's early heroes was a rodeo cowboy who won the world's calf roping championship, even though he lost three fingers in the event. "Now that's my definition of tough," he later commented.[7] Sometime around age seven, Perot began breaking horses for his father. The experience left him with the trademark of a nose flattened out by repeated fractures.

Business was a constant topic of discussion in the Perot household. From his father, cotton broker and horse trader Gabriel Ross Perot, the youngster imbibed valuable lessons in negotiating. As he recalled years later, a farmer would drive up to the Perot homestead and announce, "Gabe, I've got that horse you always wanted." Regardless of how eager he was to buy the animal, Ross's father would matter-of-factly reply, "What horse?" Then, he would ask the farmer to state his price and, no matter what the answer was, indicate that he had no interest. Having traveled 25 miles, the farmer did not want to turn right around. "Dammit, Gabe, aren't you going to look at him?" he would sputter. Strolling outside, the canny trader would compliment the horse but continue to insist that he did not want to buy it. A few days later, Gabriel Perot and the farmer would settle on a figure, perhaps a third lower than the seller's initial price.[8]

Early on, Gabriel's son displayed a talent for selling, which he employed in hawking garden seeds, Christmas cards, used saddles, and the *Saturday Evening Post*.[9] By the time he was 12, he closed his first major deal. At the time, the *Texarkana Gazette* made no effort to sell subscriptions in a mostly black slum called New Town. Depending on who tells the story, either the area was considered too dangerous or it was assumed that none of the residents could read. Perot proposed to open up the untouched territory, on the condition that he be allowed to retain 70 percent of the subscription fees, instead of the customary 30 percent. Figuring there was nothing to lose, the circulation department accepted his terms.

Beginning at 4:00 every morning, Perot covered 20 miles on horseback[10] or bicycle before heading to school. "I had a second route in the afternoon," he remembered years later. "My mother had serious reservations about the last stop—a house of prostitution. I delivered papers to the door, during the daylight hours, to these women. They were always courteous and paid me promptly."[11] Before long, he was clearing $40 a week. Alarmed by the small fortune that the lad was taking home, the circulation department unilaterally cut his payout to the standard 30 percent. Young Perot was not easily intimidated, however. He marched straight into the office of the *Gazette*'s publisher and announced, "I made a deal with your paper and here it is. I've kept my end of the deal and your paper's reneged. I just want to know if your paper is going to keep its commitments." Perot not only held the paper to the original agreement, but learned a valuable business lesson as well: "Go to the man who can say yes or no."[12]

After high school, Perot enrolled at Texarkana Junior College, expecting to move on to the University of Texas to study law. He was elected class president in 1947, but his true ambition was to attend the U.S.

Naval Academy. Determined though he was, he failed to obtain the required appointment by a member of Congress until luck intervened. An aide to W. Lee "Pappy" O'Daniel of Texas reminded the retiring senator that among his unfinished business was the filling of a vacancy at the Naval Academy. O'Daniel asked if anybody wanted the appointment, whereupon he was informed that a boy from Texarkana had been angling for a spot for several years. "Well, give it to him," replied the senator, without ever hearing Perot's name.[13]

The World beyond Texarkana

At Annapolis, Perot's grades ranked him only around the middle of his class. His energetic nature and engaging personality quickly grabbed attention, however. "What Ross lacked in physical size," observed the editors of his senior yearbook, "he more than adequately replaced by his capacity to make friends and influence people."[14] Besides excelling in debating and heading the committee that enforced the Academy's honor code, Perot won notice as coxswain of the whaleboat crew. "Perot was the smallest one in the boat as the coxswain, but we won every race with him yelping at us," one rower later remembered.[15] On the strength of his sheer dynamism, Perot was twice elected class president. (A future chief of naval operations, who was in the same class, had to be content with the vice presidency.)

Classmates regarded Perot as a shoo-in for admiral and some even speculated that he would one day be President of the United States. His ambitious nature suggested that he would not disappoint them. On a 1953 visit to Texarkana, Perot told a boyhood chum that he was thinking of volunteering for the Marines. Why on earth would he want to do that, the friend demanded to know, with junior officers being killed at a horrendous rate in the Korean War? "It's risky," conceded Perot, "but if you survive you get to be a general faster."[16]

In the end, though, Perot entered the Navy, which proved to be less than an ideal field of operations for the independent Texan. Although he got off to a good start, swiftly advancing to chief engineer of a destroyer, he soon found himself in a personality clash with a new commander. Reassigned to less prestigious duty aboard an aircraft carrier, Perot decided to leave the military at the conclusion of his tour. "The promotion system and the waiting-in-line concept were just sort of incompatible with my desire to be measured and judged by what I could produce," he later said.[17] At the time, he also complained about the immorality he observed in the Navy, a stark contrast to his own abstention from liquor, tobacco, profanity, and promiscuity.[18]

Having been exposed to primitive computers in the Navy, Perot initially planned to join Texas Instruments, then a small high technology company based in Dallas.[19] Shortly before his Navy hitch ended, however, he met an IBM executive, who urged him to apply for a sales job. Signing on as a trainee, Perot quickly adopted the company's code of fierce dedication to the customer's needs. During one problem-ridden installation, he spent several days feeding stacks of data cards into the computer. Sleeping on a cot that he had moved into the area, he awoke to feed in another stack every time the clickety-clack of the reader ceased.

After finishing at the top of his sales training class, Perot quickly began landing orders at some of the toughest accounts in IBM's Dallas sales branch. By exhaustively studying the prospect's business, Perot invariably managed to present a solid case for purchasing or leasing a mainframe computer. With the intensity of a pit bull, he sought solutions to every problem that stood in the way of a sale. To sell a huge machine to Southwestern Life Insurance Company, for instance, he canvassed until he found other customers willing to buy the computer time that Southwestern could not use.

Perot eventually became a victim of his own success, however. In 1961, IBM introduced a new commission plan. The company set a quota for each salesperson, based on an assessment of sales prospects for the year. By meeting the quota, the salesperson earned a full allocation from the bonus pool. Under the plan, the only way to earn more than the allocated bonus was to meet the quota twice over and receive a double allocation. At the start of 1962, it so happened that Perot was on the verge of selling the company's most expensive model, the IBM 7090, to an engineering school. When he closed the deal in January, he made his quota for the year. That left him no further upside in compensation, barring the unlikely event of selling another 7090 before year-end.

Contrary to the popular version of the story, achieving the IBM quota in January was not unprecedented. Thomas Watson Jr., the son of IBM's founder, once met his sales target on January 1. All the same, the new commission plan rankled Perot. Just as in the Navy, he was frustrated by a system that prevented him from advancing according to his ability. Climbing up the corporate ladder seemed an unappealing prospect, nor did senior management show interest in Perot's proposal to expand IBM's tiny computer services division.[20]

The only solution was to go into business for himself. Perot came to that realization in a barbershop, when a quotation from Henry David Thoreau, reprinted in *Reader's Digest*, caught his eye: "The mass of men lead lives of quiet desperation." Resolving that he would never let the phrase apply to himself, Perot resigned from IBM. On his 32d birthday, he incorporated Electronic Data Systems (EDS), having borrowed $1,000 from his wife's bank account for the incorporation fee. To keep some money coming in during the start-up phase, Perot became a data processing consultant to a health insurance plan, Blue Cross–Blue Shield of Texas. In addition to "keeping the back door open," as Kirk Kerkorian has described the technique of limiting risk, Perot demonstrated several other classic billionaires' methods at EDS and his subsequent ventures.

$\sim$

At the time of EDS's 1962 birth, the computer industry's services segment (as opposed to the manufacture and sale of hardware) was limited to basic processes such as billing and payroll. "Service bureaus" collected data from their customers, processed it on their own computers, and returned it the following day. Perot's innovation was to tackle more complex tasks, including installation of systems and management of the user's difficult transition from manual to automated data processing.[21] After landing a contract to develop a sales route accounting system for snack food producer Frito-Lay, Perot's young company grew rapidly and quickly became profitable.

The unique capabilities of EDS made it the right company at the right time when the federal government introduced Medicare in 1965. Not only did an unexpected flood of claims swamp health insurance providers, but fraud proliferated as a result of inadequate controls. The Texas Blue Cross–Blue Shield Medicare program, designed by EDS, became a showcase for efficient processing of claims, opening the door at health care plans throughout the country.[22]

By 1967, EDS had pioneered facilities management, another entirely new business. Perot's teams took charge of companies' faltering computer centers—equipment, staff, and all—and turned them into effective operations. Facilities management tended to retain customers for EDS for the long haul, unlike the company's original business of getting systems up and running. Frequently, the result of a successful installation was a decision by the customer to take the now smoothly running operation in-house. Far from being an inspiration of Perot's, the new, improved business model was thrust upon EDS by a corporate customer in desperate need of help. Even if Perot did not hatch the idea of facilities management on his own, however, he lost little time in recognizing its profit potential.

$\sim$

Along with his keen instinct for turning a profit, a key ingredient in Perot's success was his ability to build an organization. He recruited self-starters like himself and let them operate with a minimum of bureaucratic rules. Authority to make decisions, Perot believed, must remain in the field, rather than at a massive corporate headquarters. (Electronic Data Systems had the world's shortest procedural manual: "Do what makes sense.")[23] The company's compensation plan emphasized stock options, ultimately resulting in the creation of more than a hundred millionaires at EDS.[24] Employees responded to the work style and financial incentives with an intensity that gave EDS a powerful competitive edge. Adopting the motto "whatever it takes," they put in excruciatingly long hours on projects that sometimes kept them away from home for months at a time.

Perot's charisma accounted in part for the intense dedication of EDS engineers and salespeople. He inspired the troops with his tenacity, as well as mottoes such as, "Eagles don't flock. You have to find them one at a time." There was more to the cohesiveness of EDS than the leader's personality, however. Perot regarded loyalty as a two-way street. This was not mere corporate lip service, as he demonstrated most dramatically in Operation HOTFOOT (Help Our Two Friends out of Teheran), the 1979 rescue of two EDS employees unlawfully held in an Iranian prison. On a less spectacular scale, Perot went the extra mile to help managers through medical crises and to show appreciation for spouses who had to endure the strain created by EDS's intense work ethic. It was not unusual for Perot to show up at the maternity ward when a child was born in the EDS family.

Another key to EDS's sensational success in its early years was low overhead. The company did not own a computer before 1965, doing its processing on rented equipment until then. Its consultant teams worked on customers' premises, so EDS needed no office space. Staff meetings took place in Perot's Blue Cross office, which he rented for $100 a month. (When the fledgling company finally moved into its own head-quarters with its name out front, passersby allegedly mistook the building for a restaurant named "Ed's.")[25]

Thanks to the minimal need for capital, Perot retained 81 percent of EDS's stock until it went public in 1968. The rest did not go to venture capitalists, but to engineers whom Perot lured to the company with equity participation. As with Bill Gates several years later, creation of a wildly successful business was only half the task of climbing to billionaire status. Holding on to a large chunk of the equity was no less important.

Also significant was the enormous effort that Perot put into getting a good price in EDS's initial public offering (IPO). Unused to the ways of Wall Street, he began with the assumption that investment bankers had a standard formula for pricing new issues. To his dismay, he found a wide divergence among the 17 underwriters that submitted proposals to EDS. One firm recommended pricing the offering at 30 times earnings, while most of the others were scattered over a range of 60 to 90 times. Studying the results of a couple dozen other high technology IPOs, Perot was struck by the amount of money typically left on the table. In many cases, the stocks had been priced at 30 to 90 times earnings, but doubled or even tripled on the first day of trading. "Those companies suffered an ir-recoverable loss by offering too low," Perot concluded.[26] Puzzling as well to a Texan weaned on horse-trading ploys was the cautious language of IPO prospectuses, which seemed to him designed to dissuade buyers. Se-curities laws required disclosure of every material risk in an offering, even some that sounded far-fetched to entrepreneurs.

To put the valuation question into perspective, large run-ups in prices of new shares have remained common occurrences since the time of the EDS offering. Investment bankers and academicians explain the phenomenon in several different ways. For one thing, initial offerings typically involve only a small fraction of a company's shares. A steep price rise following the offering can sharpen investors' appetites for sub-sequent public offerings by the company. Underwriters also have to be conscious of state blue-sky laws, aimed at preventing unjustifiably high valuations on the sale of new shares. In any case, it is notoriously diffi-cult to value rapidly growing high-tech companies, as illustrated by the wild gyrations in Internet stocks during the late 1990s. Furthermore, an evaluation of EDS at the time of its IPO had to take into account not only the company's vast prospects, but also the substantial risks. Fully 64 percent of the company's fiscal 1968 revenues came from just three customers. Any one of them might decide, like EDS's first customer, Frito-Lay, not to renew its service contract. In short, even if a new issue skyrockets after its initial sale, there are few objective benchmarks by which to demonstrate that the investment bankers goofed.

Financial theorizing held little interest for Ross Perot, however. Like other billionaires who grew up far from New York, such as John D. Rockefeller Sr. and Warren Buffett, he was skeptical of Wall Street. One of the few investment bankers who impressed Perot was Charles Allen of Allen & Company. Perot paid him the supreme compliment by saying that like his own father, Allen had "the style of the great cattle traders."[27] In the end, Perot awarded the underwriting mandate to the most optimistic firm of the lot. R. W. Pressprich and Co., which he had never heard of until then, assured him that EDS could be launched at 100 times earnings.

En route to signing the papers that would seal the arrangement, Perot recalled warnings he had heard regarding investment bankers' bait-and-switch tactics. "I suppose you're now going to tell me that the deal can't be done at 100 times earnings," he grumbled to Pressprich's Ken Langone. Winking at Perot's wife, Margot, Langone replied, "Ross, you're absolutely right. It shouldn't be at 100 times earnings." Furious, Perot snapped, "You're just like everybody else." Margot interjected, "Dear, maybe you should let him finish." Perot obliged by asking Langone what the earnings multiple ought to be. "Oh, maybe 116," he answered. "There's so much demand, I think we should raise the price."[28]

Ultimately, EDS came to market at a near-record 118 times earnings, or $16.50 a share. Despite Perot's resolute drive to get top dollar for the shares he sold in the IPO, the price immediately skyrocketed in frenzied buying of high-tech stocks. Before trading closed on the day of the offering, September 12, 1968, EDS shares had risen to $23. Over the next year, EDS zoomed to $160 a share, representing a mind-boggling price-earnings multiple of 500. At the peak of the go-go market in 1969, Perot's remaining nine million EDS shares were worth $1.5 billion on paper. He had "pulled off perhaps the most spectacular personal coup in the history of American business," in *Fortune*'s estimation. "Probably no other man ever made so much money so fast."[29]

Perot achieved a remarkable financial feat of quite a different sort when the inevitable bear market arrived in 1970. In a single day, April 22, his net worth plunged by almost half a billion dollars. Perot downplayed the significance of the event, consistent with his claim that making money had never been his goal at EDS.[30] "The day I made Eagle Scout," he once said, "was more important to me than the day I discovered I was a billionaire."[31]

The year after his spectacular one-day loss, Perot suffered another setback when he attempted to save duPont Glore Forgan, a failing brokerage house. Perot's financial muscle, along with his expertise in the sort of order-processing problems that were sinking duPont Glore Forgan, seemed to make him a logical candidate for the mission. On the other hand, it was a curious undertaking for someone so suspicious of Wall Street's ways. In addition, EDS's heavy recruiting of ex-Marines had created a gung-ho ethos that struck freewheeling brokers and investment bankers as militaristic and retrograde. Perot's attempt to impose the EDS dress code and ban on facial hair added to the culture clash. "His style left something to be desired," observed *Barron's* columnist Alan Abelson. "He came across as a super–Boy Scout."[32]

Perot subsequently claimed that he had agreed to the rescue effort only out of patriotism. The regulators, he explained, told him that a failure by duPont Glore Forgan would jeopardize the financial system.[33] In any event, Perot's can-do convictions could not save duPont Glore Forgan. Equally unavailing was a merger with the Walston & Co., which created the largest retail brokerage system excluding Merrill Lynch.

In the end, the combined enterprise went down, taking with it more than $60 million that Perot had poured into the effort. Undeterred, he continued to approach his business activities with his characteristic vigor, but he did not repeat the error of making a huge financial commitment to an unfamiliar business. The next major venture he launched was a direct competitor to the business that initially put him into the billionaire category. Before reprising his success in computer services, however, he scored big with his father's tactics.

~

On his 54th birthday, exactly 22 years after he incorporated Electronic Data Systems, Perot accepted a $2.55 billion buyout offer from General Motors. His initial response to GM's overture had been to regard the automobile producer as a potentially huge new customer for computer services. General Motors chairman Roger Smith, however, was determined to effect a business combination, hoping that the acquisition of EDS's aggressive, technologically advanced spirit would galvanize his slower-moving organization. Drawing on the lessons he had learned from his horse trader father, Perot held out for a highly advantageous deal. The buyer, he recognized, was more highly motivated than the seller.[34]

Selling EDS to GM returned Perot to exactly the sort of bureaucratic environment he had found unbearable in the Navy and at IBM. On the other hand, as a director and the company's largest shareholder, he saw a possibility of revitalizing GM and the entire U.S. automobile industry. Clearly, U.S. carmakers needed a tune-up, with vigorous Japanese competition sapping their profits.

Perot and Smith clashed from the outset, however. Despite assurances that Perot would continue to have a free hand running EDS, Smith attempted to jettison the subsidiary's stock option plan. The problem, according to Perot, was that it enabled many EDS employees to earn more than Smith could.[35] Perot again ran afoul of Smith by opposing the $5.2 billion acquisition of Hughes Aircraft, displaying independence not expected from a GM director.[36] To his dismay, Perot discovered that the directors had not voted against the corporation's chairman since the 1930s. Before long, he was ridiculing the board as Smith's "pet rock." He declared in a press interview that the directors ought to buy GM cars, instead of receiving specially fixed up vehicles as perks, in order to understand the ordinary customer's situation. Perot spoke of "nuking the GM system" by exiling managers from their expensive offices to the plants, where they would be close to designers and workers.[37] He jabbed at GM's huge capital spending program: "We are spending billions to develop new cars. This isn't a moon shot; it's just a car."[38] Most of all, Perot decried GM's bureaucratic ways:

> The first EDSer to see a snake kills it. At GM, first thing you do is organize a committee on snakes. Then you bring in a consultant who knows a lot about snakes. . . . Then you talk about it for a year.[39]

Annoyed by the public airing of criticisms, Smith tried to maneuver Perot off GM's board. Perot responded by promising a battle royal, causing the chairman to shift tactics. First, Smith attempted to rid himself of the gadfly by selling EDS to AT&T.[40] When that deal fell through, he offered to buy back Perot's GM stock.

Smith's back was to the wall. Profits were at a low point, creating the otherwise unimaginable prospect of General Motors falling victim to a hostile takeover. Horse trader Perot once again pressed his advantage. "I just kept making obscene demands," he said, "and they kept agreeing to them."[41] When the dickering was finished, Perot had extracted a buyout price almost double the stock's prevailing market quotation.[42] The nearly $750 million proceeds to Perot represented a tripling of the value of his GM stake in the space of just two years (during which the company's condition markedly deteriorated).[43] In return, Perot granted the comparatively minor concessions of agreeing not to launch a hostile takeover of GM for five years or to form a for-profit competitor of EDS for three years. (He had to wait only 18 months before hiring EDS employees, however.) General Motors and Perot also consented to refrain from publicly criticizing each other, a pact that broke down almost the moment the buyout was completed. Summing up his inability to change GM's direction, Perot said, "I took a calculated gamble that failed."[44]

No longer part of the company he had founded, Perot turned his focus to investments. In addition to bonds, he emphasized Texas real estate, where he perceived great bargains as a result of the mid-1980s plunge in oil and gas prices. He also dabbled in venture capital, taking a $20 million stake in NeXT Computer, a start-up by Apple Computer founder Steve Jobs, and passing on such dubious inventions as a flying car and a water-powered engine.[45] Perot's confrontation with GM was not over, however. As soon as the noncompete agreement expired, he founded a new computer services company, Perot Systems. To the consternation of GM management, he began to raid EDS for talent, much as he had cherry-picked IBM in the early days of EDS. Contentious litigation over interpretation of the noncompete agreement ensued, perhaps not entirely to the distaste of the pugnacious Perot.

The new venture enabled Perot to demonstrate that despite the passage of three decades since the initial public offering of EDS, he still had the ability to shake up the financial world. On February 1, 1999, an initial public offering of Perot Systems was priced at $16 a share. When trading commenced the next day, demand was so strong that the exchange officials were twice obliged to halt trading in the shares until an orderly market could be reestablished. Before the session was over, Perot Systems had soared from $27.50 to $43.50 a share. Never before had an initial public offering listed on the New York Stock Exchange doubled on its first day of trading.[46]

Taking into account IPOs of all kinds, the Perot Systems takeoff represented the 10th largest first-day gain ever for a United States stock. In subsequent sessions, the price briefly climbed as high as $85.75. True to form, Perot had held on to a large piece of the company through the IPO stage. His 38 percent stake was worth approximately $2.1 billion at the first week's close of $66.

Granted, the initial boom occurred in the context of investor euphoria over Internet stocks. Perot Systems was hardly a pure play, although Perot stressed in an interview that business-to-business sales via the Internet were a key to the company's growth.[47] In the two months following the IPO, Perot Systems shares fell by more than 50 percent from the $66 peak as investors began to sort out the computer services company's business profile. Nevertheless, at the age of 68, Perot had topped his own legend-making achievements of taking EDS public and extracting a huge payment to leave GM's board.

"Call Me Ross"

From his wrangling with the *Texarkana Gazette*'s circulation department to his second fabulously successful initial public offering, Ross Perot has remained remarkably unchanged from the straight arrow who left his hometown for Annapolis in 1949. Asked by a reporter whether he preferred being called a millionaire or a billionaire, he answered, "Call me Ross."[48] A longtime acquaintance, former Democratic National Committee chairman Robert Strauss, commented, "I've seen him around Presidents and the average guy on the street. He is no different in either place."[49] Perot buys his suits off the rack and shops at mass marketers Kmart and Sears, as well as the tonier Neiman-Marcus.[50] As a candidate for the highest office in the land in 1992, he pledged to stop for red lights instead of creating traffic jams with a Presidential motorcade. His personal means of conveyance at the time was an unchauffered seven-year-old Oldsmobile acquired during his stint with General Motors.

Characteristically, Perot ceased accepting his director's perk of receiving a new car every three months once he learned that the vehicles receive extra inspections before delivery to board members.[51] To get a clearer sense of the ordinary customer's experience, he traded in a 1979 Chevrolet for the 1985 Olds, personally haggling over the price at a dealership.[52]

In one of his few breaks from his past, Ross Perot allowed the pronunciation of his last name to be altered from "PEE-row" to the more logical "puh-ROW" during his Navy hitch. "The instructors and midshipmen at the Naval Academy pronounced it 'puh-ROW' when they first saw it, and I finally got tired of correcting everybody," he said. Perot had no part, however, in the addition of the initial H (for Henry) to his name. Shortly after EDS's initial public offering, a *Fortune* reporter dubbed him "H. Ross Perot," a formation reminiscent of "J. Paul Getty." (The same article referred to one of H. L. Hunt's sons in similarly affected style as "N. Bunker Hunt.")[53] Although Perot considered the three-piece name ostentatious and never used it himself, it proved unshakable.[54]

Curiously, the press also frequently refers to another famously unpretentious billionaire, Wayne Huizenga, with the initial H (for Harry). Sometimes the styling carries a sarcastic undertone, as in articles protesting his financially motivated breakup of the Florida Marlins championship baseball team. To his professional associates, Huizenga remains just plain Wayne. In fact, on arriving for an interview with Huizenga in 1993, a journalist was greeted by a cheerful, gum-chewing receptionist who asked, "You here to see Wayne?"[55] In the late 1960s, however, Huizenga wrote a letter to the editor of the *Fort Lauderdale News*, responding to an article entitled, "Who Raises Garbagemen?" The cofounder of Waste Management proudly recounted how his grandfather, a man "with a strong back and a weak sense of smell," had founded a waste-hauling dynasty. Proud grandson Wayne signed himself, "H. Wayne Huizenga," thereby lending a touch of grandeur to the lighthearted letter.[56]

Sam Walton

Most everything I've done I've copied from someone else.[57]

Like Ross Perot and Wayne Huizenga, Sam Walton maintained the common touch during and after his rise to the billionaire ranks. No one doubted that Walton genuinely delighted in visiting his Wal-Mart discount stores to lead employees (whom he insisted on calling "associates") in the company cheer. In his relentless grassroots search for ways to improve operations, he went so far as to flag down a Wal-Mart 18-wheeler and ride for a hundred miles, pumping the driver for ideas all the way. The driver had not expected to be called upon for a briefing, but like everyone at Wal-Mart, he knew that the boss would take his suggestions seriously.

Much of Walton's personal wardrobe came from his own mass merchandise chain, which he founded and built into the largest U.S. retailer. His residence in Wal-Mart's headquarters town of Bentonville, Arkansas, was impressive but far less lavish than he could have afforded. When a childhood friend from Walton's birthplace, Kingfisher, Oklahoma, came to visit, the billionaire picked him up in "an old car that had cuts on the dashboard"; an ancient, dirty carburetor rested on the floorboards. A titled British couple who traveled to Bentonville to discuss Wal-Mart's "Buy American" campaign was treated to a ride in Walton's pickup truck, famed as the vehicle for transporting his bird-hunting dogs.[58] Not surprisingly, the press had a field day with the spectacle of an unpretentious man in an obscure town who had risen to the top of the Forbes 400 list of wealthiest Americans. "The media usually portrayed me," Walton sighed, "as a really cheap, eccentric recluse, sort of a hillbilly who more or less slept with his dogs in spite of having billions of dollars stashed away in a cave."[59]

In fairness to the media, Sam Walton supplied lots of colorful, and frequently hokey, copy in the name of building employee morale and publicizing Wal-Mart. Most famously, in 1984, he bet the company's president that management could not produce a pretax profit margin greater than 8 percent. Walton lost the bet and, true to his word, settled up by dancing a hula on Wall Street, adorned in a grass skirt and Hawaiian shirt. At each year-end management meeting, former senior vice president Ron Loveless presented the Loveless Economic Indicator Report, which was based on the number of edible dead chickens he spied on roadsides. His charts and graphs showed that when times got hard, fewer edible specimens could be found.

Walton complained that the press, distracted by the hokum, missed the real story—namely, the principles underlying Wal-Mart's phenomenal success. Investors, similarly blinded, were slow to recognize Wal-Mart's potential for growth. For the first decade following its 1962 founding,

Wall Street largely dismissed the regional, small town–oriented retailer as the "couturier of the hillbillies."[60]

As late as 1971, Wal-Mart did not rank among the 71 largest discount chains in the United States. With just 25 discount stores (plus 13 outposts of Walton's earlier variety store business), the company registered sales of only $44 million, equivalent to a mere 2 percent of the revenues generated by Kmart's 488 stores. From that position far back in the pack, Wal-Mart raced ahead to overtake Kmart as the nation's largest discounter in November 1990. Early the next year, Walton's outfit displaced Sears as the largest U.S. retailer of any kind, registering $32.6 billion in sales.

Although a large segment of the press failed to appreciate Sam Walton's genius, business experts, money managers, and even his competitors were generous with their praise. In 1980, a panel of 50 securities analysts chose him as the most outstanding chief executive officer in the United States in an annual competition sponsored by *Financial World*. The same publication's survey named him chief executive officer of the decade in 1989. In 1990, the United Shareholders Association, a nonprofit organization focusing on shareholders' rights, ranked Wal-Mart number one among 1,000 publicly held corporations, based on stock performance and management responsiveness to the interests of shareholders. Stanley Marcus of the department store retailer Neiman-Marcus called Walton "a prime exemplar of entrepreneurship."[61] Harry Cunningham, who as chief executive officer of S. S. Kresge Co. launched Wal-Mart's archrival, the Kmart discount chain, put it even more simply: "He is the greatest businessman of this century."[62]

~

In the estimation of the Reverend Billy Graham, a confidant of several Presidents, Sam Walton was not only an outstanding businessman, but also "one of the most remarkable Americans of the twentieth century" from any walk of life.[63] He seemed destined for greatness in some field from youth, during which he considered running for President and entering the insurance business. At 13, Walton became the youngest boy up to that time to attain the rank of Eagle Scout in Missouri, where his family moved in search of better opportunities during the Depression. (In other parallels with fellow Eagle Scout Ross Perot, young Sammy Walton honed his business skills by selling magazine subscriptions and operating a newspaper route.)

Standing just five feet nine, but showing fierce determination, Walton played guard on his high school's state champion basketball team and quarterbacked the football team to a state championship as well. "I didn't throw particularly well, but we were mostly a running team," he self-deprecatingly recalled. "And I was fairly slow for a back, but I was shifty, sometimes so shifty than I would fall down with a bunch of daylight in front of me."[64] (As a retailer years later, he again achieved success by relying on capable associates who compensated for his own shortcomings in areas such as accounting and technology.) Elected student body president, Walton immersed himself in a wide range of activities.

At the same time, Walton got his first direct exposure to the retailing business, working part-time in a five-and-ten-cent store. This retailing format (also known as the variety store), featured a wide range of low-priced merchandise such as housewares, toys, dry goods, and apparel. Prominent companies in the field included its originator, the F. W. Woolworth Company; S. S. Kresge, which later launched the Kmart discount chain; and the Ben Franklin chain, in which Walton began his career as a store owner.

Before going into business for himself, however, Walton spent four very busy years at the University of Missouri. He was elected president not only of his senior class, but also of a Sunday school group reputed to be the largest in the world, as well as a prestigious honor society. To help fund his education, he waited on tables in exchange for meals, worked as a lifeguard, and continued to manage his newspaper route of 160 *Columbia Missourian* subscribers. For several years running, Walton later recalled, he was the paper's top salesperson, earning an extra $500 of commissions each year by contracting for bulk sales at fraternity and sorority houses. (A few years later, Warren Buffett demonstrated similar entrepreneurial zeal in the newspaper delivery business, amassing five *Washington Post* routes and 500 customers.)

Walton hoped to go on to business school at the Wharton School at the University of Pennsylvania, but family finances were too tight. Instead, he signed on as a management trainee with J. C. Penney for $75 a week plus commissions. It was while working at this operator of junior department stores, a format that emphasized soft goods, that Walton settled on a career in retailing. He also commenced his lifelong habit of prowling competitors' stores for ideas—using his lunch hours for the purpose—and began devouring books on retailing. Walton continued these practices in his stateside military service during World War II. He checked out every retailing book in the Salt Lake City library and spent off-duty hours studying the Mormon Church's ZCMI department store.

As soon as the war ended, Walton contacted a fraternity brother who was working in the shoe department of Butler Brothers, franchisor of the Ben Franklin variety store chain, as well as the Federated Stores chain of small department stores. The pair hatched a plan to buy a Federated store in St. Louis, but Walton's wife vetoed the scheme. She disliked the idea of a partnership, based on unhappy experiences in her own family, and refused to live in a city of more than 10,000 residents. By necessity, therefore, Walton set on the course that became a cornerstone of his success, namely, an orientation to tiny towns that the major retailing chains declined to enter. On September 1, 1945, he opened his first store, a 5,000-square-foot Ben Franklin franchise in Newport, Arkansas, a cotton-farming town of 7,000.

From that humble beginning, Walton built the nation's largest retailing company and reached the top of the Forbes 400 rankings. His methods represent a veritable checklist of the techniques that can be culled from studying the careers of the most successful moneymakers. In most cases, he carried the concept far beyond limits that ordinary mortals would find reasonable.

∼

In light of Walton's role in the retailing industry's discounting revolution, it is appropriate to examine his career in a chapter entitled "Do Business in a New Way." At the same time, he proudly proclaimed that he invented almost nothing. "Most everything I've done I've copied from someone else," he acknowledged.[65] Walton humbly attributed his success to spending more time than anyone else shopping in his competitors' stores and adopting the best of what he saw there. Like Bill Gates, who turned other people's good ideas about computer operating systems into immensely profitable businesses, Walton made up in intense drive and competitiveness whatever he lacked in originality.

Borrowing the best industry practices was a key to creating the largest independently owned variety store chain in the United States, a distinction Walton attained before achieving still greater success as a discounter. He converted his operation to the self-service format after reading that two Minnesota Ben Franklin stores had introduced the concept. (Ever meticulous, Walton made the long trip north by bus to observe firsthand the new style of doing business.) From the Sterling variety store chain, he borrowed the idea of replacing the standard wooden merchandise displays with all-metal fixtures.

Despite his success with the variety store format, Walton became convinced that discounting was the wave of the future and to ignore it would be fatal. The strategy boiled down to taking small markups in order to offer low prices to consumers, thereby increasing sales volume. Large sales made it possible for a discount chain to obtain volume discounts (reductions in price per unit) from suppliers, enabling it to gain even more market share through low prices to shoppers. The huge volume could generate high profits despite the small markups, as long as the retailer held down its operating costs, such as labor, rent, and advertising.

Adapted from the supermarket business, the discounting format was introduced in hard goods (appliances, cameras, luggage, and so on) in the early 1940s. Apparel discounting began in mill stores, located in abandoned textile mills, such as the Ann & Hope store founded in Cumberland, Rhode Island, in 1953. Walton visited Ann & Hope's founders, Martin and Irwin Chase, in preparation for launching his own discounting operation in 1962. He also called on a number of other discounters, introducing himself (according to one account) as a "little country boy from Arkansas," then relentlessly pumping the stores' operators for information about the ins and outs of discount retailing.[66] Even after Wal-Mart was up and running, Walton capitalized on the fact that few discounters regarded his small, regional outfit as a competitor. By his estimate, he visited more headquarters of discounting chains than anyone else in history. Out of curiosity, if nothing else, the managers frequently let him in and freely shared information about their methods.

Recognizing the difficulties of creating a new chain from scratch, Walton first tried to persuade Butler Brothers to back him with its existing infrastructure. Rebuffed, Walton next approached Herbert R. Gibson Sr., founder of Gibson Products Company, which had built a successful discounting chain in the Southwest on the motto, "Buy it low, stack it high, sell it cheap." Walton showed up at Gibson's Dallas headquarters unannounced and waited all afternoon to see the chief. Gibson listened to Walton's proposal to buy some franchises, then asked, "Do you have $100,000?" When Walton admitted he did not, Gibson replied that it took that much capital to buy in carload lots, as his franchisees did. "You're not fixed to do business with us. Good-bye," he concluded.[67] Once again, necessity took charge and Walton started the venture that would eventually make his family the primary owners of the country's most successful discounter.

About the only original idea Walton could claim in his approach to discounting was his focus on towns of 5,000 to 25,000, which fell below the larger chains' radar screens during Wal-Mart's formative years. Having operated in small towns since 1945, Walton was convinced that they had greater business potential than the bigger operators believed. Wal-Mart's strategy proved immensely successful in the long run. The company's stores ringed large metropolitan areas and prospered as the population migrated outward from the center cities. While Walton may have arrived at the idea independently, his strategy of "thinking small" merely carried a bit further a concept that was being adopted around the same time by retailers in other parts of the country. Minneapolis-based Gamble-Skogmo began locating 20,000- to 40,000-square-foot Tempo Discount Centers in country towns in 1964. A company executive explained, "If you're first, you're apt to be alone. Most towns we're in won't take two stores of that size."[68] F. W. Woolworth's Woolco discount chain placed a few units in cities of 25,000 to 75,000, while San Diego–based Fed-Mart put stores in towns of 12,000 to 35,000. In fact, the wake-up call that alerted Walton to the threat that discounting posed to his variety store business was the entry into northeast Arkansas of Gibson Products, which focused on cities of 20,000 to 50,000.[69]

Aside from the question of the size of the targeted marketing area, almost everything about Wal-Mart was borrowed. Walton selected the chain's name, which was suggested by the manager of his original Bentonville variety store, because of its similarity to "Fed-Mart." Speaking of that outfit's founder, Sol Price, Walton said, "I guess I've stolen—I actually prefer the word 'borrowed'—as many ideas from Sol Price as from anybody in the business."[70] Two decades after the founding of Wal-Mart, Walton copied Price yet again by launching Sam's Club stores to compete in the warehouse club category. Price had introduced this deep-discount format, selling everything from food to appliances under one roof, through the Price Club chain in 1976.

The Ben Franklin chain in which Walton began his career as a store owner apparently was the source of one concept essential to Wal-Mart's successful growth, the use of distribution centers. By receiving bulk shipments at these locations, then reshipping them to its stores, the company achieved cost savings through centralization of receiving and processing procedures.[71] Earlier, Wal-Mart had adopted Ben Franklin's simple accounting system, including "beat yesterday" ledger books that facilitated day-by-day sales comparisons with year-earlier performance. "I wasn't all that great at accounting in college," Walton explained, "so I just did it according to their book."[72]

Even Walton's legendary magic touch with employees drew heavily on borrowed notions. For example, Wal-Mart got tremendous mileage out of referring to hourly employees as associates. His first full-time employer, J. C. Penney, had used the same terminology, although Walton said the more direct source of the idea was Lewis Company, an English retailer that he once visited en route to the Wimbledon tennis tournament. Penney's founder, James Cash Penney, had allowed store managers to buy small portions of the ownership of their stores, a practice sometimes misconstrued as a Wal-Mart–patented method. Penney also kept close to customers and picked up ideas for adoption throughout his chain by frequent visits to his stores. Walton updated the practice, which was essential to successful operation of a widely dispersed chain, by learning to pilot his own plane. After visiting South Korean and Japanese factories in 1975 and observing the morale-building effects of group calisthenics and company cheers, he incorporated a cheerleading session into his store visits. (Walton: "Gimme a W!" Associates: "W!" and so on through the Wal-Mart name, with Walton shouting, when he got to the hyphen, "Gimme a squiggly!" and wiggling his hips.)

"What sets us apart," Walton said in explaining Wal-Mart's success, "is that we train people to be merchants. We let them see all the numbers so they know exactly how they're doing within the store and within the company; they know their cost, their markup, their overhead, and their profit."[73] Deeply involving workers at all levels in the store's success was indeed a distinctive feature of the Wal-Mart operation. In the late 1970s, the company agreed to share with the associates the benefits of efforts to reduce shrinkage, the disappearance of inventory through damage, shoplifting, internal theft, or faulty records. By 1984, Wal-Mart had reduced shrinkage to 1.4 percent of sales, well below the industry average of 2.2 percent.[74]

Profit sharing and stock-purchase programs also served as effective motivators all up and down the organization. These fringe benefits were a testament to Walton's pragmatism and ability to learn as a businessman. In his early days in the variety store business, by his own admission, he was so obsessed with beating the competition's prices that he was stingy when it came to paying hourly employees.[75]

Aside from wringing maximum performance from its people, perhaps the most important element in Wal-Mart's overtaking of its competitors during the 1980s was its willingness to embrace new technologies. By computerizing its inventory management and being early to adopt the Universal Product Code (or bar code) scanning system, the company was able to maintain its frenetic growth without spinning out of control. Even in the area of technology, though, Wal-Mart's edge derived from the positive corporate culture created by its founder. If the environment had been less open to challenging senior management, Walton's personal reluctance to spend on new systems would have prevented Wal-Mart from embracing state-of-the-art techniques. Instead of squelching ideas through a hierarchical structure, however, Walton encouraged the internal debate that eventually won him over.

Kmart, by contrast, fell disastrously behind in computerizing its inventory system because of an organizational inability to question top-level decisions. Harry Cunningham's successor as chairman sided with the store managers, who viewed computerization as a centralizing move that threatened their authority. Given the strictly top-down culture that had always characterized the company, no other group dared to oppose the chief's decision to stick with outmoded, handwritten inventory records.[76]

Walton said that the most exciting phase of his career was Wal-Mart's period of extraordinary growth during the 1970s. Between 1970 and 1980, the company expanded from 32 to 276 stores, while sales grew from $31 million to $1.2 billion. By 1990, the totals were 1,525 stores (including Sam's Clubs) and $25.8 billion of sales. Walton remarked, "It was the retail equivalent of a real gusher: the whole thing, as they say in Oklahoma and Texas, just sort of blowed."[77]

In his race for growth, Walton personally scouted potential new store locations in the airplane he piloted on his store visits. Flying over a town that he had targeted for expansion, he identified an ideal piece of farmland to acquire by observing traffic patterns and the direction of population growth, as indicated by new residential construction. He then came in for a landing, sought out the owner, and struck a real estate deal on the spot.

Wal-Mart honed its new store opening techniques to perfection, but also made strategic acquisitions to maintain its rapid growth. For instance, the company bought three Howard Discount Centers from Howard-Gibco Corporation of Texarkana in 1975. In 1977, Walton bought a 16-store discount chain operating in Missouri and Illinois, Mohr Super Value, and converted the outlets to Wal-Marts. He added the 104-store Big-K chain in 1981, making an attractive purchase after the 71-year-old retailer overextended itself through an acquisition and construction of an expensive corporate headquarters. After entering the warehouse club segment, Wal-Mart acquired the Midwest-based, 27-store Wholesale Club chain. When the time came to begin entering larger cities, Walton bought the 21 D. H. Holmes department stores to gain a foothold in New Orleans. In short, Sam Walton's success had a touch of the industry consolidation magic for which Wayne Huizenga became famous.

Starting with more limited resources than his competitors, Walton was forced to operate differently to achieve his growth objectives. Initially, Wal-Mart built stores only within one day's driving distance of its single distribution center in Bentonville. Operationally, the key benefit was the ability to resupply stores quickly, thereby keeping the shelves stocked while also avoiding excess inventory. From a strategic standpoint, densely packing the territory with stores discouraged competition and maximized Wal-Mart's name recognition. Repeating the success formula, Wal-Mart added distribution centers in other regions and densely filled in the territory around them.

Walton got the most out of his resources by running his stores with lean staffs. Constantly in need of additional managers for his rapidly increasing number of stores, he kept his eyes peeled for entry-level workers who displayed high potential as merchandisers and managers of people. With as little as six months' experience, a go-getter could get promoted to assistant manager, a much swifter career path than other retailing chains deemed advisable.

$\sim$

Although Sam Walton was careful about spending money, he understood the need to take risks in order to achieve greatly. For a man already operating the nation's largest independent variety store chain, entering the discount store business was a high-risk/high-potential-reward proposition. In 1962, the year he opened the first Wal-Mart in Rogers, Arkansas, 146 discount retailers went bankrupt, according to Dun & Bradstreet. The following year, the number of casualties climbed to 158.

Earlier, when Walton was running his first variety store in Newport, Arkansas, he learned that his main competitor planned to expand by buying out the lease on an adjacent Kroger grocery store. Rushing to his car, Walton sped 140 miles to the Hot Springs home of the store's owner and bought out the lease ahead of his rival. At that point, he had no idea what he would do with the property. Ultimately, he opened a minuscule department store. The venture never proved very profitable, but Walton achieved his purpose of preventing his competitor from getting the 2,500-square-foot space.

The growing number of stores and expansion of Wal-Mart's market area eventually induced Walton to take a huge risk on technology. Telephone lines, with their capacity limitations, were beginning to pose a constraint in collecting the vast amounts of data required to keep tabs on operations. In 1983, Wal-Mart's computer chief proposed a solution: a private satellite system, capable of transmitting not only voice and data, but also video broadcasts of Walton leading the company cheer. The technology was not really proven and the cost was huge for a company of Wal-Mart's size at the time. Nevertheless, Walton gave the project the green light. Predictably, construction costs ran significantly over budget. When the system was finally completed, it broke down frequently until technicians worked out the bugs. In the end, however, the gamble paid off in spades. With the largest privately owned satellite communications network in the United States, Wal-Mart reaped tremendous benefits in such varied uses as tracking delivery trucks, transmitting training videos, and speeding up the processing of credit card transactions. Savings realized through detection of credit card fraud were more than enough to pay for the system.[78]

One of Walton's main reasons for taking Wal-Mart public was to get out from under the several million dollars of personal debt that he took on by 1970 to finance the company's growth. To be sure, the company almost certainly could not have grown to the scale that made him a billionaire many times over if it had not gone public. Aggressive borrowing, however, was critical in getting Wal-Mart to the stage of being a viable candidate for a public offering.

Walton got into the habit of borrowing for expansion while operating his initial variety store venture in Newport, Arkansas. He began with a bank loan of $1,800 to buy a soft ice cream machine as a traffic-builder and never looked back. At age five, Walton's daughter Alice confided to a friend, with tears in her voice, "I don't know what we're going to do. My daddy owes so much money, and he won't quit opening stores."[79]

Walton's compulsion to keep opening stores reflected an unwillingness to rest on his laurels. He repeatedly reinvented his business, switching from variety stores to discounting, then branching out into warehouse clubs. Still later, he combined his discounting format with food retailing to create Wal-Mart Supercenters. Inevitably, Walton's boldness generated some mistakes.

For example, the successful Wal-Mart Supercenters were scaled-down versions of hypermarkets, a format that the company abandoned after opening four stores. The massive (200,000 square feet) hypermarkets combined supermarket items and general merchandise under a single roof. Unfortunately, customers were fatigued by having to cover large distances to find items. Additionally, shoppers found the hypermarkets' selection too limited in categories such as electronics. They also balked at buying groceries in the large-quantity packages that the stores featured.

Other retailing concepts that proved failures for Wal-Mart included Save-Co Home Improvement Centers, Helen's Arts and Crafts, and dot Discount Drugs. Another abortive scheme involved selling new cars through Sam's Club stores at just $100 over dealer's invoice. The venture collapsed, after selling just 10 cars, when the Arkansas Motor Vehicle Commission ruled that Sam's Club was illegally acting as a broker.

In the 1950s, Walton failed in an attempt to become a shopping center developer. He was correct in seeing the potential of shopping centers, but was undercapitalized and premature with his project in Little Rock. Twenty-five thousand dollars in the hole after two years, he decided to take his whipping and concentrate on running stores. Throughout his career, Walton showed that the wisdom to admit a mistake was nearly as valuable as the wisdom to avoid mistakes in the first place.

Entering an unfamiliar business with too little capital was by no means the only fundamental business error Walton ever made. When he opened his first variety store in Newport, Arkansas, he neglected to obtain an option making his lease renewable after five years. Impressed by the young merchant's success, the landlord refused to renew the lease at any price and turned the store over to his son. Walton, in his own words, was "kicked out of town"[80] after building sales from $72,000 a year to $250,000. He had made his Ben Franklin store the most profitable in a six-state region and the largest variety store in Arkansas, yet an elementary contractual oversight forced him to start over in Bentonville.

Learning from his mistake, in true future-billionaire fashion, Walton thereafter read his leases more closely. In addition, he later reported, it was probably after the Newport affair that he began to encourage his six-year-old son Rob to become a lawyer. Rob eventually served as Wal-Mart's general counsel and ultimately its chairman. Among his contributions on the legal front was registering "Wal-Mart" as a trademark, a detail his father had overlooked for many years after the company's founding.

Walton's children grew up knowing that family vacations would include excursions to gather intelligence on competitors' stores. When he drove his daughter, Alice, to horse shows, his wife assumed that he was staying and watching. In truth, father and daughter had a pact that allowed him to go off and look at stores while she exhibited her horses. Retailer Sol Price complained that when he and his wife socialized with the Waltons, Sam unfailingly steered the conversation to such entertaining topics as how to prevent vendors from corrupting buyers with favors. "He was pretty much all business," Price lamented.[81]

Relentless observation of competitors' stores, Walton said, was "something you have to do if you want to be successful in the retail business."[82] Working weekends was another, in his view. Saturday morning meetings were an essential component of Wal-Mart's management process. Walton enjoyed rolling into the office at two or three o'clock on Saturday morning to go through each store's weekly numbers, a task that consumed approximately three hours. "When I'm done I have as good a feel for what's going on in the company as anybody here—maybe better on some days," he observed.[83]

Walton demanded similarly fanatical dedication from his senior managers, rewarding them handsomely if they obliged. According to a Wal-Mart employee, onetime president Jack Shewmaker's motto was "TGIM—Thank God It's Monday."[84] Shewmaker, it was alleged, would have preferred to have Friday flow straight into Monday and eliminate everything in between. Not surprisingly, some Wal-Mart managers wilted under the relentless regimen of flying from Bentonville to their territories to visit stores. Senior vice president Ron Loveless, for example, retired at 42, citing job-related stress. At one point, the hard-charging Walton even ordered the company pilots to put their nonflying time to good use by proceeding to the nearest Wal-Mart store to check for out-of-stock items. He reluctantly rescinded the order in response to vehement protests from the pilots.[85]

~

By the end of the 1960s, Walton felt confident that Wal-Mart had tremendous potential for expansion, but his dependence on bank financing was a constraint. He had been forced to give up five intended store sites for want of ready cash. Taking Wal-Mart public seemed the only solution, despite his wife's concerns about opening up the family's financial affairs to unwelcome prying.

As a first step, Walton consolidated his debts by obtaining a $2.5 million loan from Massachusetts Mutual Insurance Company. The terms were stiff. In Walton's words, "We agreed to give them our right arm and our left leg."[86] In more technical terms, the loan agreement called for an interest rate of 9.75 percent and 15-year options to buy 45,000 Wal-Mart shares at the initial offering price. Those shares, which were worth $742,500 in the IPO, appreciated to nearly $300 million over the next 15 years, while splitting seven times.

Despite the necessity of letting that large chunk of equity get away, brothers Sam and Bud Walton, along with their immediate families, managed to retain 69 percent of the public company's stock. The initial offering sold 23 percent of the shares to the public. The remaining 8 percent of the equity was swapped for minority stakes in individual stores. These stakes arose from Wal-Mart's corporate structure prior to the public offering. Each store was set up as a separate company, with ownership held in varying proportions by employees and Walton relatives.

The pre-IPO structure was unwieldy, but it motivated store managers effectively by giving them a stake in their stores. Moreover, Walton invited the managers of existing stores to buy small stakes in new stores. As a result, the managers had a direct interest in the success of Wal-Mart as a whole.

Tapping the savings of his managers also enabled Walton to avoid an alternative strategy for growing rapidly on limited capital, namely, franchising. Herbert R. Gibson Sr., who had brushed off Walton's request for a franchise on grounds of insufficient capital, was ultimately done in by his reliance on franchisees. The Gibson Discount Centers chain peaked in 1978 at 684 stores, the vast majority owned by franchise operators rather than the Gibson family. That year, some of its multistore franchisees, including the largest, 74-unit Pamida Inc., began to withdraw from the chain. Gibson Discount Centers rapidly went into decline.

Walton's personal frugality became a model for Wal-Mart's core strategy of holding down costs in order to deliver low prices to customers. In his memoirs, Walton was scornful of early competitors in the discounting business who lived high when there was easy money to be made. "Most of these early guys were very egotistical people who loved to drive big Cadillacs and fly around in their jets and vacation on their yachts," he recalled.[87] The reason that the majority eventually went out of business, he asserted, was their failure to follow the basic principles of running good stores.

To Walton, those basic principles included keeping an extremely tight lid on expenses. As an economy measure, he drafted assistant managers from existing stores to help set up new store openings. On at least one occasion, he avoided the cost of hotel rooms by persuading the makeshift crew to sleep on the floor of the local manager's not-yet-furnished house.[88] When Wal-Mart buyers visited New York, they stayed in cheap hotels and walked to their meetings instead of wasting money on taxicabs.

Wal-Mart's dedication to keeping costs down was apparent at its decidedly low-overhead corporate headquarters. Walton frowned on frills such as elevators and carpeting, agreeing only grudgingly to install the latter amenity in some portions of the building. President David Glass described the headquarters decor as "early bus station."[89] Lobby wall decorations included a portrait of Walton's favorite bird dog and tokens of gratitude from vendors, including a plaque memorializing Wal-Mart's placement of the world's largest order of pork and beans.

As an additional cost-saving measure, Wal-Mart maintained no regional offices. Instead, the company based all of its regional vice presidents in Bentonville, flying them out to their regional territories every Monday morning. This strategy saved the company as much as 2 percent of sales, relative to competitors Kmart and Target.[90] To economize on the cost of maintaining a fleet of planes, Walton opened a facility at a spare hangar to serve other airplane owners with fuel, storage, and maintenance. By thus demonstrating that he was in the general aviation business, he qualified to buy parts and fuel on wholesale terms.[91]

Modern distribution centers enabled the company to limit its distribution costs to 1.3 percent of sales in the late 1980s, while Kmart and Sears were spending around 3.5 percent and 5 percent, respectively.[92] Wal-Mart capped its advertising costs at approximately 2 percent of sales, below average among retailers, partly by printing its circulars once a month rather than weekly. As alternative means of generating store traffic, the company emphasized low-cost, local promotional events, such as gerbil races in its pet stores and the World Championship Moon Pie Eating Contest.

The Moon Pie gimmick began in 1985 when Wal-Mart's assistant manager in Oneonta, Alabama, accidentally ordered five times as many of the cookie-and-marshmallow delicacies as he had intended. To clear out the excess inventory, he staged an event that soon became a tradition. By 1990, when a contestant billing himself as "the Godzilla of Gluttony" set a record by wolfing down 16 of the three-and-a-half-inch-diameter confections in 10 minutes, the annual competition was attracting media coverage from all over the world.

Walton's obsession with controlling costs was an underlying theme even in some of his greatest public relations coups. For example, in 1989 Wal-Mart was widely praised for donating $1 million of goods to victims of Hurricane Hugo. Even though some of the retailer's vendors contributed to the relief effort, news reports gave the retailer all the credit because the goods were delivered in Wal-Mart trucks. When questioned about the affair, Wal-Mart officials declined to name the contributing vendors or to disclose the percentage of the $1 million that Wal-Mart itself had donated. In general, the company's zeal for beating its competitors on costs extended to philanthropy. For instance, in 1987 Wal-Mart ranked last among major discounters in charitable contributions as a percentage of pretax sales.[93] (From his personal resources, though, Walton made a number of sizable donations to educational and religious institutions.)

Wal-Mart won additional kudos by installing greeters at the entrance of every store. The innovation provided employment for senior citizens, who welcomed shoppers and handed them shopping carts and sale circulars. Customer relations benefits were just the icing on the cake, however, to the Wal-Mart store manager in Crowley, Louisiana, who introduced the idea. His original concern had been shoplifting. The manager reckoned that a greeter would be less intimidating to honest customers than a uniformed guard, but still convey the message that shoplifters would be caught.[94] Walton, always eager to reduce shrinkage, enthusiastically adopted the innovation throughout the chain.

In 1985 Wal-Mart launched a "Buy American" program with great fanfare. The impetus came partly from a 1984 visit to Central America, where Walton was reportedly disturbed by the work conditions he observed in factories producing goods for U.S. retailers. Trumpeting the adverse impact of imported goods on American jobs and the balance of trade, Wal-Mart won favorable publicity for its concerted effort to shift to domestically produced goods. Public opinion polls recorded high respect for Wal-Mart as its stores displayed red-white-and-blue banners proclaiming, "Keep America Working and Strong."

As recently as 1983, however, Wal-Mart executives had testified against U.S. manufacturers' demands for increased duties on Chinese government-subsidized textiles and apparel. Consistent with its price-conscious procurement policies, the company had sought foreign-produced goods aggressively, opening purchasing offices in Hong Kong and Taiwan in the early 1980s. Aside from the modest portion of its merchandise that the company procured directly from overseas manufacturers, Wal-Mart relied heavily on American manufacturers that moved their production outside the United States to take advantage of lower labor costs.

Beneath the rhetoric, the Buy American program arose largely from a realization that the apparent price advantage of goods produced offshore was frequently offset by other factors. These included longer required lead times for placing orders, the expense of sending executives overseas to monitor quality, and the comparative difficulty of obtaining refunds on defective goods. Once Wal-Mart developed formulas to equalize for these hidden costs, the company offered American manufacturers a shot at recapturing business, on condition that they find ways to reduce their costs. A Wal-Mart director said, concerning the Buy American program, "One of our big objectives was to put the heat on American manufacturers to lower their prices."[95]

Ironically, one way that the U.S. apparel manufacturers could lower their costs was to buy fabrics from overseas producers instead of higher-cost domestic companies. That was the strategy adopted by Farris Burroughs, a showcase example of the Buy American program. Walton awarded the company a large contract for flannel shirts at the personal request of Arkansas governor Bill Clinton. By 1988, Walton could claim that Wal-Mart had created or saved 17,000 American jobs by switching to domestic producers on goods accounting for $1.2 billion of annual sales at the retail level. The company's direct purchases of imported goods *rose* between 1985 and 1988, however, as Wal-Mart increased the percentage of merchandise that it bought directly from manufacturers (including foreign manufacturers) rather than through distributors.[96]

～

Bringing discounting to small towns was a mission suitable to only an individual who was willing to withstand intense criticism. Many established retailers closed their doors soon after Wal-Mart arrived, unable to compete with the giant chain on price. Joining the chorus of resentful merchants were social critics who decried the impact on the fabric of small-town life of essentially cloned Wal-Mart stores, controlled from afar. Walton, however, steadfastly rejected any suggestion that it was somehow unfair or immoral to offer a superior deal to consumers. Neither did he buy into the tacit agreement among the chains not to expand beyond their respective market areas.

Walton also showed his independence by rejecting the retailing industry norm of cordial relations between buyers and vendors. He insisted on hard-nosed bargaining and forbade his buyers to accept meals or gifts from sales representatives. Wal-Mart's buyers were "as folksy and down-to-earth as home-grown tomatoes," according to one executive who did business with them. "But when you start dealing with them—when you get past that 'down home in Bentonville' business, they're as hard as nails and every bit as sharp."[97] An official of another company characterized Wal-Mart more bluntly, calling it "the rudest account in America."[98]

The company turned tougher still in the early 1980s, adopting an unacknowledged policy of bypassing independent manufacturers' representatives.[99] Wal-Mart ordered goods directly from manufacturers and demanded that they reduce their prices by the amount of the representatives' commissions. In reality, the manufacturers' savings from eliminating the middleman were largely illusory, since they had to assign their own people to perform the representatives' tasks. If they refused the new terms, however, they risked being cut off by Wal-Mart.

Wal-Mart softened its stance toward suppliers after the manufacturers' representatives organized and launched a publicity campaign denouncing the company's policies. Walton's more accommodative approach did not entirely represent a backing down in the face of criticism. In part, he was responding to technological advances that made it more economical to cooperate with vendors through information-sharing agreements than to maintain an adversarial relationship.

Walton conceded that his toughness toward vendors partly reflected lingering resentment of his treatment at their hands in Wal-Mart's early years. "I don't mind saying we were the victims of a good bit of arrogance from a lot of vendors in those days," he recalled. "They didn't need us, and they acted that way."[100] As a result, he said, "We have always resented paying anyone just for the pleasure of doing business with him."[101]

Leaving aside the specific origins of his testy relations with vendors, Walton's hardheaded attitudes were at least partly inherited. His father, Thomas Walton, abandoned his early career in farming to become a mortgage lender. Farmers put up part of their land as collateral for seed, paying back their loans at harvest time. If their crops failed, they defaulted on their debt and forfeited their land. Defaults were common during the difficult economic period of the 1930s and the elder Walton repossessed hundreds of farms, often from families who had owned and farmed the land for generations. As a result of foreclosures, as well as land purchases he made with his savings, Walton's father eventually became a millionaire. At his death in 1984, his holdings included 23 farms and ranches spread across four states.[102] Given that foreclosing on farmers during the Depression was no way to win a popularity contest, the elder Walton necessarily developed a thick skin. "I worked cattle for old man Walton for fourteen years, and let me tell you, he was a mean son of a bitch to work for," said a longtime employee. "He didn't take any [*expletive deleted*] off anyone and he didn't care what people thought of him."[103] Some of his father's imperviousness to criticism appears to have rubbed off on Sam Walton, even if he managed his employee relations more smoothly.

∽

The unifying theme in Walton's work ethic, risk taking, and other principles of success was an extraordinary desire to beat the competition. That was surely the motivation that drove him to extraordinary heights, even if it would be naive to assume that he was completely indifferent to money. Had he cut back on expansion during the 1960s and worked his way out of debt, he would have been affluent enough to support the lifestyle he maintained in his later years as a billionaire. Once he recognized the spectacular expansion potential of his unique brand of discount retailing, however, the drive to be the biggest took over.

Thanks to retaining a huge portion of the equity in Wal-Mart, Walton eventually emerged from Ozarks obscurity to unwanted prominence among the richest Americans. When *Forbes* commenced publishing its list of the 400 wealthiest Americans in 1982, he showed up in ninth place with a fortune of $619 million. A year later, Walton climbed to the number two slot behind J. Paul Getty's son, Gordon. The same ranking prevailed in 1984, with Getty at $4.1 billion and Walton at $2.3 billion.

In 1985, Walton landed in the top slot with an estimated net worth of $2.8 billion, followed by Ross Perot. The chief basis of *Forbes*'s estimate was the 39 percent share of Wal-Mart's stock held by Walton Enterprises, the family investment firm. *Forbes* continued to rank Walton number one through 1988, reporting a peak net worth of $8.5 billion in 1987. Outdoing Perot's one-day loss of half a billion dollars in 1970, Walton sustained a $1.8 billion drop in the October 19, 1987, stock market crash. He appeared untroubled by the decline, telling reporters that the wealth was just paper, anyway.

When Walton Enterprises converted to a partnership to avoid double taxation in 1989, *Forbes* began counting Walton and each of his four children separately for purposes of its richest-Americans list. With $1.8 billion each in that year, the Walton clan captured places 20 through 24. Sam's brother Bud, with $415 million in Wal-Mart stock, appeared at number 172. John Kluge took over the top spot, followed by Warren Buffett.

In a strict sense, the reorganization of Walton Enterprises changed nothing, implying that Walton never should have been listed as the wealthiest American. On the advice of his father-in-law, he had divided his wealth five ways way back in 1953. The eminently sound estate-planning principle was to give away wealth before it appreciated, thereby minimizing subsequent estate taxes. Even though the ownership of the Walton family stock had not really changed, *Forbes* perceived a watershed in Walton's surrender of the chief executive officer title in 1988.

At any rate, Walton's public pronouncements all suggested that he would have preferred not to appear on the *Forbes* list at all. When the magazine first blew his cover as one of the wealthiest individuals in America, he wrote to the editor: "I could kick your butt for ever running that list."[104] To aspiring billionaires, Sam Walton's career strongly suggests that a mere desire to amass wealth is not a sufficiently strong enough motivation. Success is more likely to accrue to people who find intrinsic satisfaction in the accumulation of wealth, as opposed to the possession of wealth.

5

DOMINATE YOUR MARKET

All for one, one for all.
—Alexandre Dumas *père*

Dominating a market is a highly effective strategy for accumulating wealth. It has produced both the first self-made billionaire, John D. Rockefeller Sr., and the first self-made centibillionaire, Bill Gates. In both cases, as well, market dominance has prompted calls to break up the companies that made them rich, Standard Oil and Microsoft. Developing a thick skin is an especially important principle if you pursue this path to fortune.

Market dominance is not synonymous with monopoly. Complete elimination of competition is the ultimate form of dominance, but it is not a realistic objective. Moreover, dominating a particular market does not confer unlimited economic power, given the interdependence of suppliers, producers, and customers.

Standard Oil in its heyday controlled most of the petroleum refining industry in the United States, but never achieved remotely comparable dominance in crude oil production. Overseas, Rockefeller faced well-capitalized competition, rather than the token independent refiners that shielded him from charges of monopolization at home. Microsoft captured the lion's share of the market in operating systems, but was not similarly dominant in applications software.

Using a Dominant Position Wisely

Even when market dominance is achievable, it is not necessarily sustainable. Well before the antitrust authorities get into the act, competition and innovation typically start to chip away at market share. By the time the Supreme Court broke up Standard Oil, its control of the refining business had already begun to erode. In technologically dynamic businesses, the constant threat of obsolescence makes it difficult to preserve a product's preeminent position. Conceivably, a dominant producer might try to use its market power to stifle competing innovations. In its antitrust case against Microsoft, the U.S. government tried to make a case that Microsoft had used such tactics. It is by no means clear, however, that such a strategy can prevail over an extended period.

Aside from growing complacent about a dominant market position, the major pitfall to avoid is exploiting it in less than an optimal fashion. The simple models of supply, demand, and price equilibrium that you may have studied in an introductory economics course are not the best guides on this question. According to the rudimentary discussions of supply and demand, monopolists limit production and raise prices above the level they would reach in a freely competitive market. Extracting artificially high profits, however, is not necessarily the best long-run strategy.

This statement may be counterintuitive. After all, the excess profits obtainable through a monopoly can be staggering. The magnitude of the opportunity was shown in the mid-1990s, when New York City cracked down on a garbage collection cartel controlled by organized crime.

For decades, the crime bosses rigged prices. Commercial property owners, who were required to hire private trash haulers, had no choice of the company they dealt with and no opportunity to negotiate contracts. In consolidating local companies into Waste Management, Wayne Huizenga steered clear of the New York area to avoid any taint of mob influence.

At long last, prosecutors broke the cartel. They won convictions against three reputed mobsters and 14 owners of trash-hauling companies that participated in the scheme. A dozen companies linked to the mob either went out of business or were acquired by national operators. In addition, a new city agency called the Trade Waste Commission began denying trash-hauling licenses to companies that it found to be linked to the mob's anticompetitive conspiracy.

The resulting price reductions to the city's businesses were tremendous. In 1998, one boutique operator reported that instead of paying $40 a month and having to settle for twice-weekly pickups, she was now having her garbage removed five days a week for just $25 a month. The manager of a Fifth Avenue office tower said that he was now paying $950 a month for service that previously had cost $10,000. All told, according to prosecutors, as much as $400 million of the New York businesses' $1.5 billion aggregate garbage-collection bill represented excess profits realized by the monopolists.[1]

Inflating your profits by more than 25 percent of sales sounds wonderful. Note, however, that the trash haulers did not have to worry about new technologies that might allow dissatisfied customers to bypass the cartel. Monopolists in many other industries enjoy less insulation from new types of competitors. Furthermore, they lack the mob's means to intimidate potential new entrants.

The high-price approach produces high profits for the dominant producer, but also makes it possible for new companies to enter the business and earn attractive profits. Sooner or later, the new entrants will probably cut their prices in an attempt to gain market share. If you then attempt to run the newcomers out of business through predatory pricing, you will surely attract unwanted attention from the antitrust authorities. Their involvement could destroy a dominant market position that you have patiently built up over many years through lawful means.

Instead of creating a price umbrella that invites competition, you may be better off showing restraint. Suppose your company dominates the production of some good and sells it at a price that generates healthy, but not sensational, profits. Potential new entrants will not be able to match your production costs in the near term, because you enjoy a huge advantage through economies of scale. If you play your cards right, you may be able to deter new competition indefinitely. Meanwhile, assuming you hold on to a big piece of your company's equity, your wealth will increase as rising demand for your product results in larger sales and profits.

In short, you do not have to behave like the mob to turn a dominant market position into a billion-dollar fortune. Table 2 illustrates the power

TABLE 2　　The Benefits of Market Share Dominance

Comparative Income Statements
Year Ending December 31, 20XX

	Leader Corp.	In-Pack, Inc.
Sales (millions of units)	25	20
Price per unit ($)	100	100
Sales ($million)	2,500	2,000
Fixed production costs ($million)	850	850
Administrative costs ($million)	525	525
Total fixed costs ($million)	1,375	1,375
Fixed cost per unit ($)	55	69
Variable cost per unit ($)	20	20
Units produced (millions)	25	20
Total variable costs	500	400
Total costs ($million)	1,875	1,775
Total cost per unit ($)	75	89
Pretax profit ($million)	625	225
Pretax profit per unit ($)	25	11

of the scale economies you can obtain by becoming your industry's largest producer. By producing the largest number of units, you achieve the lowest cost per unit and the highest profit per unit.

In the table, total cost of production consists of fixed costs, which do not vary with the volume of production, and variable costs, which depend on the number of units produced. Fixed costs include such items as rent, real estate taxes, managerial salaries, and annual depreciation of plant and equipment. (Depreciation is a current charge against profits representing the future-year cost of replacing worn-out equipment.) Variable costs include materials and hourly wages. That is, the larger the number of units produced, the more man-hours will be needed and the more materials will be consumed in production. In the example shown here, Leader Corp., the dominant producer, is able to spread its fixed costs over a larger number of units (25 million) than its competitor, In-Pack, Inc. (20 million). Taking into account also the variable costs, Leader's total costs ($1.875 billion) are greater than In-Pack's ($1.775 billion). Leader's *cost per unit,* however, is significantly lower—$75 versus $89. Vigorous competition prevents Leader from obtaining a premium price for its product, which is essentially identical to In-Pack's, but its cost advantage yields a higher pretax profit per unit—$25 versus $11.

Getting a Leg Up

The toughest part of exploiting market dominance is achieving it in the first place. John D. Rockefeller Sr. and Bill Gates managed the feat through iron determination and application of classic billionaires' methods. As the wealthiest of the self-made billionaires in their respective eras, their careers are worth examining at length. You will not master, in a single reading, all of the details of Gates's bid for supremacy in computer software. As you progress along your own path to a 10-figure net worth, however, rereading this section will prove extremely useful.

THE BILLIONAIRE HOW-TO

Fundamental Strategies

- Dominate Your Market
- Do Business in a New Way
- Take Monumental Risks
- Consolidate an Industry
- Thrive on Deals

Key Principles

- Pursue the Money in Ideas
- Develop a Thick Skin
- Rules Are Breakable
- Copying Pays Better Than Innovating
- Keep on Growing
- Hold on to Your Equity
- Hard Work Is Essential

John D. Rockefeller Sr.

I believe it is my duty to make money and still more money and to use the money I make for the good of my fellow man according to the dictates of my conscience.[2]

John D. Rockefeller Sr. is remembered today as much for his philanthropy as for his creation of a staggering personal fortune through domination of the oil industry. His munificence was largely responsible for the establishment of the University of Chicago, Rockefeller University, Spelman College, the Rockefeller Foundation, and the Peking Union Medical College, as well as the development of a yellow fever vaccine, the eradication of hookworm disease, and the suppression of the boll weevil. In November 1917, Rockefeller estimated that if he had not given away such vast sums to charity and to his heirs, his net worth would have grown by then to $3 billion.

Even after these substantial subtractions, Rockefeller died in 1937 with a net worth of $1.4 billion, an amount equivalent to one-65th of the gross national product (GNP) of the United States at the time. By that measure, admittedly only one of several methods for comparing wealth in different eras, he was the richest American of all time.[3] Remarkably, too, Rockefeller's brainchild propelled no fewer than five other men onto the list of wealthiest Americans of all time, as measured by percentage of GNP. Henry M. Flagler, Oliver H. Payne, Henry H. Rogers, and John D. Rockefeller Sr.'s brother, William, all struck it rich as partners in Standard Oil. In addition, Edward Stephen Harkness reached the wealthiest-ever list by inheriting a large stake in the company from his father. This extraordinary creation of net worth is traceable to methods that Rockefeller's successor billionaires would employ again and again.

After earlier success as a Cleveland produce dealer, John D. Rockefeller Sr. was drawn into the infant industry of oil refining. It took him little time to recognize and exploit the power of market share. The benefits of size first became apparent in connection with a critically important expense, the shipment of crude oil to refineries and of refined oil to markets around the country.

In the late 1860s, the Pennsylvania Railroad attempted to monopolize shipments of crude oil from the Pennsylvania producing regions by promoting the interests of the New York and Philadelphia refineries, which lay along its routes. Most of Cleveland's oil refiners panicked, fearing their access to crude would be cut off. Rockefeller, in contrast, capitalized on the situation in his negotiations with the two railroads that continued to rely on Cleveland's business, the New York Central's Lake Shore line and Jay Gould's Erie Railroad. Rockefeller and his associate Henry Flagler extracted secret discounts of 30 percent to 75 percent from the railroads' officially posted rates. In return, Rockefeller and Flagler promised a huge volume of regular shipments. This steady, predictable business enabled the carriers to achieve substantial operating efficiencies.[4] Rockefeller had ended the Pennsylvania's threat to the other railroads' oil-shipping revenues while also gaining an immense cost advantage.

Although Rockefeller was already the world's largest refiner, his output was not big enough to meet the shipping volumes he had promised in return for rebates on rail rates. Accordingly, he undertook to coordinate his shipments with those of the other Cleveland refiners. Rockefeller's inclination to replace competition with coordination accelerated as high profits and low entry costs lured many new players into oil refining. By 1870, refining capacity had ballooned to three times the volume of crude oil being produced. As a result, Rockefeller estimated, 90 percent of refiners were losing money.

Rockefeller's solution to the profit squeeze was to end the prevailing "ruinous competition"[5] through consolidation of the refining industry. He began by incorporating his partnership as the Standard Oil Company (Ohio), making it easier to raise the vast new sums required for his scheme. Then, early in 1872, Standard Oil forged an alliance with the three dominant oil-shipping railroads, the Pennsylvania, the New York Central, and the Erie, which were weary of intense price competition among themselves. The alliance among shippers and carriers, known as the South Improvement Company (SIC), drastically raised freight rates for all refiners, but granted rebates of up to 50 percent for SIC members. Even more outrageously, to critics of monopoly capitalism, the railroads gave its refining members rebates *on each barrel of oil shipped by nonmembers*. In addition to these tremendous cost advantages, Rockefeller received detailed information from the SIC about nonmembers' shipments, which helped immeasurably in undercutting his rivals' prices.

Within two months, opposition from New York refiners broke up the

South Improvement Company. By then, however, Standard Oil had acquired 22 of its 26 hometown competitors, an operation thereafter remembered as the "Cleveland Massacre." The sellers had a clear sense that if they refused to sell out, they would be driven under by Rockefeller's huge shipping cost advantage. By the middle of 1872, Standard Oil dominated the oil business in Cleveland, which had meanwhile become the nation's largest refining center. Still, the boom-and-bust nature of the oil business, with its depressing effect on profitability, offended Rockefeller's sense of order. Some new plan of organization was needed, in his view.

Pittsburgh's refiners rejected Rockefeller's first plan, based on voluntary limitation of production. Another possible means of maintaining profit margins in refining was for crude oil producers to manage production, in order to control price swings in the commodity they sold to refiners. To Rockefeller's disgust, however, the crude producers proved incapable of colluding to stabilize prices.

~

Ultimately, Rockefeller concluded that the only practical solution was to gain control of refining capacity on a national scale. Capitalizing on the depression that followed the stock market panic of September 18, 1873, Standard Oil started to acquire competitors outside of Cleveland. Among Rockefeller's tactics was granting the target companies a peek at his books. Once they realized his operations were so efficient that he could sell below their cost and still make profits, they lost their inhibitions about joining the fold.

Under terms of its incorporation, Standard Oil Company (Ohio) could not lawfully own assets outside its home state. John D. Rockefeller Sr., however, was not one to be deterred by such details. He instructed the acquired companies to continue operating under their established names and to make no written reference to their affiliation with Standard Oil.

In a secret meeting in 1874, Rockefeller gained control of the leading refineries in Philadelphia and Pittsburgh. His new allies in turn proceeded to acquire their local competitors. Within two years, the number of Pittsburgh-based refiners fell from 22 to one. Over the next few years, Standard Oil consolidated its covert control of all major refining centers, including New York, West Virginia, and Baltimore, as well as the refineries located close to the Pennsylvania crude-producing regions. By 1877, Standard Oil accounted for almost 90 percent of refined petroleum products in the United States.[6]

Standard Oil extended its monopolistic power by investing aggressively in oil transportation. The railroads, cowed by geologists' predictions that the nation's oil fields would soon be exhausted, balked at huge outlays tailored to the industry's needs. Rockefeller exploited this fear by taking over the Erie's Weehawken, New Jersey, terminal on condition of modernizing it to handle oil shipments. In the process, Standard Oil obtained preferential rates, as well as valuable information about other refiners' shipments, and even secured the power to block the shipment of competitors' oil. When the railroads refused to invest in the newfangled tank cars that were replacing the oil barrels formerly employed, Standard Oil created its own fleet. Capitalizing on his ability to withhold its tank cars from the railroads, Rockefeller extracted concessions that increased his transportation cost advantage over smaller refiners. Finally, as pipelines became increasingly important in oil transportation, Standard Oil created its own system. Rockefeller also bought an interest in another pipeline network that pretended to operate independently of Standard Oil. Before long, the Rockefeller pipelines and their ostensible competitors had formed a cartel to allocate production and fix prices.

Unfortunately, for those who would copy John D. Rockefeller Sr.'s methods, certain of his tactics were ethically questionable or downright illegal. For example, Standard Oil persisted in collecting rebates from railroads long after they were outlawed in 1887, using accounting legerdemain to disguise the practice. When called upon to testify in court regarding the company's practices, Rockefeller feigned befuddlement or gave technically correct but misleading answers. Rockefeller even perjured himself in an affidavit concerning the ownership of South Improvement Company.[7]

Standard Oil showed especially sharp elbows when it sought to prevent the construction of a competing pipeline in the Pennsylvania oil fields. The company planted newspaper stories alleging that oil leaks would ruin the crops of any farmers who sold rights of way to the proposed Tidewater Pipe Line. Rockefeller took the high road only when, in spite of Standard Oil's concerted efforts, the detested Tidewater project was completed. Turning statesmanlike, he rejected a subordinate's proposal to smash the pipeline to smithereens. Rockefeller instead tried to sabotage Tidewater by savagely undercutting its rates, while also attempting to block both the pipeline's access to crude and its outlets to independent refineries. In the end, Rockefeller's allies took advantage of dissension within Tidewater's board to purchase a minority interest in the pipeline. Standard Oil and Tidewater then formed a cartel to divide the pipeline business in Pennsylvania.[8]

Despite the rough edges around John D. Rockefeller Sr.'s strategy for amassing wealth, you can adopt its essential elements without resorting to criminality. One of Rockefeller's key principles was to keep his mind open to change. He was slow to appreciate the importance of oil pipelines, yet once he came to understand the issue, he moved decisively into the business. Similarly, Rockefeller overcame his initial aversion to substantial investments in the highly volatile business of crude production. Fearing that Standard Oil might become dependent on foreign sources that it could not dominate, Rockefeller built the company's crude operations to a 33 percent share of U.S. production.

~

Standard Oil's entry into crude production highlighted another of Rockefeller's strong points, namely, a willingness to take risks. New oil fields had been discovered near Lima, Indiana, but the crude produced in that region had a high sulfur content, which produced an unbearable stench. Rockefeller nevertheless proceeded to acquire oil properties and build pipelines, gambling that chemist Herman Frasch could devise a process for making the Midwestern "skunk oil" marketable. (The risk was only slightly mitigated by Standard Oil's ability to market the evil-smelling oil as boiler fuel, a less profitable line than kerosene, the key product of that pre-automobile era.) Rockefeller even offered to underwrite the Lima venture out of his own pocket. The gesture so impressed Standard Oil's previously hesitant directors that they gave him the go-ahead. Ultimately, Rockefeller's gamble paid off as Frasch's patented process produced immense profits for Standard Oil.

The same openness to risk exhibited itself in Rockefeller's later venture, outside the Standard Oil framework, in the Mesabi Range. Much like the Indiana crude oil, the iron ore discovered in Minnesota had little commercial value, given existing technology. Unlike the conventional hard rock ore extracted from underground mines, the Mesabi ore was a fine powder that clogged blast furnaces. In another parallel to his previous exploits, Rockefeller took advantage of financial distress, namely, an iron price slump precipitated by the Panic of 1893. Leonidas Merritt and his family, early developers of the Mesabi Range, became financially overextended in their zeal to create mining infrastructure. Bit by bit, Rockefeller began to provide cash in exchange for a growing share of the Merritts' operations. Eventually, when steelmakers figured out how to adapt their blast furnaces to the Mesabi ore, the value of Rockefeller's investment skyrocketed. (Rockefeller made so much money, in fact, that the Merritts claimed they had been swindled and extracted half a million dollars in an out-of-court settlement.)

~

As for building a business organization, Rockefeller consistently sought alliances that genuinely benefited both parties. In acquiring companies for the Standard Oil empire, he preferred persuasion to coercion, exercising patience and turning on his personal charm with considerable effect. Unlike the masters of the art of buying low (see Chapter 7), Rockefeller did not invariably try to acquire assets at the cheapest possible price. Rather, he reckoned the value of acquisitions in terms of their strategic importance, which in certain cases involved the benefits to be obtained from shutting down inefficient, redundant capacity. Recognizing the advantages of retaining existing managers and keeping them on friendly terms, the otherwise cost-conscious Rockefeller even tolerated a few executives who failed to pull their weight.

Playing to Win

If the soft sell ever failed, however, Rockefeller was prepared to shift to the exercise of naked power. This characteristic carried over into his personal affairs. For example, he decided at one point to increase the seclusion of his Pocantico Hills, New York, estate by acquiring a small adjacent property. The owner declined Rockefeller's generous offer, which included a nearby piece of land to which he could move his house. Thwarted in his effort to act magnanimously, Rockefeller instructed his superintendent to enclose the neighbor's property with gigantic cedar trees. Seeing he would be condemned to perpetual darkness, the owner finally yielded to the oil magnate's will.[9]

Clearly, a tough-minded attitude is essential for anyone hoping to follow in John D. Rockefeller Sr.'s footsteps.

Bill Gates

It's possible, you can never know, that the universe exists only for me. If so, it's sure going well for me, I must admit.[10]

The names of William H. Gates III and John D. Rockefeller Sr. became inextricably linked in 1998. By chance, the publication of a best-selling biography of Standard Oil's founder (*Titan*, by Ron Chernow) coincided with the Justice Department's decision to launch an epic antitrust case against Microsoft, the computer software producer that Gates cofounded. Like Rockefeller, Gates achieved spectacular success while comparatively young and became far and away the wealthiest American of his era. Measured by inflation-adjusted dollars, Gates's net worth comfortably exceeded Rockefeller's.[11] One economic commentator calculated that Gates's fortune was equivalent to the net worth of the least-affluent 120 million Americans—nearly half the population.[12] As the late-1990s bull market boosted Microsoft stock to new heights, Gates surpassed the Sultan of Brunei to become the world's richest man.[13]

Both Rockefeller and Gates responded to inevitable charges of monopolization by correctly pointing out that far from gouging consumers, they steadily brought down the prices of their products. When called upon to testify in antitrust proceedings, Gates responded to prosecutors' questions in a hairsplitting manner reminiscent of Rockefeller's cagey style on the stand. At one point, Gates professed not to understand the term "market share." Industry wags suggested that the part of the phrase he did not understand was "share."

The similarities between the two titans extended even to record-setting achievements in philanthropy. Early in 1999, Gates and his wife gave $3.3 billion to two charitable foundations that they had established, bringing the institutions' combined assets to nearly $5.5 billion. At the age of 43, Gates had given away more money than any other living American. The William H. Gates Foundation, focusing on world health, population, and education, ranked among the 10 largest U.S. foundations in assets and was the only one in that category with a living donor. Not since the time of Andrew Carnegie and John D. Rockefeller Sr. had a living philanthropist donated such substantial assets to a foundation.[14]

In yet another parallel noted by Rockefeller biographer Chernow, Gates repeated his predecessor's tactical error of being slow to mount a public relations response to the criticism that inevitably arose from his dominant market position.[15] If Microsoft's publicists were tardy in addressing the antitrust allegations head-on, however, they had long since succeeded in making Gates a well-known, and largely sympathetic, figure. Thanks to a public relations campaign launched in 1982, Gates was widely seen as a brainy computer techie, the fabulously successful hero of a *Revenge of the Nerds* tale.

People included Gates in its year-end 1983 list of the "25 Most Intriguing People." (Exaggerating his legitimately solid record as a Boy Scout, the magazine reported that he had reached the Eagle rank. Billionaires Ross Perot and Sam Walton, by contrast, earned the distinction the hard way.) At the end of 1984, *Esquire* listed Gates among the "Best of the New Generation." Perhaps the most unusual accolade was Gates's February 1985 selection for *Good Housekeeping*'s list of 50 most eligible bachelors, along with entertainers Warren Beatty, Michael Jackson, Burt Reynolds, and Tom Selleck. "They are all wealthy and charming and waiting for the right woman to come along," gushed the editors.[16]

Fame and Controversy

Even quirks of Gates's personality became familiar fare to followers of his remarkable career. These included his unkempt ways, his hacker-like love of junk food, and his penchant for rocking while engrossed in thought. *Young Jump*, a Japanese comic book about a boy modeled on Gates, took its title from the Microsoft chairman's habit of spontaneously leaping toward the ceiling.

Over the years, Gates has occasionally embellished his own legend. He long claimed that his first 13 software customers had gone bankrupt, a tale that underscored the fierce competitiveness of the computer industry. "I made that up," he subsequently conceded.[17] Gates also said that between 1970 and 1974, he and Microsoft cofounder Paul Allen developed a computer program that was eventually used in about half the elevators in the United States. This "never happened," he later acknowledged.[18] Additionally, Gates maintained that it was during the 1970–1974 period that he and Allen began using the phrase that they later repeated endlessly as Microsoft's creed: "A computer on every desk and in every home, running Microsoft software." In reality, no such company name existed at the time. The famous phrase, which apparently was not heard around Microsoft until the mid-1980s, evolved from a January 1975 *Popular Electronics* article heralding "the era of the computer in every home."[19]

Gates's bona fide achievements make hyperbole superfluous. His preeminent role in the software industry inspires envy and occasionally loopy outbreaks of hostility. Jeffrey Papows, chief executive officer of Microsoft competitor Lotus Development, proudly proclaims that he and Larry Ellison, founder of database producer Oracle Corporation, are "co-captains of the I-hate-Bill-Gates fan club."[20] They share the title, Papows explains, because they cannot decide who hates Gates more. Ellison, for his part, has sought to fire up his employees by displaying a massive computer-created image of Gates giving them the finger. Detractors target not only Gates, but also the extremely bright programmers (internally referred to as "Bill clones") assiduously recruited by Microsoft. When the Justice Department launched an antitrust case against Microsoft in 1998, a newspaper cartoon portrayed a dweebish figure peering at a computer monitor. The screen read, "Our beloved leader, Mr. Gates, is under attack. Leave your possessions. Go to the desert. Await the spaceship."[21]

Numerous web sites are devoted to hatred of Microsoft's chairman. They depict him being shot, peppered in the face with darts, and unmasked as Satan. There is even an International Anti-MS Network of web sites dedicated to denigrating Microsoft. Also intended with malice is the Bill Gates Personal Wealth Clock, which tracks his net worth, minute by minute. Following a Microsoft stock split early in 1999, the figure soared to a mind-boggling $94.6 billion. The Wealth Clock reported that Bill Gates became the world's first centibillionaire.[22]

Like Rockefeller before him, Bill Gates has helped many others achieve wealth and mega-wealth. The 1998 Forbes 400 ranked Microsoft cofounder Paul Allen third among America's wealthiest. (To be sure, Allen also profited from other ventures after leaving Microsoft in 1983.) In fifth place was Steve Ballmer, a college classmate of Gates who joined the company in 1980. A January 1994 magazine article commented, regarding Microsoft's Redmond, Washington, headquarters, "Nowhere on earth do more millionaires and billionaires go to work every day than do so here." At the time about 2,200 out of 15,000 employees owned at least $1 million worth of Microsoft stock.[23] By early 1999, the number of millionaires within the company had grown to 5,000, propelled by Microsoft's expanding head count and rising stock price.[24]

Early Bloomer

Microsoft's success has exceeded anything Bill Gates could have foreseen at its founding, but he never lacked big dreams. Born in Seattle in 1955, Gates was a precocious child. By the age of eight or so, he had read *The World Book Encyclopedia* from cover to cover. At 11, Gates astounded his pastor by flawlessly reciting from memory the entire Sermon on the Mount.[25] He later scored a perfect 800 on the mathematics section of the Scholastic Aptitude Test and won a National Merit Scholarship.

Gates's entrepreneurial ambition also manifested itself early on. As a sixth grader, he received an A on a paper outlining his future plans to form Gatesway Incorporated, a company that he envisioned marketing a coronary care system to hospitals.[26] In high school, Gates confidently told a friend that he would be a millionaire by the age of 20.[27]

Legend has it that Gates solidified his credentials as an entrepreneur while serving as a Congressional page in the summer of 1972. According to Gates's account, he spotted a great moneymaking opportunity when the news broke that Senator Thomas Eagleton, running mate of Democratic presidential nominee George McGovern, had once received electric shock treatment for depression. Correctly foreseeing that McGovern would drop Eagleton from the ticket, Gates and a fellow page snapped up thousands of McGovern-Eagleton campaign buttons for a nickel each. A few weeks later, so the story goes, they sold the same buttons as rare collector's items for $10 to $25 apiece.

Research into the affair has corroborated the view of Gates's sister, Kristi, that the story has gotten somewhat inflated over the years. For one thing, the pages recruited by Gates to sell the buttons do not recall receiving prices anywhere close to $10. At the time, commercial vendors were advertising McGovern-Eagleton buttons at around one dollar.[28]

Even in Gates's most vivid re-creation, however, the campaign button caper was only a tiny bit as fabulous as the true story that began with his youthful introduction to computers. Worried that the Seattle public schools could not adequately challenge their mathematically gifted son, Gates's parents enrolled him in Lakeside, a private prep school. During Gates's year in eighth grade, Lakeside became one of the nation's first schools with computer capability by acquiring an ASR-33 Teletype. The primitive electromechanical device enabled users to hook up by telephone line to a minicomputer in downtown Seattle owned by General Electric. Computing quickly became an obsession for Gates, as it did for Paul Allen, a Lakeside student two years his senior.

Gates soon began exploring the financial dimensions of his new hobby. Computer time was extremely expensive and the Lakeside students were using a lot of it. Together with some friends, Gates cracked the security system of Computer Center Corporation (informally known as "C-Cubed"), which had joined General Electric as a provider of computer time to Lakeside. The boys capitalized on their successful bit of hacking by altering the accounting files to reduce the amount of time charged to them. Although apprehended and severely scolded for their trick, Gates and his friends were later hired by C-Cubed to help debug (remove programming flaws from) the company's system. In exchange for unlimited free computer time, the boys worked a night shift, finding and documenting procedures that caused the system to crash. Gates became so consumed with the work that he would sneak out of his house at night and spend most of the night at C-Cubed.[29] Over six months, the crew filled more than 300 pages with descriptions of system bugs that they found, most of them discoveries of Gates or Allen.

When Paul Allen moved on to Washington State University in 1971, he and Gates created a new venture called Traf-O-Data. The idea was to computerize the handling of traffic-flow data collected by municipalities from rubber hoses laid across roadways to count cars. Traf-O-Data's program reduced the work involved in translating the raw data into usable information for the engineers.

Gates next earned $4,200 creating a class-scheduling program for Lakeside, aided by Allen, who was on summer break from college. The politically astute partners made certain that the headmaster's daughter always received exactly the schedule she requested. In addition, Gates geared the program to schedule himself in classes with the school's prettiest girls.

Capitalizing on the knowledge acquired from the Lakeside project, Gates landed a contract to design a scheduling program for the student-run Experimental College at the University of Washington. He netted only about $500 on the job, however. The affair also led to accusations of nepotism when the campus newspaper discovered that the contract had been awarded to the brother of a student government officer, Kristi Gates.

During Gates's senior year at Lakeside, he took time off from school and Allen dropped out of college to work full time as $165-a-week programmers for defense contractor TRW Inc. The Gates-Allen collaboration then moved across the country to Massachusetts. While Allen worked for Honeywell, Gates attended Harvard, where he devoted considerable time to playing poker and met future Microsoft president Steve Ballmer. Already veterans in the emerging industry of software, which mainframe computer manufacturers had largely viewed as an afterthought, Gates and Allen were ready to act on the event that set the course of their careers. Tried-and-true billionaires' methods immediately came into play.

In January 1975, *Popular Electronics* ran a cover story on the Altair 8800 microcomputer, manufactured by Albuquerque-based Micro Instrumentation and Telemetry Systems (MITS). Other organizations had designed personal computers, but MITS was the first to make one available commercially. The Altair retailed at $397, a price that did not include software to make the computer perform its wonders. As Gates and Allen immediately recognized, the long-awaited revolution in personal computing had begun. For the time being, however, the only enlistees in the revolutionary forces were dedicated hobbyists with the patience to program the keyboardless Altair by flipping switches in lengthy sequences.

Ed Roberts, MITS's founder, believed that the key to expanding the Altair's user base was to enable it to run BASIC (Beginners' All-purpose Symbolic Instruction Code), an easy-to-learn programming language originally developed for larger computers. From a technical viewpoint, that was a tall order. The breakthrough that had made the Altair possible was semiconductor manufacturer Intel's introduction of the 8080 chip. Intel's engineers, who had not developed the chip with microcomputers in mind, doubted that it was possible to make it run BASIC.[30]

Bill Gates and Paul Allen thought otherwise and set their sights on the contract to supply software for the Altair. Their business plan was simple. From Gates's room at Harvard, they called Ed Roberts and proudly informed him that they had developed a BASIC program that would run on the 8080 chip. Roberts gruffly replied that the mandate was theirs if they could successfully demonstrate a BASIC program sooner than the 50 other groups making similar claims.

Gates and Allen's audacious tactics qualified them as pioneers in the production of vaporware. This term refers to the tactic of announcing a software product before it exists, typically to discourage rivals from proceeding with development of competing versions. Over the years, vaporware would become a characteristic Microsoft technique. One biography of Gates described his use of it thus:

> Announcing a product that didn't exist, developing it on the model of the best version available elsewhere, demonstrating an edition that didn't fully work, and finally releasing the product in rather buggy form after a lengthy delay.[31]

Now the challenge was to write computer code for the program that Gates and Allen claimed they had already created. The intrepid pair's confidence was buoyed by the belief that they had a head start over competitors. Their previous effort at Traf-O-Data had given them experience with a predecessor of the Intel 8080 chip. Extension of that work, they felt sure, would enable them to perfect a BASIC program for personal computers.

Despite Gates and Allen's confidence, the obstacles proved formidable. In developing their program, they were unable to test it on an actual Altair computer. The machines were in such short supply that the "computer" photographed on the famous *Popular Electronics* cover was actually a dummy, an empty metal shell festooned with switches and lights. Gates and Allen had to rely on a manual that described the Altair, knowing that if it contained errors, or if they misread it, their program would be flawed.[32]

With no Altair to work on, the team developed its software at the Harvard computer center, aided by freshman Monte Davidoff. A flap subsequently arose over the fact that Gates was not only using Harvard's resources to develop a commercial product, but was also regularly bringing nonstudent Allen into the late-night code-writing sessions at the computer facility. Gates later denied claims that he was threatened with expulsion over the incident, although he was quite concerned at the time, according to his roommate.[33] In the end, he received only a strong reprimand, a fair resolution given that the university had not yet established clear guidelines for use of computer time.

Birth of an Industry

As it turned out, the Gates-Allen team truly was ahead of the competition and MITS was eager to see a demonstration of its BASIC software. Still not certain that the program would actually run on an Altair, Allen flew to Albuquerque. En route, he suddenly realized that he and his partner had forgotten to write a "bootstrap," a program that would instruct the Altair how to load BASIC. Allen hurriedly created the necessary code, finishing just as the airplane landed. The following day, he loaded up the program and asked the computer to solve the problem 2 + 2. As the Altair printed out "4," Bill Gates and Paul Allen took their places in the vanguard of the personal computer revolution.

Not long afterward, Allen quit Honeywell to become MITS's director of software. During summer break following his sophomore year in 1975, Gates joined Allen in Albuquerque to pursue further development of the BASIC program. Now that they had a product to license, the duo formed a partnership, initially called "Micro-Soft" (short for "microcomputer software"). Profits were to be split 60/40 (later amended to 64/36), with Gates receiving the larger share in recognition of his greater contribution to the original development of the BASIC software. Gates returned to Harvard in the fall, but eventually dropped out to work full time with Microsoft. Within a year of Microsoft's founding, its BASIC program had effectively become the standard for microcomputers. Manufacturers planning to introduce their own personal computers began making the trek to Albuquerque to contract with Microsoft for creation of their own BASIC languages.[34]

With the birth of the personal computer software industry, an issue immediately arose that is essential in placing subsequent controversies surrounding Bill Gates in context. The Altair was an instant success, generating far more sales than founder Ed Roberts had dreamed possible. Moreover, Microsoft had crafted a licensing agreement with MITS that carefully protected its interests, helped by Gates's father, a prominent attorney. For some reason, though, what should have been a torrent of royalty payments to Gates and Allen was proving to be a trickle. The reason turned out to be computer hobbyists who were circulating pirated copies of Microsoft's BASIC program.

At first, Gates was so discouraged that he offered to sell Microsoft's BASIC outright to MITS for around $6,500. It was not the last unconsummated transaction that, had it happened, might have prematurely ended Bill Gates's ascent to the billionaire ranks. In 1979, he turned down an offer to sell Microsoft to Ross Perot's Electronic Data Systems. Gates did not see eye to eye with EDS on business strategy, yet the deal might have happened if the parties had diverged less widely in their estimates of Microsoft's value. Perot later characterized his failure to step up and pay Gates's price as one of his greatest business mistakes.[35]

Recovering from his initial despair over the pirating of BASIC, Gates took the offensive. He wrote an open letter to Altair users, denouncing hobbyists for stealing his software. The letter sparked a furor and commenced the popular association of arrogance and greed with Gates's name, which until then was not widely known in computer circles.

To Gates's accusers, circa 1975, "greed" was not far removed from the notion of being in business to make a profit. Suffused with anticapitalistic sentiments of the 1960s, many of the early enthusiasts viewed personal computers primarily as instruments of liberation. The BASIC program ought to be in the public domain, they believed. Gates, on the other hand, had envisioned himself as a successful entrepreneur even before he first encountered a computer. *Fortune* was a staple of his reading when he was in high school and as a Harvard undergraduate he devoured books on business management. To Gates, the challenge of creating software had intrinsic appeal, but it was also a means to realize his financial ambitions.

Gates's argument against pirating software amounted to nothing more or less than the core notion of the free enterprise system. Microsoft could not continue to create products for the benefit of hobbyists unless it had a reasonable chance of recouping its investment. By Gates's reckoning, the royalties he had received on the BASIC program, as of the date of his tirade against software pirates, placed a value of less than $2 an hour on the time he and his associates had spent writing the code. Entrepreneurs, not to mention aspiring billionaires, are bound to feel sympathy for Gates's desire to be rewarded for creating value, regardless of what they think of his personality or the later allegations of monopolization by Microsoft.

The business opportunity that enabled the tiny Gates-Allen firm to grow to a scale that made monopolization charges sound plausible arose from IBM's 1980 decision to enter the personal computer field.[36] "Big Blue" wanted Microsoft, which by then had relocated from Albuquerque to Seattle, to develop programs for BASIC and three other computer languages for a machine designed around the new Intel 16-bit[37] 8088 chip. One of IBM's critical needs was an operating system, the program that arranges for computer hardware to execute software commands. Unfortunately, Microsoft lacked the resources to create an operating system as quickly as IBM needed it. Therefore, Gates helpfully told IBM's people where they could find a 16-bit operating system nearly ready to go. Digital Research, based in Pacific Grove, California, was at work on a refinement of its CP/M (control program for microcomputers) operating system, the CP/M-86. Gates set up a meeting between IBM and Digital Research that would prove fateful.

Gary Kildall, Digital Research's founder, did not attend the meeting.[38] According to popular accounts, he chose instead to go flying and missed the opportunity of a lifetime. Gates biographers Stephen Manes and Paul Andrews claim that in fact he flew to the Bay Area on business, while Kildall asserted that he merely arrived at the meeting while it was already in progress. Kildall customarily left business negotiations to his wife, a vice president of Digital Research, who rejected IBM's terms as too onerous. In addition, Digital Research had fallen far behind schedule in its development of the CP/M-86. Had the product been ready in time, IBM simply could have licensed it.[39] As things stood, however, the lack of an operating system was stymieing production of IBM's personal computer, which represented a potentially vast new market for Microsoft software.

Fortunately, Paul Allen knew of another 16-bit operating system. A small manufacturer called Seattle Computer Products had developed a central processing unit based on a 16-bit chip. The company was losing potential sales because of delays in Digital Research's introduction of the operating system that Seattle Computer planned to use, the CP/M-86. Tim Paterson, a Seattle Computer engineer, solved the problem by creating a near-clone of the Digital Research product. He dubbed it QDOS, an acronym for "quick and dirty operating system." Kildall later accused Paterson of "ripping off" CP/M, a charge that has shadowed Microsoft because of its subsequent purchase of QDOS.[40] Paterson countered that he never saw Kildall's code. Using Intel and Digital Research manuals, he said, he created an operating system that performed the same functions as the original CP/M operating system on a 16-bit chip. "Making the recipe in the book does not violate the copyright on the recipe," said Paterson. "I'd be happy to debate this in front of anybody, any judge."[41] Paterson also differentiated QDOS from CP/M by devising improved approaches to storing data and organizing files.

Under pressure from an IBM deadline, Allen contacted Seattle Computer with news of a Microsoft customer with a possible interest in licensing QDOS. He asked whether Microsoft could act as licensing agent, never mentioning that the customer was the world's biggest computer manufacturer. In January 1981, Seattle Computer granted Microsoft nonexclusive rights to market QDOS. Microsoft paid $10,000 upon signing of the agreement and agreed to pay $10,000 each time it sublicensed the product (or $15,000 if the sublicense included the source code). Allen and Gates then turned around and sublicensed QDOS and the source code for the first and only time under their contract with Seattle Computer. Microsoft reportedly received just $15,000 from IBM for the sublicense.[42] The transaction kept development of the IBM personal computer on track, however, thereby ensuring that the sale of Microsoft's languages would move forward as well.

It is likely that no one fully appreciated how valuable the operating system that became known as DOS would ultimately become. IBM sacrificed immense profits by adopting a hands-off policy toward all software developed for its personal computer, the PC. As a hardware manufacturer, the company probably did not foresee that in years to come, software would become the more important element of computer systems. Moreover, in its negotiations with Microsoft, IBM was reacting to past lawsuits. When the company failed to keep well clear of software vendors' activities, vendors had a habit of accusing IBM after the fact of stealing their ideas. Neither did Seattle Computer understand the sales potential of QDOS. (Management may have guessed who Microsoft's customer was, however, based on information that was beginning to leak out about IBM's top-secret personal computer.) Finally, few if any market participants foresaw the proliferation of competitive clones of the PC, which created another vast market for the original's operating system.

~

Bill Gates, however, apparently did have some inkling that QDOS might prove to be a gold mine. Two weeks before IBM launched its personal computer, Microsoft bought the operating system outright from Seattle Computer Products for $50,000. Allen initially discussed only an exclusive licensing agreement, but when the contract arrived at the office of Seattle Computer founder Rod Brock (reportedly after being personally revised by Gates),[43] the terms called for Microsoft to own the product.

Microsoft had approached Seattle Computer after learning that a software distributor was offering $250,000 for the rights to QDOS. The source of that information was the distributor himself, who felt that in good faith he had to disclose the offer to Microsoft, with whom he had a business relationship. Brock accepted Microsoft's lower cash offer, perceiving that the difference in price was offset by other terms of the deal.

These advantages included a 50 percent discount on licensing of Microsoft languages, as well as Microsoft's promise to provide updated versions of QDOS to Seattle Computer. The latter represented a substantial benefit because Tim Paterson, the creator of QDOS, had left to join Microsoft, leaving Seattle Computer no ability to update QDOS on its own.

To clinch the deal, Allen brought in Paterson to read over the contract. Paterson knew about Microsoft's arrangement with IBM, but his employment contract precluded him from sharing the information with Brock. He duly assured his former boss that the agreement was fair.

Paterson later said that he was surprised by the huge success of the PC, considering that IBM was a newcomer to the personal computer market. He characterized the outlay of $50,000 for QDOS as "a massive gamble on Microsoft's part, a 50/50 chance."[44] The perspective of others within Microsoft may have been different, however. For one thing, Japanese companies were beginning to ask Microsoft about sublicensing QDOS. This was a clue that the operating system represented more than a way of getting Microsoft's languages into one particular line of computers. In addition, Brock subsequently suggested that Microsoft must have been anxious to close the deal. The evidence was the company's dispatching of Steve Ballmer, who "tried to get us to hurry up and agree to the thing and sign it."[45] According to Ballmer, the Gates college buddy who had joined Microsoft from Procter & Gamble a year earlier:

> I went down there [to Seattle Computer's offices] . . . as part of the process to get the license signed, get the license signed, get the license signed. Bill had been pushing on me. . . . We knew the IBM Personal Computer and MS-DOS [the new name applied by Microsoft], not 86-DOS [Seattle Computer's designation] but MS-DOS, would be announced sometime in the not-too-distant future from the end of July. And I wanted to have this agreement signed before the IBM PC was introduced.[46]

If Gates was expecting a bonanza, he was not disappointed. The IBM PC featured an open system, that is, its design specifications were not kept secret. Software makers consequently queued up to design products for users of the PC and its clones, in each case obtaining a license for MS-DOS. Microsoft's operating system became an industry standard, eventually employed in more than 80 percent of personal computers.

Gates characterized Microsoft's resulting advantage in words that he would come to regret:

> Standards increase the basic machine we can sell into. . . . I really shouldn't say this, but in some ways it leads, in an individual product category, to a natural monopoly: where somebody properly documents, properly trains, properly promotes a particular package and through momentum, user loyalty, reputation, sales force, and prices builds a very strong position within that product.[47]

On the strength of its strong position in operating systems, Microsoft quadrupled its sales in one year, 1981, to $16 million. A decade later, the company was earning more than $200 million annually from the sales of MS-DOS alone. Sorting out charges of monopolization would prove a legal thicket, but there was no doubt about the profitability of market domination.

By Gates's admission, Microsoft focused too exclusively for too long on its languages and operating systems. As a result, the company neglected the larger segment of applications, the software that instructs computers in carrying out such functions as word processing and financial analysis. Once Gates recognized the need for a change in direction, however, he pursued the applications with characteristic fanaticism.

Working with Steve Jobs of Apple Computer, a team of Microsoft programmers began development of software for a new kind of personal computer. Called the Macintosh, it successfully commercialized the graphical user interface, a technology originally developed by Xerox Corporation. Abbreviated "GUI" (pronounced "gooey"), the new technology did away with the letter codes that computer users had been obliged to memorize and tap into keyboards in order to enter instructions. In place of the bland codes were lively icons, pictorial representations of desired computer functions. For example, Xerox's commercially unsuccessful Star computer introduced a trash can icon for erasing files, which the Macintosh adopted. By pointing to icons with a hand-manipulated control (mouse), the Macintosh user could run the computer with the intellectual ease of moving papers from a desktop to a file drawer.

Microsoft's task was to supply the Macintosh with a spreadsheet, a business graphics program, and a database. In crafting the agreement,

Jobs took into account the possibility that Microsoft might exploit the experience gained in its Macintosh work and beat Apple to market with its own software for mouse-driven computers. The contract barred Microsoft from marketing any such products before January 1, 1984, or a date one year after the Macintosh's first shipment, whichever came first. Once again, it turned out, Gates had struck an advantageous bargain. Microsoft did, in fact, leverage off its Macintosh development work to create a competing graphical user interface product. When Jobs objected, Gates pointed out that he was not competing in any of the three specific applications that the contract covered and would not do so before January 1, 1984. Jobs wound up with less of a head start over Microsoft than he had expected when he drafted the contract, thanks to his own excessive optimism about the length of time required to ready the Macintosh for market.

Microsoft's own GUI product had been in development since late 1981. Initially called Interface Manager, the program was designed to be sandwiched between the software applications and Microsoft's DOS operating system. As Gates envisioned it, Interface Manager would reduce the difficulty of switching between applications with dissimilar designs. A key feature was the ability to divide the computer's screen into "windows," which permitted users to view several different applications simultaneously. Hoping to create an industry standard for the IBM PC in the interface category, as it had in operating systems, Microsoft finally settled on a generic name for the product: Windows.

Gates then began lobbying computer manufacturers to sell Windows with their machines and software companies to begin writing applications programs for his not-yet-available interface. Unfortunately, Microsoft's competitors were further ahead in the development of GUI applications. Hoping to rally support, Gates suggested to reporters (in January 1983) that Microsoft would launch Windows before competitor VisiCorp introduced its VisiOn program. That prediction was refuted in October, when VisiCorp announced that VisiOn was ready to ship. Striking back, Microsoft formally announced Windows. Like the original Allen-Gates pitch on BASIC for the Altair, it was a case of vaporware, even though the term still had not been coined. Computer manufacturers and software developers should not gear their efforts toward VisiOn, Gates was saying, because Microsoft would soon be in the market with something better. By the end of 1984, he proclaimed, Windows would be running on more than 90 percent of all IBM-compatible computers.

Despite long hours in college honing his poker skills, Gates had overplayed his hand. The technical challenges of creating a graphic environment on top of the DOS operating system proved formidable. Again and again, Microsoft was forced to delay the shipment of Windows. When the product finally debuted, two years late, there was little for Microsoft to do but poke fun at itself in a "Windows Roast" for media and industry pundits. Gates joked that Ballmer had proposed accelerating development by eliminating features. "He came up with this idea that we could rename this thing Microsoft Window," he said, "and we could have shipped that thing a long time ago."[48]

Even then, Gates's travails with Windows were not over. The initial product was "a pig," in the words of a Microsoft programmer who spent nearly two years on the project.[49] As a matter of fact, one observer ticked off a veritable menagerie of unflattering comparisons:

> When Windows first appeared, it was widely viewed as a kludge (a dog): it was buggy (it had glitches) and was a memory pig (it used up a lot of space in the computer's hard drive), and it was generally less elegant than Apple's GUI.[50]

Most personal computers in use in 1985 had too little speed or memory to take full advantage of Windows's capabilities. Furthermore, as a consequence of the long delays in getting the program to market, few application programs had been written for Windows.

On top of everything else, Apple threatened to sue Microsoft for allegedly violating its copyright in creating Windows. Apple backed down, however, when Gates indicated he would halt development of Excel and Word for the Macintosh. Apple needed the programs badly in order to bolster the Macintosh's disappointing sales. The settlement of the suit required Microsoft to make the modest concession of acknowledging that its visual displays were derivatives of visuals developed by Apple. In return, Microsoft received a royalty-free license to use the graphical display technology that had been developed for the Macintosh. Gates thought the issue had been laid to rest, but in 1988, Apple sued Microsoft for allegedly stealing Macintosh features for its Windows 2.03 update. In the end, the court rejected Apple's claim of copyright infringement, ruling that "the look and feel" of the Macintosh desktop was not covered by the company's copyright.

Only in 1990, with the introduction of version 3.0, did Microsoft finally win over the Windows critics. This time around, all major software producers supported the product, in sharp contrast to the 1985 experience. Windows 3.0 became the hottest software product of all time, selling a million copies within four months. Bolstered by the program's belated success, Microsoft became the first software maker to reach a billion dollars of annual revenue in 1990. Gates also achieved his objective of creating another industry standard in the interface category. By the late 1990s, more than 90 percent of all personal computers in the United States were using the Windows 95 update of his original GUI vision.

Bill Gates and Paul Allen received additional gratification in 1990 as Allen rejoined Microsoft's board of directors. The company's cofounder had stepped down in 1983 following a bout with Hodgkin's disease. Clashes between the two strong, but contrasting, personalities were also said to have contributed to Allen's departure, although Gates stated that heated disagreements had been a productive element in their relationship from the outset. In any case, the two longtime friends teamed up to provide the funds for construction of the Allen/Gates Science Center at Lakeside, where their collaboration began. "We like to talk about how the fantasies we had as kids actually came true," Gates remarked.[51]

Indeed, the reality far exceeded anything that Gates fantasized. By 1998, Microsoft had 27,000 employees and was logging $14 billion of sales. In the early days, Gates speculated that if the company proved truly successful, it might someday employ 20 people.[52] Around 1981, Steve Ballmer wanted to alleviate an acute shortage of programmers by hiring 50 people. Gates refused to authorize such an aggressive plan, fearing that the added costs would bankrupt the company. Shortly before Microsoft's annual revenue quadrupled to $16 million in one year with the introduction of the IBM PC, Gates insisted that it was impossible for a software company to grow to more than $10 million in sales. The market was too small, he claimed, and growth was constrained by limits on the number of programmers who could collaborate effectively on a project. After that theory was disproved by the spectacular success of the DOS operating system, Gates told venture capitalist David Marquardt, "You cannot build a software company bigger than a hundred million. And I will prove it to you."[53] Later, he confided to Ann Winblad, a successful entrepreneur who was Gates's romantic interest for a time:

> I think I can get this company to half a billion dollars in sales. I think. And everyone's counting on me to do that. Now in my mind, if I really stretch my mind, I can get the company to half a billion dollars in sales. Then everybody will expect more, and I don't have a clue how we'll ever get past half a billion dollars in sales.[54]

Investment bankers saw a brighter future, however. By the early 1980s, they were urging Microsoft to make an initial public offering (IPO) of its stock. Apple Computer had gone public in 1980, suddenly making founder Steve Jobs worth $250 million on paper. Two of Microsoft's competitors, Lotus and Ashton-Tate, sold stock to the public in 1983, raising a total of $74 million. Three more producers of microcomputer software went public in 1984–1985.

Notwithstanding the market's ravenous appetite for software IPOs, Gates was cool to the idea. To begin with, he worried that a stock offering would distract employees. Publicly traded stock, he observed, created confusion because its value did not always correspond to short-run financial performance. "And to have a stock trader call up the chief executive and ask him questions is uneconomic," Gates added. "The ball bearings shouldn't be asking the driver about the grease."[55] Furthermore, with net profits running at 19 percent of revenues in the 12 months ended June 30, 1985, Microsoft could easily finance itself from internally generated funds. Unlike its competitors, Microsoft was under no pressure to go public from venture capitalists seeking to cash in their investment. To be sure, Gates and Allen had mildly diluted their stakes by selling a 5 percent stake to David Marquardt's venture capital firm, Technology Venture Investors (TVI), shortly after converting the Microsoft partnership into a private corporation in 1981. (Future billionaires Gates, Allen, and Ballmer received the largest slices of stock: 53 percent, 31 percent, and about 8 percent, respectively.) The $1 million generated by the TVI sale was not needed in the business, however. Microsoft simply added the funds to its already large cash hoard.

Despite Gates's misgivings about going public, Microsoft's growth and its need to attract top talent forced the issue. By 1987, the company estimated, more than 500 managers and programmers would own stock as a result of grants of options and sales of shares to employees. At that point, Microsoft would be required to register with the Securities and Exchange Commission. Registering would effectively create a public market, albeit a narrow one, for Microsoft's stock. By selling a substantial number of shares to the public, the company could create a liquid trading market.

Bill Gates's initial approach to pricing the Microsoft IPO contrasted sharply with Ross Perot's determined effort to obtain the highest possible price in Electronic Data Systems's 1968 offering. (See Chapter 4.) With a bull market underway and price-earnings multiples for software companies soaring, the lead underwriters recommended a price range of $17 to $20 a share. Gates argued successfully for a *lower* range of $16 to $19. At that level, he argued, the underwriters would not risk embarrassing Microsoft by being obliged to drop below the lower bound to sell the stock. Even at $16, Microsoft's price-earnings multiple would rank in between the prevailing multiples of other personal computer software producers and the higher multiples accorded mainframe computer software producers. Besides, at $20 a share, Microsoft's market capitalization (the aggregate value of its shares) would top $500 million, a level that made Gates uncomfortable.[56]

Once institutional investors saw management's presentation, however, it became clear that the Microsoft IPO would be a hot deal. Encouraged also by the continuing stock market rally, Gates reconciled himself to the eventual offering price of $21. On the first day of trading, March 13, 1986, ferocious demand drove Microsoft's shares to $27.75. Gates had sold about $1.7 million worth at the initial offering price, retaining a stake worth more than $300 million at the close of trading. *Fortune* reckoned that at the age of 30, Bill Gates ranked among the 100 richest Americans.[57] A year later, on March 19, 1987, Microsoft shares closed at $91.25, $.50 above the price required to make Gates a billionaire. At the time, he was the youngest person ever to have achieved that status. In the high technology area, he shared the distinction of being a self-made billionaire with only Ross Perot and Hewlett-Packard's David Packard and William Hewlett.

From a net worth point of view, it was a great time for Gates, but fate was laying the groundwork for future travails. The month after he officially became a billionaire, IBM and Microsoft announced OS/2, a new operating system that they expected to become the new standard for personal computers. Unfortunately, the product ultimately failed, in part because personal computer users balked at the expense of switching from DOS. Even though OS/2 faded from the scene, however, it left an enduring and troublesome legacy on the antitrust front. At a November 1989 trade show, Gates and the head of IBM's desktop computer division made a joint statement to software dealers about the already troubled OS/2. A related press release implied that Microsoft would add features to OS/2, which would be designed to operate only on the most powerful personal computers. At the same time, the press release suggested, Microsoft would limit the capabilities of its potentially competitive Windows program and aim it at less powerful machines.[58] To Federal Trade Commission (FTC) lawyer Norris Washington, it sounded as if the two companies were colluding to divide the market for operating systems.[59] That would be a clear violation of the antitrust laws, enforcement of which the FTC shared with the Justice Department. Thus began a determined effort to pin an antitrust rap on Microsoft.

Long after the OS/2 became a dead letter, federal prosecutors' attempt to mount an antitrust case against Microsoft continued. When the FTC abandoned the enterprise in 1993, the Justice Department's Antitrust Division took the unusual step of obtaining the records of the FTC's investigation in hopes of breathing new life into the case. The matter did not end with a 1995 consent decree, in which Microsoft agreed to refrain from certain practices that the Justice Department deemed anticompetitive. Prosecutors took Microsoft to court in 1998, charging that the company had violated the terms of the consent decree.

The aspect of the Microsoft antitrust case that is important to you, as an aspiring billionaire, is not the legal hairsplitting. Operating within the bounds of the law is a given, as is hiring competent legal counsel to deal with the inevitable need to define those bounds as new circumstances arise. Subject to such constraints, your objective is to overcome the leveling impact of competition in order to earn exceptional profits. Microsoft unquestionably achieved that goal, vaulting Bill Gates, Paul Allen, and Steve Ballmer to the top ranks of American billionaires. The antitrust case provides an invaluable glimpse into the company's successful business tactics. Concepts gleaned from the following sketch of the case can be applied and modified to create tomorrow's great fortunes.

Case Study: The Microsoft Antitrust Case

As the antitrust case evolved, the prosecutors' thesis shifted from their original notion that Microsoft was conspiring with IBM to divvy up the market for operating systems. That concern became irrelevant as the two companies moved from an uneasy collaboration to fierce, head-on competition in which IBM allied itself with Oracle and Sun Microsystems. The government accordingly turned its focus to two types of alleged anticompetitive practices.

First, the investigators searched for evidence of tying, illegal transactions in which customers were compelled to buy one Microsoft product if they wished to buy another that they truly desired. In particular, the government objected to Microsoft's requirement that personal computer manufacturers include Microsoft's browser (software for searching the Internet) whenever they installed Windows 95. To the extent that manufacturers complied with Microsoft's demands, users of personal computers would not see icons for competing browsers such as Netscape's when they initially turned on their monitors. As an example of alleged coercion in enforcing the policy, Compaq's software procurement director stated in a deposition that Microsoft threatened to terminate its licensing agreement if Compaq displayed Netscape's browser icon on the "desktop" (main screen) of its Presario line of computers. Microsoft's critics charged that such tactics were designed to "cut off the air supply" to competitors.

In support of the antitrust case, Microsoft's critics cited the 1951 *Lorain Journal* precedent. It involved an Ohio daily newspaper that enjoyed a substantial monopoly in local print advertising. The United States Supreme Court ruled it illegal for the paper to refuse to sell advertising space to businesses that also advertised on radio. To Microsoft's opponents, this precedent applied to such exclusionary practices as forbidding Internet service providers to promote non-Microsoft browsers. Microsoft's leverage arose from the service providers' need to deal with the company on account of the dominance of Windows in personal computers.[60]

Microsoft countered that adding a browser to Windows was a natural product innovation that the government should not impede. The company likened it to product enhancements originally offered as options by automobile manufacturers, but which eventually became standard equipment. In effect, the company sought to expand the definition of "operating system" in reaction to charges that it was illegally bundling other products with Windows. (Indeed, Windows itself had gradually come to be viewed as part of the operating system, even though it was originally conceived as the interface between the DOS operating system and applications software.)

The company even contended that Windows and the browser were inseparable. One technology columnist disputed that claim, saying that a purchase of Microsoft's Internet Explorer along with Windows was "like buying a bottle of shampoo with a bottle of conditioner taped to it."[61] Another commentator labeled as "transparently untrue" Microsoft's claim that Windows and Internet Explorer constituted a single, integrated product. He pointed out that Microsoft had earlier sold the two separately and continued to list Internet Explorer among its "products," along with Excel and Barney Goes to the Circus.[62] In proceedings arising from a Justice Department complaint that Microsoft had violated its 1995 consent decree, Federal District Judge Thomas Penfield Jackson further undercut Microsoft's assertion of inseparability. In a matter of minutes, he removed Internet Explorer from the screen of a new computer running Windows, then demonstrated to the court that Windows continued to work satisfactorily. On the face of it, a self-proclaimed layman in computer technology had succeeded in a feat that Microsoft's programming experts contended was impossible.[63] Michael Caton, technical director of PC Week Labs in Medford, Massachusetts, backed up the judge's position. His organization's tests, he said, disproved Microsoft's claim that removal of Internet Explorer 3.0 would make it impossible to "boot" (start up) its operating system.[64] On the other hand, *Business Week*'s technology commentator, Stephen H. Wildstrom, upheld Microsoft's argument that the browser should be regarded as an integral part of the operating system. He found, upon trying out a test version of Windows 98, that it integrated Internet Explorer more effectively than previous versions had.[65]

For you, the aspiring billionaire, the essential point does not involve the details of the embedded browser issue. What you need to absorb is the spirit in which Microsoft contested the issue:

> *The keys to battling antitrust claims are ingenuity and tenacity.*

At one stage, Microsoft offered, as a concession, to give consumers three options:

1. A two-year-old version of Windows.
2. A current version of Windows with Internet Explorer removed, a modification that Microsoft claimed would totally cripple the system.
3. The current Windows/Internet Explorer bundle.

Computer users immediately grasped that if the claim of total crippling was true, the choice was really a nonchoice between the bundled product and an outmoded operating system. Later on, Microsoft executives attempted to shift the terms of the embedding debate by ceasing to refer to Internet Explorer as a browser. That phraseology made the product sound too much like the separate entity that the prosecutors contended it was. Testifying in the antitrust case brought by the Justice Department and 20 state attorneys general, company executives instead referred to "bits of browsing technologies."[66]

The Microsoft defense team pulled out all the stops in fighting the Justice Department's antitrust charges. Defense witness Richard Schmalensee, a Massachusetts Institute of Technology economist, cited a survey that found that 85 percent of software developers believed Microsoft's integration of Internet functions with Windows would benefit their companies. The prosecution then produced a February 1998 e-mail message from Bill Gates that read:

> It would HELP ME IMMENSELY to have a survey showing that 90 percent of developers believe that putting the browser into the operating system makes sense. Ideally, we would have a survey before I appear at the Senate on March 3rd.[67]

Other e-mail messages from Microsoft employees explained how they could pose questions to elicit the responses that Gates desired.

A few days later, Microsoft attempted to rebut a prosecution witness's claim that he had created a program capable of separating Internet Explorer from Windows without degrading Windows's performance. The company presented a videotape demonstration showing, the defense team said, that the procedure in fact slowed down the operation of a computer running Windows. During cross-examination, the prosecution pointed out that on the videotape, a title bar (a label indicating which program was running) showed that the Internet Explorer had not, in fact, been removed. On the face of it, the poor performance captured on the tape was not the fault of the program designed to remove the browser. Caught by surprise, Microsoft's witness insisted that the company had not meant to mislead the court and had "probably just filmed the wrong screen shot."[68] After the lunch recess, the witness reported that he had learned that the videotape did in fact show a computer running Windows with the browser removed, but that the title bar for some reason did not change as it was supposed to. Government lawyer David Boies commented that Microsoft had provided no real explanation for what it claimed to be a mistake. "All we do know," he added, "is that the tape they put into evidence is not reliable."[69]

Some industry observers and legal experts contended that Microsoft hurt its case by its uncompromising stance on the integration of Internet Explorer and Windows. Therefore, it is not clear how far would-be billionaires should go in emulating Microsoft's antitrust counterattack. By the same token, imperviousness to just this sort of criticism, combined with willingness to defend a competitive edge relentlessly, has served Bill Gates well on balance.

Another benefit of reading the Microsoft case study is the insight it provides on defending a dominant market position. If you achieve such a position, you can expect competitors to fight ferociously to take it away. While staying within the bounds of the law, you must be prepared to respond in a manner that can be summed up in three words:

Play to win.

The second category of anticompetitive practices for which federal prosecutors searched were attempts to thwart development of potentially competing products through coercion, financial inducements, or acquisitions. For example, in 1985 Apple's new chairman, John Sculley, gave in to Gates's demand to discontinue development of the MacBasic language for Macintosh and sign over rights to the MacBasic name to Microsoft. According to Sculley, Gates indicated that if Apple did not give up the project, he would suspend Apple's license to use the competing Microsoft language on its popular Apple II computer. "[Gates] insisted that Apple withdraw what was an exceptional product," claimed an Apple software engineer. "He held the gun to our head."[70] In a similar vein, internal documents of Intel indicated that at an August 1995 meeting, Gates made "vague threats" to support competitors of the semiconductor producer if it did not cease development of software that he viewed as a danger to Microsoft's interests. Intel did in fact, delay the project. Chairman Andrew Grove characterized that decision by saying that his company "caved in" to Microsoft's demands.[71]

On the defense side of the case, Microsoft and a number of sympathetic journalists maintained that the allegations of antitrust violations originated with rival software producers. Having failed to compete effectively by the ordinary route of creating superior products, said Microsoft's defenders, these companies lobbied to have Washington clip Bill Gates's wings. Moreover, Microsoft's competitors chose an inappropriate vehicle for their nefarious purpose. In the view of Gates and his supporters, the antitrust laws had little application to the knowledge-intensive software business. The legislation was designed in the nineteenth century with capital-intensive industries such as steel in mind. Surely, the reasoning continued, it served no legitimate public purpose to shackle America's conspicuously successful software industry with new regulations. Government bureaucrats could not possibly keep up with the computer world's constantly changing technology.

In the late 1990s, as the likelihood increased that the Justice Department would charge Microsoft with monopolization, Gates passionately argued the merits of his case. Ridiculing the allegations against him, he stormed:

If we weren't so ruthless, we'd be making more creative software? We'd rather kill a competitor than grow the market? Those are clear lies. Who grew this market? We did. Who survived companies like IBM, ten times our size, taking us on?[72]

Gates also pointed out that his supposed monopoly had not enriched itself through price gouging. On the contrary, consumer prices had fallen at the same time that the power of software was rising. The parallel with John D. Rockefeller Sr. was striking. Both titans of wealth had sought to create an industry standard (with Rockefeller even incorporating the notion into his company's name), which in itself could be fairly portrayed as a benefit to consumers, while steadily bringing down the cost to users.

On some of the later versions of Windows that it introduced, however, Microsoft raised its prices to manufacturers of personal computers. Granted, the updates provided additional value through new features, but Microsoft's dominant market share facilitated its ability to boost prices. A similar strategy was evident in the market for suites, or packages of programs such as word processing and spreadsheets, a segment in which Microsoft's Office had attained an 87 percent market share by 1998. In 1997, Microsoft stopped allowing corporate customers to use Office at home at no extra charge. The company also phased out "concurrent" licensing, in which a company could pay for fewer licenses than one per employee, provided no more than the licensed number of employees would be using Office simultaneously. Given the difficulty of switching from Office after building applications for it, companies argued that they had little choice but to accept the cost increase resulting from the policy change. "I wish we had an alternative," said the president of one Microsoft corporate customer, "but we really are in a captive position."[73]

Also worthy of careful study by aspiring billionaires is Microsoft's Internet browser pricing policy, namely, giving it away for nothing. Mitch Stone, a personal computer user with no industry affiliations, characterized Microsoft's zero-price policy as a deliberate effort to destroy Netscape, a much smaller competitor. Stone, who created the "Boycott Microsoft" web site, said that he saw no benefit to consumers from such tactics.[74] Notwithstanding Stone's evident passion on the subject, his interpretation of Microsoft's intent was not an outright fantasy. Commenting in 1997 on the Microsoft-Netscape rivalry, Steve Ballmer said, "We're giving away a pretty good browser as part of the operating system. How long can they survive selling it?"[75]

In his effort to head off antitrust action, Gates did not limit himself to intellectual arguments. Microsoft, which along with many other high technology companies had previously paid little attention to Washington, beefed up its governmental relations effort. (Sun Microsystems and Netscape, regarded in some quarters as instigators of the antitrust initiative, had been quicker to escalate their political activities.)[76] Some onlookers discerned a conscious public relations effort by Microsoft to counter the demonization of Bill Gates. Microsoft's $150 million investment in now-struggling Apple Computer, according to these observers, was a "clever ploy" designed to defuse monopolization charges by propping up Apple's "token resistance" in the market for operating systems.[77]

On the question of the applicability of nineteenth-century antitrust laws to Microsoft's competitive environment, Gates contended that Moore's Law made the computer industry unique. Named after Gordon Moore, one of the founders of Intel, the law states that microprocessing power doubles (and therefore becomes half as costly) every 18 months. In such a competitive environment, Gates argued, no company could maintain undue control of the market for long, as evidenced by the high mortality rate of computer and software companies over the years. Commissioner Christine Varney of the FTC, which deadlocked on the question of bringing an antitrust action, acknowledged that it was difficult to apply existing legislation in such a dynamic environment:

> My concern is with the law's ability to keep pace with market conditions in fields that change so rapidly. Once it's clear a practice is anticompetitive, the issue may already be moot.[78]

Yale professor of law and economics George L. Priest sounded a similar note. Because of the high costs of entering the steel industry, he observed, U.S. Steel's monopoly had taken 30 years to erode. In the low-barrier-to-entry software business, by contrast, "market share can be overturned in a very short period."[79]

Certainly, Sun Microsystems's Java language had to be regarded as a credible challenge to the lock on customers that Microsoft enjoyed through its domination of operating systems. Java offered a cost-effective means of distributing upgrades through a server (a central computer feeding a network) or over the Internet, rather than relying on armies of technicians for installation. Additionally, the new, flexible language ran on a variety of computer architectures, potentially helping corporations that were still dependent on mainframe computers to make the leap to the Internet. In short, Java represented a technological end run that might undermine even as well entrenched a position as Microsoft maintained through DOS and Windows.[80] The existence of Java bolstered Gates's argument that in an industry as dynamic as software, no government intervention was required to prevent companies from establishing and maintaining monopolies.

Bolstering Gates's argument was a study by economist Stan Liebowitz and his collaborator, Stephen Margolis. The researchers found that Microsoft products had succeeded in the marketplace when they achieved superior ratings in computer magazine reviews and had failed when they did not. Liebowitz further noted that Microsoft achieved dominance in word processing and spreadsheet applications on Macintosh, where it did not control the operating system, before it reached comparable market shares on DOS-driven personal computers. This undercut charges that Microsoft had triumphed by leveraging one monopoly into another.[81]

There was also ample support for Microsoft's claim that its rivals were the impetus behind the government's antitrust case. Oracle and Sun Microsystems were members of a coalition, ostensibly focused on promoting competition in electronic commerce, that was formed by former Senate majority leader Bob Dole. Dole lobbied against Microsoft, which he accused of using its monopoly in operating systems to "stifle competition, slow down innovation, and leverage itself into monopolies in other markets."[82] Another Microsoft rival, Netscape, retained Robert Bork, an antitrust expert and onetime nominee for the Supreme Court, as an adviser on legal strategy. Notwithstanding his past reputation for advocating a low level of antitrust intervention by the government, Bork proceeded to pen opinion pieces supporting the case against Microsoft. (Bork answered the charge of inconsistency by pointing out that he had long ago stated that the Supreme Court had decided the aforementioned *Lorain Journal* case correctly.[83])

If you achieve a dominant market position, then judging by Gates's experience, you must be prepared to be demonized with comments like the following. Each came from an executive of, or an attorney for, a Microsoft competitor; not all were willing to be quoted by name:

> Hey, I think the guy is truly dangerous. Bill is the most surprisingly conscience-free individual I've ever met, and that amount of power in the hands of a guy without a conscience is dangerous.[84]

> The question is, are we looking forward to the Information Age, or will it be the Microsoft Age? It's kind of like Microsoft vs. mankind—and mankind is the underdog.[85]

> Theirs is a praying-mantis business model: they have sex with you, and then they eat you.[86]

> Sometimes Microsoft seems like the fox that takes you across the river and then eats you. There isn't any part of the market they don't want.[87]

> They have a game plan to monopolize every market they touch.[88]

Ironically, the "underdog" quotation came from Oracle's Laurence J. Ellison. The chief executive officer of Netscape, James L. Barksdale, said Oracle was the first company that he recalled using the phrase "choke off their air supply," later associated with Microsoft. Oracle, according to Barksdale, was promising to apply the treatment to one of its own competitors.[89]

Gates's Lifelong Application of Billionaires' Methods

The "air supply" example of the pot calling the kettle black raises a key point to emphasize in summarizing Bill Gates's lessons for future billionaires. The high-growth industries that most often spawn vast personal fortunes tend to be characterized by fierce struggles for survival. No one is likely to emerge from such battles without a willingness to push the envelope. Gates showed the requisite instincts early on, cracking the C-Cubed code to cut his charges for computer time, marketing a vaporware BASIC language, and exploiting the vagueness in Harvard's rules on use of its computer center.

Similar gray areas in the antitrust rules were invitations to play extremely hard to win. Without attempting to interpret the law, you can observe that Microsoft fought its way into new markets by aggressive pricing, calculating that it could outlast less well capitalized competitors. Critics might assert that such tactics were predatory, but, as the saying goes, you cannot make an omelet without breaking eggs. To put it another way:

> *In high-stakes businesses such as computer software, making billions without making enemies is probably impossible.*

While Gates had a natural inclination to test boundaries, he further prepared himself for the software wars through precocious experience in negotiating contracts. While still in high school, he learned to bargain effectively in selling programming services to corporate executives, school administrators, and municipal officials. "If anybody wants to know why Bill Gates is where he is today, in my judgment it's because of his early experience in cutting deals," says the father of one of the billionaire's high school years collaborators.[90]

Another lesson reinforced by Gates's career is that originality is not essential to creating a vast fortune. "Bill Gates is the leader of the parade," one software industry veteran observed, "because he sees where the parade is going and gets in front of it."[91] To be sure, Gates was a highly talented programmer before switching to a full-time management role, where he continued to provide invaluable strategic guidance to product development. Microsoft's dominant position, however, arose from an operating system closely modeled on a Digital Research product and the graphical user interface technology invented at Xerox.

Like Sam Walton, Gates exemplifies the success achievable by those who do not fall victim to the not-invented-here syndrome. As with tactics designed to choke off competitors' air supply, adopting the best features of competitors' products must be viewed through the prism of industry practice. In 1988, when Apple Computer sued Microsoft for alleged copyright violations involving the Macintosh's visual display features, software analyst Lawrence Magid criticized Apple for trying "to thwart the obvious direction of the industry."[92] Dan Bricklin, developer of the VisiCalc spreadsheet program, added that the nature of writing software was to build on what was there before. Gates's most valuable talent was his ability to turn good ideas into dollars by translating them into commercially successful, and frequently dominant, products. Even at that, it was software distributor Vern Raburn who gave Gates the idea of entering the market for retail software, which eventually became Mirosoft's largest source of income.[93]

Fierce dedication has been another principle of Gates's financial success. During summer break after his senior year in high school, all-night sessions became the norm in his programming work on TRW's massive Bonneville Power Administration project. As he later recalled:

> We had contests to see who could stay in the building like three days straight, four days straight. Some of the more prudish people would say, "Go home and take a bath." We were just hardcore, writing code.[94]

Gates's climb also underscores the importance of retaining as much ownership of an enterprise as possible. As noted, he owned nearly half of Microsoft's stock at the time of its initial public offering. By insisting on extremely conservative financial policies, he kept the company out of the position of being compelled by a downturn in business to raise outside capital.

Finally, and to tell the complete story, luck took a hand in Gates's success. Specifically, Microsoft benefited from a number of strategic errors by competitors. For example, Digital Research drove too hard a bargain with the vastly more powerful IBM and handed Gates and Allen the mandate to furnish an operating system for the PC. Apple opened a vast opportunity for Microsoft by not emulating IBM's open architecture strategy, thereby discouraging software developers from designing products for the Macintosh. "Microsoft," according to Vern Raburn, "has been the single greatest beneficiary of inept competition of any company in the world."[95] Learning to be lucky is clearly a tougher challenge than copying the other elements of Bill Gates's success formula. At a minimum, though, you should learn this lesson of Microsoft's success:

> *Don't be too proud to take advantage of undeserved good fortune.*

6

CONSOLIDATE
AN INDUSTRY

In union there is strength.
                    —American proverb

Consolidation consists of reducing the number of firms in an industry. In automobile manufacturing, for example, a large field of American producers at the beginning of the twentieth century eventually narrowed to three major competitors, General Motors, Ford, and Chrysler. By the 1990s, the industry was consolidating on a global basis, highlighted by Chrysler's merger with Germany's Daimler-Benz.

The usual rationale for consolidation is increased efficiency. In some cases, the efficiencies arise from spreading fixed costs of production over a greater number of units than a small operator can produce. Spreading administrative costs or advertising expenses over a larger sales volume is another basis for consolidation. Yet another type of savings arises through obtaining volume discounts on the purchase of raw materials or goods for resale. One more impetus for consolidation is the desire of corporate customers to control their costs by limiting the number of suppliers with which they deal.

To be sure, large organizations often become inefficient as a result of cumbersome controls, unduly long lines of communication, and redundant overhead. Smaller, more streamlined companies may then be able to enter the industry and compete successfully. In other instances, a new entrant may prosper by cream skimming, that is, concentrating solely on a highly profitable segment of the business. Long before any of these new entrants appear, however, young industries follow a predictable pattern of consolidation. Mom-and-pop operators sell out to well-capitalized, professionally managed outfits capable of doing business on a regionwide or nationwide scale. Opportunities for amassing riches exist for those who recognize the potential for the process to repeat itself in yet another industry.

The financial benefits of consolidation are enormous and have arisen in countless industries. It is therefore surprising that consolidators are not more prominent among the all-time leaders in wealth accumulation. The outstanding example is the banker J. Pierpont Morgan, who ranked 23d in Michael Klepper and Robert Gunther's 1996 ranking of the wealthiest Americans of all time.[1] Morgan masterminded the consolidations that produced such industrial giants as American Telephone & Telegraph, General Electric, International Harvester, United States Steel Corporation, Westinghouse Electric Corporation, and Western Union. According to a cartoon published in *Life* magazine, the answer to the question "Who made the world?" was "God made the world in 4004 B.C., but it was reorganized in 1901 by James J. Hill, J. Pierpont Morgan, and John D. Rockefeller."[2] Hill, too, was a consolidator. He focused on railroads, an industry that Phil Anschutz helped to consolidate further a century later. Rockefeller carried consolidation to the limit by establishing an effective monopoly in petroleum refining. There was likewise an element of consolidation in the formation of the largest U.S. retailer, Wal-Mart. Sam Walton grew the company primarily by building new stores, but he also bought out several competing chains. Wayne Huizenga stands out among contemporary billionaires, however, in his primary reliance on consolidation as a business strategy. Perhaps the reason lies in the immense challenges involved not only in making a consolidated enterprise gel, but also in clearing a large personal profit in the process.

To begin with, a consolidator must forge a coordinated enterprise out of many separate companies. As with any corporation built through acquisitions, there is a practical argument for retaining the former owner-operators to stay on and run their businesses. There may be no other way to recruit a sufficient number of experienced managers quickly enough. The drawback is that independent operators do not make an easy transition to employee status. Keeping too tight a rein on the former entrepreneurs may destroy their motivation, while too loose a rein may prevent the consolidated company from providing consistent quality.

Managing the managers is just one of several organizational problems of fashioning an effective organization out of disparate enterprises. An individual who excels at the deal making required to put the company together may lack any skill or interest in the administrative routine of preventing it from falling apart. The classic example was William C. Durant, the genius chiefly responsible for melding the independent automobile producers Buick, Cadillac, Chevrolet, Oakland (later Pontiac), and Olds (later Oldsmobile) into General Motors. Durant's limitations as a manager caused him to lose control of his creation just two years after its founding, and then again, permanently, a decade later. It fell to Alfred P. Sloan Jr. to devise the necessary organizational methods for running a complex, multidivisional automobile manufacturer.

In the end, Durant's consolidation proved phenomenally successful, with General Motors surpassing Ford as the largest automaker. Unlike Henry Ford, however, neither Durant nor Sloan became a billionaire. Durant ultimately lost his fortune in stock market speculation. Sloan died a wealthy man, but did not qualify for Klepper and Gunther's list of the wealthiest Americans of all time. Two individuals who did make the cut were the brothers John and Horace Dodge, who built a successful carmaker of their own, in addition to bankrolling Ford in his early days. From a personal wealth standpoint, entrepreneurs fared better than consolidators in the auto business.

Many decades after the nationwide consolidation of car manufacturing, an effort to consolidate the automobile dealership business represents a formidable challenge even for Wayne Huizenga. His success in building national organizations in the formerly fragmented businesses of waste hauling and video rentals gives many investors the assurance to take the leap of faith with him. In any industry, however, the feasibility of consolidation is obvious only after it has been accomplished. Economies of scale that look tantalizing on paper sometimes prove elusive in practice.

Aside from a firm grasp of the potential operating efficiencies, considerable financial sophistication is needed to consolidate a business and emerge with a large personal profit. The consolidator must raise vast amounts of capital, which in turn requires convincing lenders and investors that the business plan will work. Another group to win over consists of the sellers of the companies that will form the new entity, who may be asked to swap their businesses for the acquirer's stock. Unless the consolidator can overcome a mountain of skepticism, the cost of acquiring companies, in terms of equity given up, will be extremely high. Without hanging on to a big chunk of the equity, there is little chance of personally clearing a billion dollars.

In short, consolidation is a plausible path to colossal wealth, but one for which you must stretch your talents in several different directions. Learning to love the deal is paramount, but once you have completed the

---

THE BILLIONAIRE HOW-TO

Fundamental Strategies

- Consolidate an Industry
- Outmanage the Competition
- Thrive on Deals

Key Principles

- Keep on Growing
- Make Mistakes, Then Learn from Them
- Develop a Thick Skin
- Use Financial Leverage
- Hard Work Is Essential
- Copying Pays Better Than Innovating

lengthy round of acquisitions, the consolidated company will flounder without the application of superior organizational skills. If you are not keen on running a complex organization, it may be sufficient to bring credible, professional managers into the picture. Do not, however, imagine that you will be able to cash in immediately and potentially leave behind a house of cards. Investors are wise to that one. A more likely path to success is to copy Wayne Huizenga's methods, with a particular emphasis on his extraordinary work ethic.

Wayne Huizenga

Money is how you keep score.[3]

Wayne Huizenga has capitalized on consolidation in a variety of businesses. The range is remarkable, encompassing waste hauling, videotape rentals, automobile sales and rentals, security alarms, professional sports franchises, hotels, portable toilets, lawn care, bottled water, pest control, billboards, and machine-parts washing service. In general, though, he has operated within the services category, favoring rental businesses that generate recurring revenues. "If I rent something," he explains, "basically I'm selling the same thing over and over again."[4] Even in waste hauling, Huizenga identified Dumpster rentals as the most profitable part of the business and emphasized it.

After dropping out of college, Huizenga (pronounced "HIGH-zeng-uh") took a job managing a small garbage collection business owned by a family friend. If not a glamorous business, waste hauling was one that Huizenga knew and respected. It had provided the livelihood of Huizenga's grandfather, his father, three uncles, and five male cousins. In the Chicago community of Dutch descendants from which they all sprang, people liked to say they "had garbage in their blood."[5] Before long, Huizenga was applying the tried-and-true methods that underlie most billion-dollar fortunes.

Wayne Huizenga had learned from his father that he would not go far by working for someone else. Almost immediately, he was on the lookout for an opportunity to become his own boss. In 1962, the 25-year-old

Huizenga got his chance. With $5,000 borrowed from his father-in-law, he bought a used garbage truck and a list of 20 customer accounts in Fort Lauderdale, Florida. After hauling waste from 2 A.M. until noon, Huizenga would go home, shower, don his only suit, and solicit additional business. By 1968, he had expanded his operations in a fiercely competitive industry from a single truck to more than 40.

From this modest start, Huizenga built the world's largest trash-hauling business. Together with Dean Buntrock, who had married into the Huizenga clan, he founded Waste Management Technologies (now WMX). A few years earlier, Browning-Ferris Industries, led by Tom J. Fatjo Jr., had conceived the idea of creating a nationwide waste-hauling company. Buntrock and Huizenga set themselves a similar objective and a breakneck timetable, acquiring 100 companies within the first two years. Waste Management went public in 1971 with an aggregate share value of $5 million. By 1984, the company's valuation had grown to $3 billion.

Explaining that he was weary of commuting from his Florida home to the company's Chicago headquarters, Huizenga retired from Waste Management in 1984. (The friction inherent in sharing senior management duties with the equally strong-minded Buntrock probably influenced his decision, as well.) Huizenga began investing in a variety of service businesses, but found his next great opportunity in a Dallas videotape rental chain. When first persuaded over his strong objections to investigate the opportunity, he was no movie fan, did not own a videocassette recorder, and had previously perceived the video rentals as a sleazy business dominated by pornographic titles. To his surprise, however, Blockbuster had legitimized the young industry. Quickly recognizing the company's potential for generating recurring revenues, Huizenga and his partners bought a 60 percent stake and launched a breakneck expansion program. Through a combination of acquisitions and internal growth, Blockbuster added stores at the rate of one every 17 hours over seven years.[6] By 1992, the operation was larger than the next 300 video store chains combined and had more cardholders than American Express.[7] Under Huizenga's guidance, the company's stock market value skyrocketed from $32 million in 1987 to $8.4 billion in 1994, when he sold out to Sumner Redstone's Viacom.

Having built two billion-dollar companies, Huizenga already boasted a record nearly unparalleled in the annals of American industry. Nevertheless, he was eager to move on, spurred less by the trappings of wealth than by the challenge of increasing it. "Wayne always keeps the carrot far enough out in front of him and he never really wants to catch it," observes Dean Buntrock. "That's his personality. He's never satisfied."[8] Huizenga next undertook to consolidate the huge but fragmented automobile dealership industry, using as his base a conglomerate called Republic Industries. By 1997, Huizenga controlled the largest U.S. auto retailer, along with two of the leading rental car companies, Alamo and National.

Over the course of three decades, Huizenga has engineered an astonishing 1,000 acquisitions.[9] By continually refining his basic strategy of consolidating fragmented service industries, he has amassed a net worth estimated at $1.8 billion in 1998.[10] Along the way, he has overcome the obstacles, setbacks, and criticism that cause most fortune builders to top out well below that level.

To begin with, Huizenga's original waste-hauling business took a wrong, although not fatal, turn in the mid-1960s. Several operators had begun to complement their business with pig farming. The less-than-obvious synergy involved separating the edible garbage, cooking it, and feeding it to the pigs. Huizenga copied the idea, but was forced to abandon the sideline when his pigs bred poorly and inexplicably became diseased. The problem was not their food supply, Huizenga insisted, correctly pointing out that other garbage collection companies had implemented the strategy successfully.[11] Since this unfortunate experience, in any case, he has become known for his disciplined approach to industry selection.

Subpoenas and fines for harassment of competitors and price-fixing dogged Waste Management during its spectacular growth period. The violations occurred in just a few of the company's many regional operations and neither Huizenga nor Buntrock was directly implicated. Nevertheless, regulators and prosecutors relentlessly investigated Waste Management, inspired by previous revelations of organized crime's control of commercial waste hauling in southern New York and northern New Jersey. Huizenga steadfastly refused to make waste-hauling acquisitions in those locales, saying that they were the only parts of the United States where the mob had infiltrated the otherwise respectable business. Despite his precautions, however, the stock market valuations of Waste Management and its competitors probably suffered from popular perceptions of underworld links.[12]

In a similar vein, Blockbuster's stock market valuation was perennially held down by the specter of cable television operators introducing video-on-demand. (Huizenga rejected the argument that video rentals would be obsolete within a few years. "People go to the bathroom," he observed. "With pay-per-view, they'll miss part of the movie. With videos, they can just stop them, and start again.")[13]

When Huizenga moved on to the automobile business, Toyota and Honda sued to block his acquisition of dealerships. Skeptics questioned the plausibility of cost savings he hoped to achieve through increasing the scale of operations. Despite Huizenga's previous successes in industry consolidation, critics argued that previously independent auto dealers would not mesh in a unified operation. As for the car rental business, the naysayers disparaged it as hopelessly price-competitive.[14]

Not only his business strategies, but also his financial practices generated criticism. Observers objected to the prices he paid in certain acquisitions, arguing that they exceeded industry norms. "With individual companies, we're looking for premium people," Huizenga replied, "and to get them we'll pay a premium price."[15] On the opposite side of the coin, some Blockbuster shareholders expressed dissatisfaction with Huizenga's sale of the company to Viacom for stock. The problem was that Viacom's share price slid during the course of the lengthy negotiations.[16]

Huizenga also had to endure the accusation that the companies he created through consolidation fared poorly after he left the scene. The implication was that the entities that emerged from his rapid-fire mergers did not really hang together from an operational standpoint. According to mutual fund manager Mario Gabelli, "There's a real question about whether Wayne is an entrepreneur who bails out and then moves on to the next target."[17] Huizenga answered the charge by pointing out, more than a decade after leaving Waste Management, that he still held his stock.[18] That was hardly the expected behavior of someone who thought he was leaving shareholders with an empty bag. By the same token, Huizenga frankly acknowledged that he sold out of Blockbuster at an advantageous time:

We could see the potential that the Internet, superchannels, and other forms of technology could change that industry too much, and we were concerned that it was headed downhill.[19]

Finally, critics lambasted Huizenga's practice of acquiring businesses for stock. On the basis of his reputation, Huizenga's acquisition vehicle typically commanded a high price-to-earnings (P/E) ratio. Even though some of his acquisitions were made at premium valuations, as noted, many of his targets were mom-and-pop operations that sold for less lofty multiples. As illustrated in Table 3, a company can potentially boost its earnings per share, and by extension its stock price, by buying a low-multiple company with its own high-multiple stock. Recognizing the potential for abuse in stock-based acquisitions, one anonymous source cited in *Fortune* went so far as to label Republic Industries a chain letter. An investment banker, speaking on the record and for attribution, described Huizenga's venture into the auto business as "a financial jitterbug."[20]

In Table 3, Consolidator Corp. sports a high price-earnings multiple of 25×, reflecting the stock market's expectation that management will achieve rapid earnings growth through industry consolidation. Applying that earnings multiple to the company's $2 per share earnings produces a share price of $50. Consolidator's market capitalization (the

TABLE 3 BUILDING MARKET CAPITALIZATION THROUGH AN ACQUISITION FOR STOCK

	Consolidator Corp. (Preacquisition)	Mom & Pop Co.	Consolidator Corp. (Postacquisition)
Earnings ($million)	$100	$10	$110
Shares outstanding (million)	50	—	53
Earnings per share ($)	$2	—	$2.08
Price-earnings multiple	25×	15×	25×
Price per share ($)	$50	—	$52
Market capitalization ($million)	$2,500	—	$2,756
Acquisition price ($million)	—	$150	—
New shares issued (million)	3	—	—

Transaction costs not included.

By dominating the market for petroleum refining, John D. Rockefeller Sr. made enough money to enjoy such luxuries as having his valet push him around his estate on a chainless bicycle. *Source:* Corbis/Bettmann-UPI

In his younger days, H. L. Hunt played for high stakes at the poker table as well as in the oil fields, but a late marriage turned him toward clean living, exercise, and health food. *Source:* Corbis/Bettmann-UPI

J. Paul Getty recommended buying low as the road to riches and claimed that milk was his favorite beverage. *Source:* Corbis-Bettmann

The founder of the Wal-Mart discount store chain, Sam Walton, once vowed that he would dance the hula on Wall Street if his managers met an ambitious performance goal. *Source:* Corbis/Bettmann-UPI

After making a billion dollars in computer services, Ross Perot started his own political party and ran for President. At a press conference, he was greatly amused by a questioner's suggestion that he spent his time investigating people. *Source:* Corbis/Reuters

Richard Branson has generated millions of dollars worth of publicity with stunts such as modeling the product line at the launch of his Virgin Bride retail operation. *Source:* Virgin Management, London

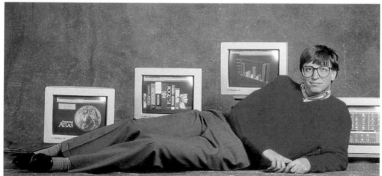

Bill Gates combined exceptional mathematical aptitude with a precocious interest in amassing wealth to become the world's first centibillionaire. *Source:* © Alan Levenson, Corbis

aggregate value of its outstanding shares) is 50 million times $50, or $2.5 billion.

Mom & Pop Co., a privately held concern, agrees to sell out to Consolidator. As a small player with unexceptional earnings growth, it fetches a price equivalent to just 15 times its $10 million of earnings. Consolidator pays the $150 million purchase price in $50-a-share stock, necessitating the issuance of three million shares.

Instead of *diluting* Consolidator's earnings (reducing earnings per share), the transaction is *accretive*. That is, the postacquisition Consolidator has earnings of $2.08 per share, up from $2 before the acquisition. Applying Consolidator's 25× multiple to the combined earnings produces a stock price of $52, up from $50. Market capitalization now comes to $2.756 billion, which exceeds by $106 million the sum of Consolidator's market capitalization prior to the acquisition and the $150 million that it paid for Mom & Pop. By extending its own high multiple to the earnings of the newly acquired, less glamorous company, Consolidator has created a whole that is worth more than the sum of its parts.

Note that at this point, Consolidator's management has not demonstrated that any cost savings or other synergies will arise from the business combination. On the other hand, repeating the acquisition-for-stock procedure dozens of times will generate sustained, rapid growth in reported earnings per share. The high earnings multiple granted to Consolidator will seem to be vindicated. The true test, however, will come as management attempts to meld the operations of many formerly independent companies. If genuine, operationally derived earnings gains fail to materialize at that point, Consolidator's multiple probably will tumble, bringing down its artificially elevated stock price.

The practice of acquiring companies for stock does not invariably create a misleading impression. If combined with aggressive accounting methods, however, it can present an exaggerated picture of the acquirer's earning power. Accordingly, on April 21, 1999, the Financial Accounting Standards Board (FASB) voted unanimously to prohibit pooling-of-interests accounting for mergers and acquisitions, the method illustrated in the Consolidator/Mom & Pop example. Subject to further regulatory procedures, the rule change was scheduled to become effective on January 1, 2001.

Even before FASB decided to ban the technique, pooling-of-interests was in principle permitted only in mergers of equals. Exceptions to the rules, however, often allowed combinations of unequals akin to Consolidator's acquisition of Mom & Pop to qualify for pooling. Aspiring billionaires must always be on the lookout for such loopholes, regardless of the specific rules in effect at any given time.

Under the "purchase method," the alternative to pooling-of-interests accounting, an asset called goodwill is created. It essentially represents the difference between the purchase price and the acquired company's tangible assets at the time of the acquisition. Subsequent to the acquisition, the combined company must write off a portion of goodwill against its earnings each year. Typically, this annual charge eliminates the earnings-per-share gain shown in the Consolidator/Mom & Pop example.

To get around the difficulty posed by the purchase method, the acquirer may be able to charge off the bulk of the goodwill immediately following the purchase. That gambit eliminates annual goodwill write-offs and restores the magical boost in earnings per share afforded by a pooling. If the auditors or regulators do not permit the slate to be wiped clean right away, the acquirer can potentially minimize the impact on earnings by writing off the goodwill over an extremely long period. (In 1989, a prominent Wall Street analyst accused Blockbuster of precisely this ploy in a research report that precipitated a sharp, although temporary, drop in the company's stock price.)

The bottom line is that by jumping through a few hoops, the acquiring company can often qualify for the pooling method or obtain equivalent benefits through the purchase method. An entrepreneur who has a significant stake in the acquiring company can create substantial paper wealth just by making acquisitions. As a rule, lasting wealth does not get created by randomly buying companies that fail to mesh as consolidated enterprises. By the same token, making acquisitions for stock can dramatically leverage the wealth-building efforts of a consolidator with a sizable personal stake in the acquiring company.

Although many unscrupulous financial operators have used stock-financed acquisitions to manufacture earnings and artificially inflate share prices, the transactions do not invariably have nefarious motives. In Waste Management's case, a mid-1970s Securities and Exchange Commission inquiry found no fault with the accounting for its stock-financed acquisition spree. The most common alternative to a stock purchase, namely, paying with borrowed cash, creates interest costs that may strain the acquirer's finances if business turns down.

In fact, Waste Management's decision to go public was necessitated by the company's voracious appetite for capital, which was dangerous to satisfy entirely with debt. From the outset of his career in waste hauling, Huizenga had borrowed aggressively. According to the son of one of his early competitors, it was his willingness to utilize debt, in addition to his tireless work, that enabled him to surpass other operators:

> Wayne learned back then how to leverage money, how to use income from one operation to buy another operation. He lived very simply and every cent he made he would pour back into the business.[21]

Not only Huizenga's father-in-law, but also his aunts and uncles supplied credit before he began relying on banks and finance companies. In his first two acquisitions, Huizenga persuaded the sellers to take back paper. He paid a percentage of the purchase price up front, then liquidated the balance over three or four years. These were "the ultimate leveraged buyouts," in Huizenga's phrase.[22]

Financial savvy has played an indisputably essential role in Wayne Huizenga's amassing of wealth. When assuming an active part in building a company, he has made certain to obtain a large enough personal stake to ensure a big payoff. By one account, he has sometimes chided Dean Buntrock for his failure to capture a larger portion of the wealth created by Waste Management.[23] (Extending the notion that it is nearly impossible to become rich by working purely as an employee, Huizenga has strongly encouraged his key managers to buy stock in his enterprises. The ownership mentality, combined with Huizenga's well-attested, genuine concern for his associates, has proven a successful motivator in practice, as well as in theory.)

~

As important as his financial astuteness is, it does not come close to fully explaining Wayne Huizenga's knack for accumulating wealth. Vital strategic insights have enabled him to leapfrog competitors, as exemplified by his early recognition that owning a landfill is essential to achieving a dominant role in waste hauling. (Ownership brings in incremental revenue from other operators, while also eliminating the risk of getting squeezed by a hike in dumping fees at a municipally owned site.) Another arrow in Huizenga's quiver is his fierce dedication to networking. Trade associations have been a key source of his operational innovations, as well as many acquisition opportunities. When a contract to haul manure from the Pompano Beach harness track accounted for a substantial portion of his revenues, he encouraged his father to get into the flow by buying a string of trotters.[24]

The most important nonfinancial factor in Huizenga's climb to the ranks of the wealthiest Americans, however, is his extraordinary capacity for hard work. Asked to account for his record of becoming the consolidator in industries where he faced many rivals, Huizenga modestly replies:

> We operate under the philosophy that we're no smarter than our competitor. To accomplish twice as much, you have to work twice as hard, and we have a lot of hardworking people who don't mind making a sacrifice to see the company grow.[25]

Cynics might consider such comments disingenuous, but Huizenga unquestionably leads by example. In building his first waste-hauling business, he says, he consistently worked 20 hours a day. "And I never drove main streets," he adds. "I always drove down the alleys and the side streets trying to find out what was happening."[26] During Waste Management's phase of frenetic acquisitions, Huizenga typically spent Sunday evening to Friday evening on the road, seeing his family only on weekends. His idea of cutting back on work, following the sale of Blockbuster, was to arrive at his office at 6:45 A.M. instead of 4:30 A.M. (He also began taking Saturdays off to play golf on his private course, but continued to work Sundays.)[27] One time, a business associate pointed out that he had scheduled a business trip to England over the Fourth of July weekend. Huizenga replied that he saw no problem, because the British did not celebrate the holiday.[28]

The intensity suggested by Huizenga's work habits comes out also in his competitiveness. He once remarked that auto sales and rentals represented a trillion-dollar market and that he only wanted his fair share: half.

Later, he explained that he had been joking; even 1 or 2 percent of such an immense market would represent a lot of business.[29]

~

Winning is no laughing matter to Huizenga, however. Associates report being sent back to the negotiating table 15 times or more until they emerge with terms that satisfy him. In purchasing a portable toilet business for $4 million, Huizenga rejected the sellers' demand that they retain $100,000 cash in a bank account. Unwilling to yield on the issue, which his colleagues thought too trivial to be a deal killer, he abruptly said, "Okay, boys, let's go home." Huizenga's team stood up and left the room, but as he expected, the sellers did not let them get down the elevator before conceding the point and closing the transaction.[30] "A deal," Huizenga once told an interviewer, with a smile, "it's like chasing a girl. You work at it until she says yes." Then the smile disappeared. "You keep putting the pressure on them. Hit 'em right between the eyes. . . . You kill 'em."[31] According to one participant in many of Blockbuster's acquisitions, Huizenga often told reluctant sellers that delaying would only reduce the eventual sales price. While they dallied, he elaborated, Blockbuster would open more stores and become a greater competitive threat.[32]

As many observers have attested, however, Huizenga's negotiating success is not entirely a matter of pressure. His down-to-earth manner immediately establishes rapport, reducing the tension inherent in a bargaining session. Huizenga is also a master at divining the other party's objectives, aside from money. For example, an entrepreneur selling out to an industry consolidator may want to stay on as chairman, even with no real duties, in order to continue having an office to go to every day.[33]

Would-be emulators of Huizenga's methods should note that his interpersonal skills represent yet another product of his extraordinary capacity for work. Despite an innately unpretentious personality and a genuine interest in others, the hard-charging Huizenga displayed a few rough edges early in his career. For example, a 1960 altercation over a bill brought him a $100 fine for assault, plus $1,000 damages in a related civil suit. Associates report that in earlier years, he let his impatience show when they disagreed with statements that he considered self-evident.[34]

Determined to realize his vast ambitions, Huizenga labored hard to master his emotions and channel his immense energy productively. He freely acknowledges that he has learned a great deal from others, including competitors. For example, Browning-Ferris's management, which tried to buy out Waste Management in 1971, provided him a valuable model for handling himself professionally, even in an ultimately unsuccessful negotiation.[35] Much like an athletic champion, Wayne Huizenga has capitalized on his natural talents while eagerly adopting nonoriginal techniques of demonstrated value.

7

Buy Low

Frugality is a fair fortune.
—American proverb[1]

"Buy low, sell high" is the simplest formula imaginable for amassing wealth. What could be less complicated than purchasing an asset when nobody wants it, then selling it when no one can live without it? Making a killing in stocks, say the sage market commentators, is merely a matter of buying straw hats in the wintertime. Best of all, the opportunities for buying cheap and selling dear crop up frequently. The most casual observer of the business scene will notice dramatic fluctuations from year to year in such assets as office buildings, crude oil, and common stocks.

Before concluding that you have found The Secret, however, you would be wise to ask, "If it's truly as simple as that, why isn't everybody rich?" The standard answer offered by financial gurus is that most investors lose their nerve when they see the crowd rushing toward the exit. Rare are the individuals who think for themselves and "buy when the blood is running in the streets." Lore has it that the market's few genuine contrarians become immensely wealthy, as evidenced by such self-made billionaires as J. Paul Getty, Laurence Tisch, and Warren Buffett. This standard explanation, however, does not stand up under close scrutiny.

The notion that any intelligent person can recognize when an asset is cheap, but only a few possess the courage to act on their convictions, presupposes that thoroughly objective standards exist for determining cheapness. Such standards do exist, but only in textbooks of finance. Quantitative valuation standards are tricky to apply in practice.

Stocks, for example, can be evaluated against one another on the basis of various financial ratios. Best known among these measures is the price-earnings multiple. Unfortunately, while there is little dispute about a company's stock price at a given moment, the relevant earnings figure can be more devilishly difficult to pin down.

If the stock price is low relative to the past year's earnings, it may reflect an expectation on the part of securities analysts that earnings will decline. Measured relative to next year's lower projected earnings, the company's multiple may be right in line with multiples of its industry peers. The stock would then be deemed fairly valued, rather than cheap.

Alternatively, the company's stock price may be low relative to analysts' consensus forecast of earnings in the coming year. Suppose, however, that the forecast is subject to huge uncertainties. For instance, the company might be facing a possible strike or a potentially unfavorable judgment in ongoing litigation. Either misfortune would cut deeply into profits. In such a case, investors would be prudent to assign a lower multiple to the company's forecasted earnings than they award to peer companies facing fewer uncertainties. Again, the conclusion that the stock is cheap, based on its price-earnings multiple, is by no means clear-cut.

In the popular mind, these are quibbles. According to the financial mass media, the renowned contrarian investors regularly swoop down on stocks that have gotten cheap by any reasonable standard. Then, when the crowd abruptly shifts from fear to greed, the titans of finance sell into the hysteria and reap spectacular capital gains. This oft-repeated tale, however, is a gross simplification of reality.

The complete story includes innumerable cases of stocks that vindicated the supposedly sheeplike majority. To cite just one case, Westinghouse Electric was trading at $25 a share during the bear market of late 1990, down from a $38 peak. At a mere seven times earnings, while the average stock was selling at a price-earnings multiple of 13, the electrical equipment manufacturer was ridiculously cheap. Various other standard financial measures, including the company's dividend yield and its market-value-to-book-value ratio, confirmed that Westinghouse was a bargain. In fact, said financial writer and money manager David Dreman, the stock "scored high by every contrarian strategy."[2] Nervous Nellies worried about real estate exposure in the company's financial division, yet management had boosted earnings steadily for a decade and a half. Westinghouse looked like a bargain hunter's dream, right up until management announced a real estate–related write-off of more than a billion dollars in 1991. From the ostensibly depressed price of $25, the price plummeted to $17 and bottomed out below $10 in 1992.

Billionaires are not exempt from the phenomenon of supposedly cheap stocks (or real estate or commodities) getting cheaper. For example, Warren Buffett has made many astute purchases over the years, but he has not prospered by investing in sure things. From time to time, as he candidly acknowledges when reviewing his performance with shareholders, the scenario has not played out the way he expected.

In 1989, Buffett's investment vehicle, Berkshire Hathaway, invested in USAir through a specially designed convertible preferred stock. The airline was attempting to create a nationwide route system connecting midsized cities, but investors were not yet convinced that the strategy would succeed. Almost as soon as Buffett bought the stock, a fare war erupted. The following year, air travel plummeted in response to the outbreak of the Persian Gulf War.

With the benefit of hindsight, the previously cheap valuation of USAir began to look like awareness that if revenues fell, the airline would be hammered by its high employee costs. Over the next few years, USAir racked up $3 billion in losses. The carrier also suspended the dividend on Berkshire Hathaway's convertible preferred stock. In the end, Buffett cut his losses and bailed out of USAir.[3]

Contrarians will quickly point out that in picking cheap securities, Buffett has been right more often than he has been wrong. His ascent to billionaire status has depended on much more than a good eye for bargains, however. The plain fact is that confirming that an asset is cheap by some standard financial ratio is not the sort of rare talent that produces a 10-figure net worth. Neither does anybody reach the billionaires' club by patiently waiting for the rest of the world to recognize the bargain. After all, if it takes an asset 10 years to double in price, the annual rate of increase in value is only 7.2 percent. In some periods, investors have done better than that by owning super-safe United States Treasury bonds.

The time-horizon problem is magnified when the buyer of a supposedly cheap asset employs financial leverage. While the clock ticks, cash flows out in the form of interest payments. Some types of assets, such as rental properties, generate income that covers at least a portion of the debt service. In contrast, raw land and undeveloped mineral reserves are examples of investments that may consume cash for years. If you play the game, you take a large risk that you'll run out of cash and lose control of the properties before the expected surge in value occurs. All in all, making money on the simple proposition of buying low and selling high is anything but simple.

As the stories of the legendary bargain hunters show, the key to making shrewd purchases pay off is to be proactive. To make that first billion, you need to do more than identify underexploited assets. You must also take steps to bring about fuller exploitation of the assets. That may mean cutting wasteful corporate overhead, capitalizing more effectively on a well-known brand name, or, in the case of a rental property, increasing the rent roll. Depending on the circumstances, bringing about more effective exploitation may require you to prod management, oust management, or take direct charge of operations. Once profits go up, the market valuation generally will take care of itself.

John Kluge illustrated the technique of turning dross into gold with WTTG, a Washington, D.C., television station that he acquired along with the moribund Dumont network in 1959. In 1962, Kluge described the money-losing station as a "garbage pail." His formula for increasing the property's value consisted of programming reruns of once-popular shows such as *I Love Lucy*, *The Dick Van Dyke Show*, and *Perry Mason*, along with movies of a bygone era. An entire generation had never viewed this material and as Kluge remarked, "The new is not necessarily as good as the old product."[4] His strategy transformed WTTG into one of the nation's most successful independent stations, sometimes outdrawing the Washington and Baltimore network affiliates during the non-prime-time hours of 4:30 P.M. to 8:00 P.M.[5]

Proactive behavior is one common theme to watch for as you read the following sketches of champion bargain hunters. Observe as well the two distinct ways in which billionaires squeeze pennies until they scream. Not only do they pay as little as possible for the assets they buy, but they relentlessly strive to reduce the operating costs of their properties. Each dollar added to profits in this manner translates into several dollars, based on the price-earnings ratio, when the buyers of cheap assets sell.

John D. Rockefeller Sr. demonstrated the power of pinching pennies in the early 1870s, when he observed a machine in a Standard Oil plant that soldered caps to five-gallon tin cans of kerosene marked for export. The future billionaire asked the resident authority how many drops of solder were applied to each can. Told that the number was 40, Rockefeller asked the man to try 38 and see what happened. Leaks developed in a few of the cans sealed with only 38 drops of solder, but not in cans sealed with 39. Reducing the number of drops of solder by one saved $2,500 in the first year, Rockefeller estimated, and as the kerosene export business grew, the savings mounted to many hundreds of thousands of dollars.[6]

If you choose to follow the path of obsessively cutting costs, be warned that the habit may cross over into your personal life. J. Paul Getty's parsimonious habits were legendary, as you will read shortly. John D. Rockefeller devoted inordinate time to scrutinizing grocery bills and knocked down a doctor's $3,000 fee to $500 by threatening to sue. At the time, his annual income, all tax-free, exceeded $50 million.[7] Rockefeller, an avid golfer, insisted on switching to old balls whenever he and his foursome approached a water hazard. Amazed at those who risked losing new balls in such circumstances, he commented, "They must be very rich!"[8] Warren Buffett likewise hates to squander even modest sums. Traveling on one occasion with Katherine Graham of the *Washington Post*, he landed at New York's La Guardia Airport. Graham, wanting to make a telephone call and pressed for time, asked Buffett whether he had a dime. Buffett, by then a millionaire many times over,

THE BILLIONAIRE HOW-TO

Fundamental Strategies

- Buy Low
- Thrive on Deals
- Take Monumental Risks
- Do Business in a New Way
- Outmanage the Competition

Key Principles

- Keep on Growing
- Keep the Back Door Open
- Pursue the Money in Ideas
- Frugality Pays
- Develop a Thick Skin
- Use Financial Leverage
- Make Mistakes, Then Learn from Them

discovered that he had only a 25-cent piece. As he headed out for change to avoid wasting 15 cents, Graham shouted, "*Warren*, give me the quarter!"[9]

J. Paul Getty

The meek shall inherit the earth, but not the mineral rights.[10]

To J. Paul Getty, buying investments on the cheap was a natural outgrowth of his tightfisted personal habits. Even though he was the son of a self-made millionaire and quite willing to enjoy assorted luxuries, he embodied the billionaires' principle "Frugality Pays." Once, Getty arrived at a London dog show, with three friends in tow, at 4:50 P.M. Noticing a sign indicating that the five-shilling admission would fall to half price at 5:00 P.M., he insisted that his companions walk around the block for 10 minutes so he could save two shillings and sixpence a head.[11] Another time, Getty asked his dinner date to wait outside a restaurant until the orchestra finished playing, enabling him to avoid a cover charge for music.[12]

In the mid-1930s, Getty was smarting from unfavorable publicity surrounding his fourth divorce. Partly to restore his social standing, he set out to build a reputation as a collector of fine art. Coincidentally (perhaps), prices then stood at their lowest level of the century, thanks to the 1929 stock market crash. Tapestries were down by 75 percent from pre-Depression levels, he estimated, while furniture could be had for 10 or 20 percent of the prices paid 20 years earlier.

Getty hired experts to school him in such specialized areas as eighteenth-century decorative arts and busts of Greek and Roman heroes. He soon set his sights on a sixteenth-century Persian carpet that had once been deemed too beautiful "for Christian eyes to gaze upon." The owner, a prominent art dealer, was dying of cancer. Getty persuaded him to part with the treasure for a gain that amounted to less than 20 percent over 20 years.

Capitalizing on fears of an impending world war, Getty grabbed a Gainsborough portrait for exactly the same price it had fetched 10 years earlier. In a 1938 sale of the Rothschild collection, he obtained two secretaries at just 36 percent of their 1930 value. The same year, an early Rembrandt portrait fell into Getty's hands for one-third the price it had fetched in 1928. Not surprisingly, the art market's subsequent rebound earned Getty many times his original investment in these works.[13]

Getty's aversion to unnecessarily parting with a dollar extended to dealings with his family. Following his father's death, Getty's mother established an "irrevocable spendthrift trust" for the benefit of her son and his children. Sarah Getty donated $2.5 million to the trust on condition that her son contribute $1 million in cash. Claiming to be short of liquid funds, Getty instead made his contribution in stock. He valued the shares at $1.2 million and withdrew a $350,000 note from the trust as his change. In short, Getty expended no cash and contributed less than the required $1 million. "I just fleeced my mother," he boasted to his publicist, Howard Jarvis, who was later to win fame as a champion of tax reductions in California.[14]

In like spirit, Getty took pride in getting the better of an English peer when he acquired Sutton Place, a lavish estate outside London. The property included 60 acres of parkland, as well as a Tudor mansion with 14 principal bedrooms and a hall reputed to be the largest in Great Britain. In 1959, British landowners were reeling under tax rates as high as 98 percent. Sutton Place's owner, the Duke of Sutherland, was further strained by the expense of operating his grossly overstaffed farms. Capitalizing on the duke's predicament, Getty picked up the property for £50,000 ($140,000 at then-prevailing exchange rates). The sum represented less than half the price paid by the duke 40 years earlier.

By Getty's conservative estimate, he bought Sutton Place for less than 5 percent of its replacement value. A friend professed embarrassment that Getty had obtained the historic property from the previous owner "for the price of two swimming pools." Better still, Getty told the newspaper columnist Art Buchwald, living expenses at Sutton Place were considerably cheaper than in his former digs at the Ritz Hotel. For example, Getty explained, he could serve the drinks they were enjoying at the moment—a tomato juice and a rum and Coca-Cola—for 10 cents, while they would cost a dollar at the Ritz.[15]

According to the most famous legend concerning Getty's cheapness, the billionaire installed a pay telephone in Sutton Place to prevent guests from making long-distance calls at his expense. Stung by the derision that this act provoked, Getty claimed that the coin-operated phone had been put in only temporarily during renovations. Various workers and certain journalists, he explained, had been helping themselves to his private phones, calling relatives all around the world and running up bills of as much as £100. Getty attributed the whole pay phone incident to the directors of a company he had established to manage the mansion. Never, he intimated, had he meant to force his wealthy friends to forage for coins when placing telephone calls. Whatever the facts may have been, the celebrated pay phone was the first item visitors demanded to see whenever Getty opened his historic home to the public.[16]

Parsimony was not merely a peculiarity of Getty's, but a cornerstone of his approach to business. What seemed like penny-pinching, he pointed out, could translate into a major cost savings. Getty cited approvingly the example of a huge corporation that conducted a study of its wastebaskets. For one week, a team of workers collected the perfectly usable paper clips, rubber bands, erasers, and pencils that employees had thoughtlessly discarded. Toting up the value of these items and multiplying by 52, management calculated that $30,000 was being wasted every year.[17]

Even in the context of huge transactions, Getty could be amazingly careful with his money. In one instance, a longtime friend offered $17.5 million in cash for New York's Pierre Hotel, which Getty had bought for $2.35 million. Agreeing that the price was fair, Getty contacted his lawyer to draw up terms. Notwithstanding the large gain he stood to realize, Getty insisted that his friend pay for the cable.

While dictating the terms to his attorney, Getty inserted a clause releasing himself from the sale if a higher offer materialized within 90 days. He then used his friend's unsolicited bid to shop the hotel around for a better price. In the end, a superior bid emerged; there is no record that Getty reimbursed the original, disappointed bidder for the cost of the cable.[18]

Getty's lucrative involvement with the Pierre exemplified his knack for creating a fortune out of his instinctive bargain hunting. The luxury hotel had been built on Fifth Avenue in 1930, just as America began to sink into the Great Depression. Getty picked up the money-losing property in 1938 for less than a quarter of its original construction cost. He quickly set about enhancing the value of his purchase by persuading a prominent socialite, William Rhinelander Stewart, to stay at the hotel. Stewart's presence turned the Pierre into a center for New York society and its reputation was made.[19]

Although he made many shrewd purchases in real estate and art, J. Paul Getty put his bargain-hunting instincts to their highest and best use in the oil business. In 1914, he set up as a wildcatter, or independent operator, in Oklahoma. In his own words, the oil fields were then ruled by a "lusty, brawling pioneer spirit." The region's "primitive boomtowns" carried "bare-knuckled frontier-era names such as those of the four 'Right' towns: Drumright, Dropright, Allright, and Damnright."[20] In this rough-and-ready setting, Getty began to apply the methods on which many billion-dollar fortunes have been built.

~

Bankrolled by his father at a subsistence level, Getty struggled through his first year. His only advantage in the fierce competition was being more open to newly developed geological methods than the old-time wildcatters. Finally, in the fall of 1915, Getty spied his opportunity as a half-interest in the Nancy Taylor Allotment in Muskogee County came up for sale at a public auction.

According to his later account, Getty considered the Nancy Taylor prospect promising, but knew that older and better-established operators would be able to outbid him. Accordingly, he persuaded a bank to send one of its executives to bid in his name, without revealing his identity. Some of the wildcatters assumed that the banker must be bidding for one of the major oil companies, which would be prepared to top all offers. Others owed money to the bank and were therefore unwilling to bid against its representative. Thanks to his ruse, Getty recounted, all of his potential competitors sat out the auction, allowing him to obtain the lease for the pittance of $500.

That, at least, is how Getty told the story. Independent evidence suggests that the other wildcatters passed on Nancy Taylor simply because it seemed a poor prospect. Perhaps Getty embellished the story over the years, but there is no question that he struck oil on the property. He then sold it to a refiner, reaping $11,850 as his 30 percent share of the profit.[21]

When the oil boom moved on to southern California, Getty and his father investigated the territory surrounding a major strike by Union Oil. The experts generally agreed that the best prospects lay to the east of Union Oil's find, resulting in furious bidding for leases in that area. Other surrounding terrain appeared perfectly flat, a topography not ordinarily associated with oil. In the course of their inspection, however, George and Paul Getty happened to notice a locomotive laboring to reach a crossing at Telegraph Road, south of the Union Oil well. As the train reached the crossing, the engineer eased up on the throttle and began to pick up speed. Both father and son immediately realized that the crossing sat at the top of a dome, the precise spot where oil was most likely to be found. For $693, the Gettys purchased a lease on Telegraph Road that no one else wanted. Over the next 17 years, the property produced profits totaling $6,387,946.65.[22]

Meanwhile, in 1929, the stock market crashed. While others despaired, Getty recognized the debacle as a golden opportunity to satisfy his predilection for paying bottom dollar. Thanks to the plunge in oil company shares, petroleum could be found more cheaply on Wall Street than in the oil patch. "It was foolish," Getty reasoned, "to buy oil properties with 100-cent dollars when you could buy them indirectly with maybe 50-cent dollars."[23]

For starters, Getty purchased stock of Pacific Western Oil Company, a large California oil producer, at $3 a share. At one time, the stock had traded as high as $17. The company boasted a book value of more than $15 a share, which understated the true value of its reserves. In 1931, after stretching his personal credit to the breaking point in pursuit of Pacific Western, Getty gained control. The penny-conscious oilman promptly took advantage of the Depression by firing every single employee, then hiring them back at reduced salaries.

Getty next undertook to realize his dream of expanding his activities from exploration and production to transportation, refining, and marketing. With a fully integrated operation, Getty Oil could end its dependency on the majors as outlets for its crude production. Such arrangements generally worked to the disadvantage of wildcatters.

Getty identified a refiner and marketer, Tide Water Associated Oil Company, as a logical fit. He launched his campaign in March 1932, when the stock market was reeling from the suicides of Ivar Kreuger, the Swedish match king, and George Eastman of Eastman Kodak. Getty acquired his initial shares at $2.50, just a fraction above the stock's all-time low. Over the next five years, Tide Water rose to more than $16 and ultimately to many times that price. Following a series of proxy fights and legal struggles, the tenacious Getty captured control of the company.

~

After World War II, Getty multiplied his fortune by obtaining a drilling concession in a desolate region of the Middle East known as the Neutral Zone. Lying between Kuwait and Saudi Arabia, the area was devoid of vegetation and wildlife. In fact, the territory had certain characteristics that might suggest it had become a buffer zone because neither country wanted it:

- Summer temperatures as high as 165 degrees Fahrenheit.
- Humidity frequently reaching 100 percent along the coast.
- Persian Gulf waters, tempting to swimmers but infested with sharks and stinging jellyfish.
- Sand dunes filled with giant scorpions and vipers.
- Dust storms lasting several days.
- Hailstorms that turned the desert green overnight, attracting massive swarms of locusts.[24]

The truth was that Kuwait and Saudi Arabia had squabbled over the Neutral Zone for centuries before agreeing to share control of the territory, as well as the associated mineral rights. Getty's Pacific Western Oil Company won the bidding for the Saudi half of the drilling privileges in 1949, while Kuwait granted its own, separate concession. As a result of this peculiar arrangement, the fiercely independent oilman was forced into an uneasy joint venture.

Getty's partner was the American Independent Oil Group (Aminoil), a consortium of midsize and smaller U.S. companies. Aminoil, claiming superior technical resources, insisted on operating control of the project. Getty agreed, against all his instincts, largely because he was confident that the Neutral Zone contained an extension of the rich Burghan field to the north, in Kuwait. This confidence was based on no personal examination of the Neutral Zone, where he did not set foot until several years later. Rather, Getty maintained his longstanding faith in geology. Paul Walton, a 32-year-old Pacific Western geologist, not only described domed geographical structures that strongly suggested the presence of oil, but also allayed his boss's bizarre fear that these features were extinct volcanoes with no economic value.

Aminoil rejected a proposed Getty strategy of drilling for easily recoverable "garbage" oil. Lying a mere 800 to 1,000 feet below the surface, this high-sulfur crude could be produced cheaply, but it was costly to refine. Aminoil instead decided to concentrate on locating the Burghan extension. The consortium's team quickly identified the correct physical structure, but commenced drilling off to the side, rather than on the formation's apex. Getty's son George, dispatched by his father to protect Pacific Western's interests, helpfully pointed out that the rigs were deployed too low on the dome to produce oil. Unimpressed, Aminoil persisted in its error for three more years.

The operator's mistake cost Getty dearly. Saddled with payments on debt incurred to purchase the Neutral Zone concession, Pacific Western was forced to suspend cash dividends in 1950. Rumors began to circulate within oil circles that Getty had finally overextended himself and would land in bankruptcy. Nearing 60, he turned morose and began to question his own business sense, all the while conducting an ego battle with Aminoil's chief.

Then, just when conditions looked bleakest, Aminoil belatedly heeded the advice of George Getty and his geologists. The operator drilled a well near the top of the dome and in March 1953 struck oil in the Burghan extension. *Fortune* described the discovery as "somewhere between colossal and history-making." Pacific Western stock soared from $23.50 to $47.50 a share, doubling Getty's net worth in a single month.

According to a participant in the venture, only J. Paul Getty's determination could have produced the miracle of finding oil in a region run by two different countries, with the heads of the two concessionaires virtually at war. All the same, the venture tested Getty's tenacity to the utmost. Shortly before Aminoil finally found the Burghan extension, he was at the point of throwing in the towel after shelling out $30 million for a share in five dry holes.

Ironically, the venture that crowned Getty's career defied his lifelong strategy of buying low. In addition to offering King Ibn Saud an immediate $9.5 million in cash to pay his civil servants' salaries, he promised to pay $1 million a year as an advance against royalties, whether or not any oil was found. Getty also acceded to Saudi demands that he underwrite housing, schools, medical care, and a mosque for the oil workers' families, as well as a telephone system, postal service, and a water utility. To top it all off, Pacific Western consented to a royalty of $.55 a barrel at a time when the major oil companies were paying $.22 a barrel in other Middle Eastern concessions.

The Saudis were reportedly flabbergasted by Getty's bid. Competitors were outraged, correctly reasoning that Pacific Western's largesse would drive up the cost of other concessions. One executive called Getty's bid "completely insane."[25]

In retrospect, of course, the price wasn't crazy at all. Largely thanks to the Neutral Zone discovery, *Fortune* in 1957 proclaimed J. Paul Getty America's richest man. ("Remember," he told a reporter who marveled at his wealth, "a billion dollars isn't what it used to be.") And perhaps Getty was simply farsighted, recognizing that crude prices would inevitably rise from the prevailing $2 a barrel. Furthermore, Middle Eastern production costs were low enough to make the business profitable, even assuming no future price increases. (Getty characteristically improved the odds in that regard, ferociously fighting Aminoil over every minor expenditure.) Finally, Pacific Western's seemingly astronomical bid may have represented an acknowledgment that the Saudi Arabian government had grown more sophisticated in its negotiations with Western oil companies.

Getty's own explanation of the Neutral Zone matter was that he offered generous terms from the outset so that he wouldn't have to duck into an alley out of shame every time he saw an Arab coming.[26] Whatever his actual motivation may have been, J. Paul Getty appreciated the value of flexibility. When the potential for gain was great enough, he had the fortitude to deviate from his tightfisted habits.

Laurence Tisch

I find business very relaxing. I look forward every day to going to the office.[27]

For three decades following the downturn that enabled J. Paul Getty to pick up the Pierre Hotel for a song, new hotel construction was almost nonexistent in Manhattan. In 1961, the drought ended with the erection of the $25-million Summit at Lexington Avenue and 51st Street. Previously, Loew's Theatres had operated an unprofitable movie house on the site. Recognition that the real estate had greater value with an alternative use was one reason that the hotel's builder, Laurence Tisch, acquired a controlling interest in Loew's in 1959.[28]

The Summit, in short, came into being in an unconventional way. Laurence Tisch rarely chooses the conventional way, however. He has approached businesses ranging from insurance to cigarettes to watches with an avowed strategy of rejecting the received wisdom about value and the means of extracting it. His long career has provided him lots of opportunities to apply classic billionaires' methods. [Note that in November 1998, Laurence and his brother and cochairman Preston (Bob) officially handed over day-to-day operating control of Loews Corporation to Laurence's son, James, in conjunction with an office of the presidency consisting of three other members of the next Tisch generation.]

~

Tisch's independent thinking became apparent in his first hotel venture. In 1946, his parents had just sold their business, a New Jersey summer camp, and were hoping to plow the $125,000 proceeds into a Florida resort hotel. They correctly perceived that the Florida tourist trade was due for a boom, but so did countless other operators. The Tisches' 23-year-old son persuaded them to look closer to home, in the winter resort area of Lakewood, New Jersey. While speculators had driven up the prices of Florida hotels to $10,000 to $12,000 a room, the 300-room Laurel-in-the-Pines in Lakewood was on the market for $375,000, or just $1,250 a room.

This disparity did not arise from any lack of basis arithmetic skills on the part of investors. Rather, the owner had allowed the property to run down rather than invest heavily in renovation. According to Christopher Winans's *The King of Cash: The Inside Story of Laurence Tisch* (1995), the owner of the Laurel-in-the-Pines feared that business would slump with the end of the World War II prosperity. His fear was validated by a recent dip in the hotel's profits.

Rejecting both the feverish enthusiasm for Florida hotels and the pessimism of many businesspeople who expected a postwar depression, Tisch proceeded with a combination of high hopes and caution. Instead of buying the Laurel-in-the-Pines, he and his family leased it. This hedged approach was conceptually similar to Kirk Kerkorian's "keeping the back door open" by buying an airplane with an option to sell it back to the manufacturer.

Foreshadowing his later successes, Tisch showed that it was important not only to recognize value, but also to know how to capture it. Razzle-dazzle was an essential ingredient. Tisch enhanced the hotel's appeal with big-name entertainers, as well as amenities that were unusual for the day, including an indoor swimming pool and an outdoor skating rink. The rink provided a setting for attention-grabbing stunts such as scheduling games of basketball-on-ice and importing reindeer from Finland to pull a sleigh. By 1948, the Tisches were able to purchase the Laurel-in-the-Pines largely from the profits they had earned by operating it for two years.

Profits from the Lakewood winter resort also bankrolled the creation of a year-round revenue stream through purchase of a summer resort in the Catskill Mountains. In 1950, Tisch Hotels added the Traymore Hotel in Atlantic City, again employing the strategy of initially leasing instead of buying. Once more, the success of the investment rested on more than buying at the right price. To turn the money-losing Traymore into a profitable operation, Laurence and his brother Bob cut personnel and entertainment costs, installed an ice rink and swimming pools, refurbished the lobby and most of the rooms, and upgraded the food service. Profits soared as the improvements in service enabled the Tisches to hike room rates by 25 percent. After one year of operating the Traymore, the Tisches purchased it for $4.35 million. They sold in 1955 for a profit of nearly $11 million. (That excludes a further gain on some land they retained, which soared in value when casino gambling was legalized in Atlantic City.)

The Tisch brothers repeated their success by coaxing unrealized value out of the McAlpin Hotel in Manhattan, which they leased in 1952. They cleared $1.5 million in two years by investing $1 million in renovations, enabling them to boost occupancy by 20 percent while raising room rates by 30 percent. Razzle-dazzle, a vital ingredient in the early coup at the Laurel-in-the-Pines, again played a role when the Tisch organization built the lavish Americana Hotel in Bal Harbour, Florida. On the ground floor was a rock pool featuring live alligators, some of whom became martyrs to postwar affluence by ingesting coins and plastic toothpicks that guests tossed into the pool.[29]

Plainly, operating skill was essential to the success of all these hotel ventures. Nevertheless, there is a widespread impression that Laurence Tisch's immense wealth derives mainly from buying low and selling high. Observers commonly overlook the negotiating skill that has enabled him to obtain bargains that otherwise might have gone to his rivals. A typical assessment runs along these lines:

To triumph as often as he has, Tisch has thumbed his nose at conventional wisdom. He buys companies or stocks when they are wildly unpopular and shuns anything that is remotely in vogue.[30]

In many such comments over the years, the press has celebrated Tisch's knack for *finding* value, while obscuring his effectiveness in *adding* value.

By way of example, financial writers have cited Tisch's astuteness in buying offshore oil drilling rigs during the late 1980s, when boom turned to bust in energy exploration. Rigs were available for far less than the cost of constructing new ones. Thanks to the inevitable rebound in energy prices, along with new technology that improved the economics of drilling, the day rates for hiring rigs rose sharply. Rigs that Tisch had bought for $5 million now pulled in $25 million of annual profits. Diamond Offshore, the drilling subsidiary that the Tisch-controlled holding company Loews[31] Corporation took public in 1985 at $12 a share (adjusted for a later stock split), was trading at $54.50 a share in mid-1997. Keeping in mind the "sell high" side of the famous dictum, Tisch capitalized on the unit's lofty price-earnings ratio of 27 to float a Diamond Offshore convertible debenture.[32]

Tisch reinforced his image as a value investor, in the manner of Benjamin Graham, through his well-publicized boycott of the 1990s bull market in stocks. He famously steered New York University's endowment into bonds as equity prices soared to levels he deemed unsustainable. In 1997, his strategy of selling stock indexes short reduced Loews Corporation's pretax earnings by 40 percent. A steep drop in stock prices during 1998 vindicated his judgment, however, and encouraged legions of investors to imagine they could replicate his success by shrewdly timing the stock market.[33]

Further contributing to Tisch's reputation for buying assets on the cheap is his personal indifference to the trappings of wealth. "Your standard of living doesn't change after the first million," he has said. "I don't want to become possessed by my possessions."[34] Tisch's son, Daniel, recalled, concerning his childhood, "We did not live in a flashy style. Our home was situated on less than an acre. We never had an alarm system. Our phone was always listed."[35] One writer described

Tisch's unprepossessing corner office at Loews headquarters as "reminiscent of a Howard Johnson's motor inn."[36]

Tisch's disdain for extravagance became more widely known after he won a dominant role in CBS, a famously free-spending network. Upon arriving at headquarters on his first day as chief executive officer in 1986, his first impression was of the waste associated with having too many uniformed security guards in the lobby.[37] In short order, he banned the use of limousines and rented typewriters, as well as messenger services, excepting emergencies.

~

All in all, Laurence Tisch has earned his reputation for buying stocks at knockdown prices. He has done far more, however, than passively wait for the market to find its way back to the proper valuation. His signature tactic has been to achieve effective control of an underperforming company, then force it to cut costs and shed money-losing operations. Both in the acquisition stage and in harvesting gains, he has played it close to the vest.

In March 1974, for example, Loews purchased a 5 percent stake in CNA Financial, disavowing any plans for a hostile takeover. By May, however, Tisch said he would seek a controlling interest, explaining that he had belatedly identified mismanagement as the source of the insurance company's undervaluation. He succeeded in acquiring a majority stake, after first dropping his initial bid when CNA's earnings deteriorated. Once in place, Tisch swiftly fired the company's chairman and eventually cut employment by 12 percent. He closed down CNA's three floors of lavish executive suites and downsized or dumped poorly performing businesses that management had previously acquired in an effort to diversify. By the end of 1975, Tisch's shock treatment had transformed a $207 million annual loss to a $110 million profit.[38]

At CBS, Tisch added value partly by being more thick-skinned than the previous management. The old guard feared that eliminating jobs would generate unsympathetic press coverage. Tisch, in contrast, was willing to bear the criticism in order to enhance the bottom line.[39] Here again, Tisch's strategy involved much more than buying a cheap asset. In fact, the purchase did not fit the usual Tisch pattern of acquiring assets that others disdained. At the time, broadcasting networks were subjects of acquisition interest by investors including General Electric.[40] CBS itself had begun 1985 at $73 a share and had risen sharply on the strength of takeover attempts by Ted Turner and Marvin Davis, to which the company responded with a 21 percent stock buyback. Nevertheless, Tisch began buying at $118 a share. As in the CNA affair more than a decade earlier, he disavowed hostile intentions but subsequently acquired enough stock to oust incumbent management.

Perhaps reflecting Loews's deviation from customary strategy of buying clearly out-of-favor assets, its investment in CBS performed only a little better than the stock market averages until Westinghouse Electric made a premium takeover bid in 1995.[41] Along with whatever hidden value Tisch had perceived in 1986, there was a subtle source of erosion in value. Cable television was about to end broadcasting's monopoly-like status in home entertainment.[42] Not even Tisch's hardheaded cost reductions could entirely offset the dual disadvantages of a not-so-cheap purchase price and an adverse industry trend.

A Closer Look at Tisch's Buy-Low Strategy

Superficially, Laurence Tisch's admirable success upholds the possibility of amassing great wealth by coolly applying well-known valuation measures such as price-earnings ratios, while others react emotionally to market upheavals. On closer examination, however, such a view does not do Tisch justice, for his success has depended on fixing problems as much as on astute timing.

Ordinarily, a company gets cheap for good reason and rebounds in value only if somebody, or some change in conditions, fixes the problem. Sometimes, the business problems prove more intractable than they appeared from the outside. This sort of hazard helps to explain why apparant bargains materialize with some frequency.

To be sure, buying offshore oil rigs during a drilling slump is not a strategy premised heavily on superior operating skills. It is a gambit, however, that depends on being sufficiently well capitalized to wait for the turnaround. Tisch has long maintained large cash reserves, precisely to obtain the strategic advantage provided by a strong balance sheet. Note, however, that there is a substantial opportunity cost in keeping sizable amounts of cash uninvested.

For the most part, Tisch has limited his downside, just as his legend suggests. The risks have not always been as small as they seemed, however. His earliest success in the hotel business is a case in point.

Tisch, as noted, steered his family toward New Jersey because the emerging Florida market had gotten too pricey. Laurel-in-the-Pines was available at a more reasonable price, according to the lore, because its owner feared a downturn in the economy. Tisch was certainly not alone, however, in his more optimistic view. The speculators responsible for the elevated Florida prices clearly were not expecting a depression. Could it be that the paucity of competing bids for a New Jersey winter resort hotel had more to do with microeconomic considerations than with a gloomy view of the United States economy?

As Winans reports in *The King of Cash*, Lakewood died as a winter resort destination once airlines began offering affordable, three-hour flights to Florida and Puerto Rico. Whether Tisch realized it or not in 1946, the chance to profit by renovating Laurel-in-the-Pines represented a short-lived opportunity. As it turned out, the only viable exit strategy was to demolish the luxury hotel to make way for inexpensive townhouses. Notwithstanding Tisch's impressive achievement in boosting profits while he owned the property, the whole venture might have concluded less favorably if Laurel-in-the-Pines had not burned down in 1967. According to Winans, the Tisches "were never questioned about the cause of the fire" and recovered the loss through insurance.[43] In short, the Lakewood operation was not quite the limited-risk undertaking that legend would have it.

Low Prices Don't Always Mean Good Value

The pitfalls of buying cheap were demonstrated even more forcefully in the 1973 Equity Funding affair. According to the numbers, the insurance company's stock was dirt cheap. Equity Funding's financial reporting, however, was anything but clean.

Tisch began buying Equity Funding shares after they fell precipitously from $28 to a fraction less than $20 a share. He was aware that rumors of fraud were circulating about the company, but perceived no fundamental reason for the price drop. A 20-minute meeting with Equity Funding's chairman, Stanley Goldblum, convinced him that the stock price decline was unrelated to the company's condition.[44]

Unfortunately, the rumors proved true. Two-thirds of the outstanding amount of Equity Funding insurance policies had been falsified. Goldblum later pleaded guilty to five felonies. Tisch managed to unload only about 20 percent of his 490,000 shares, at a small loss, before the Securities and Exchange Commission suspended trading. By then, the stock had plummeted to $14.375. Less than a month after Tisch began investing in Equity Funding, the company filed for bankruptcy. A reorganization plan proposed later that year optimistically projected that stockholders' claims would eventually be worth about $2.50 a share.

"There are a lot of geniuses after the fact," Tisch commented in the wake of the debacle. "But there's no way to adjust for massive fraud in analyzing a stock. There's just no answer to it. Either you believe the whole system of investing is based on fraud or you do business on the basis of audits, insurance regulation, and other safeguards. The idea of massive fraud never entered our minds."[45]

In fact, though, a very rigorous analysis could have turned up hints that something was amiss at Equity Funding. For one thing, insurer's sales and earnings somewhat inexplicably bucked the industry trend by maintaining a steady growth rate during the 1970 recession. Another intriguing clue arose early in the company's life, when it operated only as a sales agency, rather than as an insurance underwriter. Equity Funding stated in a 1967 prospectus that it had placed the "greater part" of the $226.3 million face amount of life insurance that it sold in 1966 with the Pennsylvania Life Insurance Company. One month later, however, a Penn Life prospectus indicated that it had underwritten only $58.6 million of Equity Funding policies in 1966.[46]

No one appears to have picked up the discrepancy between the two prospectuses until years later. Accordingly, Laurence Tisch cannot be faulted too harshly for accepting the auditors' seal of approval on Equity Funding's earnings. All the same, the incident highlights the dangers of relying on the judgment of experts. That group includes the securities analysts whose job ostensibly includes uncovering such problems as the disparity between the Equity Funding and Penn Life financial disclosures.

More broadly, the Equity Funding affair underscores the fact that buying when others appear to be panicking sometimes proves nothing except that there was good reason to panic. Tisch's success ratio has been higher when, in addition to buying a company's stock on the cheap, he has bought enough shares to gain control. In those situations, the bargain has been available because of a genuine problem that Tisch's management team was able to fix once it got inside.

Warren Buffett

I look for businesses in which I think I can predict what they're going to look like in ten or fifteen or twenty years. Take Wrigley's chewing gum. I don't think the Internet is going to change how people are going to chew gum.[47]

Not all of Laurence Tisch's passive investments have worked out favorably, but he has never had reason to regret a gamble he took in 1961. On a tip from Howard Newman, a son of the onetime partner of "Father of Security Analysis" Benjamin Graham, Tisch put $100,000 into an investment partnership managed by Graham's star pupil. Since launching his own money management business in 1957, young Warren Buffett had outperformed the Dow Jones Industrial Average in every single year. After Tisch climbed on board, Buffett continued to beat the Dow unfailingly before dissolving his partnership in 1969. Over its full life, the Buffett partnership produced a compound annual return of 29.5 percent, yielding a net profit after management fees of $150,270 on a $10,000 initial stake. The comparable figures for the Dow were 7.4 percent and $15,260.[48]

A 1994 book devoted to Buffett's investment methods noted that the Forbes 400 listing of America's wealthiest people included 69 individuals with estimated net worth exceeding one billion dollars. According to author Robert G. Hagstrom, that year's richest American, Warren Buffett, was "the only one who obtained his wealth from the stock market."[49] In a similar vein, the financial writer George G. W. Goodman, who writes under the pseudonym "Adam Smith," stated several years earlier, "Buffett has made $1 billion in the market, more than anyone else."[50] In reality, though, not even Buffett amassed a billion dollars purely by investing in stocks for his personal portfolio.

This is not to downplay Warren Buffett's extraordinary record as a money manager, which has turned him into a veritable cult figure. Buffett devotees pore over the nuggets of investment wisdom he dispenses in the Berkshire Hathaway annual report. Aspiring money masters turn out in droves to hear him speak. They name their children, and even their dogs, after him. When a certain Omaha woman went into labor, her stockbroker husband read aloud to her an account of Buffett's investment strategies, "as though his wisdom might explain the cosmic mysteries of their daughter's birth."[51]

No doubt, small investors can benefit from adopting Warren Buffett's uncompromisingly rational investment philosophy. Anyone who hopes to reach the Forbes 400 list, however, will be better off studying how Buffett built a vast industrial and financial empire on the foundation of a struggling textile company. On May 10, 1965, the day he gained control, Berkshire Hathaway's closing share price was $18. The stock ended 1998 at $70,000 a share. (One of many conventional ideas that Buffett rejects is stock splits. "I've never really felt," he explains, "that if I went into a restaurant and said, 'I want two hatchecks instead of one for my hat' I'd really be a lot better off.")[52] Massive wealth has rained down on Buffett's early investors, as well as entrepreneurs who sold him their companies for stock. *Forbes* has estimated that there are scores of families that own $100 million or more of Berkshire Hathaway shares.[53]

Buffett's Purchases of Controlling Interests

In assembling the remarkable money machine known as Berkshire Hathaway, Buffett has invested successfully in stocks, bonds, and commodities. When the circumstances have warranted it, however, he has not merely bought some shares of a company he likes, but instead has acquired a controlling interest. In some cases, this has meant purchasing a big enough stake to exert a positive influence on the company's direction. Like Laurence Tisch, another billionaire who is widely misperceived as merely an expert bargain hunter, Buffett has often enhanced the value of his investments by becoming an active member of the board of directors. Notable beneficiaries of such intervention have included Capital Cities/ABC, Government Employees Insurance Company (GEICO), Salomon Inc., and the Washington Post Company. In many other instances, Buffett's acquisition of a controlling interest has consisted of buying a public or private company lock, stock, and barrel. Examples include Borsheim's, an Omaha jewelry retailer; the *Buffalo Evening News*; Illinois National Bank & Trust, International Dairy Queen, a fast food restaurant chain; Nebraska Furniture Mart; See's Candy Shops; and the Scott & Fetzer Company, marketer of such brands as *World Book Encyclopedia* and Kirby vacuum cleaners. (Buffett, who is renowned for his simple lifestyle, has not sought glamour in his acquisitions. When he bought the decidedly nonchic Dairy Queen, one writer commented that "Wall Streeters almost gagged their sushi.")[54] Dispelling the notion of Buffett as merely an extremely smart passive investor, investment counselor and financial writer John Train comments:

> Over and over again, we see Buffett buying a company in its entirety or, via share repurchases, in part, that he knows is worth more to a private buyer than it is selling for at the moment, *particularly if a few changes are made*. (Emphasis added.)[55]

One might imagine that Buffett's predilection for purchasing companies outright, with an eye toward improving their profitability, arose at a mature stage of his career. After all, the classic problem encountered by a successful money manager is rampant growth in funds under management, as investors seek to get in on the good thing. Before long, it becomes difficult for the manager to buy enough of a stock to have a material impact on the portfolio's overall investment. A strategy of swallowing companies whole, then enhancing their value, might solve the problem. This was not how Buffett evolved into an industrial magnate, however. He began buying entire businesses near the beginning of his stint as a money manager, long before his assets were great enough to pose a problem.

In 1961, the investment partnerships managed by Buffett had total funds under management of just $5 million. Risking one-fifth of the entire portfolio, he acquired 70 percent of Dempster Mill Manufacturing, a rundown windmill and farm implement manufacturer based 90 miles south of Omaha. After appointing himself chairman, Buffett imported an operating manager from Los Angeles. His man quickly improved Dempster's profitability by trimming inventory, slashing expenses, and laying off workers. By 1963, Buffett was able to sell the company for a net gain of $2.3 million.

Thanks to the terms of the partnership agreement, which entitled him to a 25 percent share of annual partnership profits above 4 percent of capital, Warren Buffett was entering the ranks of the well-to-do by the mid-1960s. In 1966 and 1967, the Buffett operation (by now consolidated into a single partnership) acquired two retailers outright for about $15 million. As Buffett biographer Roger Lowenstein notes:

> In each case, Buffett bought not liquid shares of stock but the entire business. Among fund managers, this was unheard-of.[56]

Buffett fared poorly with Baltimore department store operator Hochschild, Kohn & Co., ultimately getting out even in a sale to Supermarkets General. A Chicago dress store chain, Associated Cotton Shops, worked out more favorably. Renamed Diversified Retailing, it was one of the two investments that Buffett retained when he wound up his money management business in 1969. The other was a threadbare Massachusetts textile manufacturer, Berkshire Hathaway, which he acquired in 1965.[57] As Buffett moved on from managing money to building a vast industrial and financial enterprise, Berkshire Hathaway became the vehicle through which he successfully implemented classic methods of the self-made billionaires.

During the life of his investment partnership, Warren Buffett's personal wealth had grown to $25 million through his override on the profits.[58] While $25 million is scarcely a sum to sneeze at, it pales next to his $29 *billion* net worth as of 1998.[59] During the three decades in which this more-than-thousandfold increase occurred, Buffett was better described as an industrial magnate than as an investor in stocks. To be sure, he labored exhaustively at buying and selling securities for the

Berkshire Hathaway portfolio. Additionally, for a few years during the 1970s, he managed FMC Corporation's pension fund as a sideline. The spectacular growth of his personal financial statement, however, depended heavily on strategies not available to a mere securities investor. To replicate these strategies, one would first have to gain control of a vast insurance business. (Note that Buffett enjoyed no special advantage, other than his acute financial perception, in getting himself into this enviable position.)

An insurance company's potential as the base of an industrial empire has three sources, namely:

- Use of funds that will eventually belong to others.
- Tax benefits.
- Financial leverage.

The opportunity to use other people's money arises from cash reserves created by insurance premiums. Eventually, the reserves must be paid out in claims, but until then, the insurance company can invest the funds. Moreover, the earnings generated by those investments are heavily tax-favored. The third benefit of investing through an insurance company, financial leverage, arises from the ability to generate annual premiums several times as great as the equity invested in the business. Consider, for example, a company capitalized with $200 million and generating $800 million of annual premiums. If the insurer earns 6 percent on the resulting investment portfolio of $1 billion, or $60 million, its return on investment (before expenses and taxes) is $60 million over $200 million, or 30 percent. This leverage is particularly powerful in Berkshire Hathaway's case. Typically, bonds represent the bulk of an insurance company portfolio, but Buffett has emphasized equities, which produce higher rates of return over time. Further magnifying the power of leveraging Berkshire Hathaway's portfolio are Warren Buffett's exceptionally high investment returns.

Recognizing that an insurance company could be turned into (in John Train's words) "a sort of super margin account,"[60] Warren Buffett got into the property and casualty business soon after switching his focus from money management to enterprise building. In 1967, Berkshire Hathaway acquired National Indemnity, a specialized underwriter that commenced business during the Depression. The founder, Jack Ringwalt, focused on a variety of risks that were scorned by other companies and were therefore comparatively lucrative to insure. In addition to his main business of auto insurance for high-risk drivers, Ringwalt issued policies to bootleggers and lion tamers.[61] Buffett added to this base by entering the reinsurance business in 1969 and forming Cornhusker Casualty Company (1970), Lakeland Fire & Casualty (1971), and Texas United Insurance (1972). Berkshire Hathaway also purchased Home & Automobile Insurance Company in 1971 and, in 1994, acquired all shares of GEICO that it did not already own.

The financial leverage inherent in these subsidiaries produced a staggeringly high compounded growth rate in Berkshire Hathaway's securities portfolio. Leverage also proved invaluable whenever Buffett spotted an attractive opportunity to acquire a company whole, notwithstanding the control premium[62] ordinarily associated with such transactions. The purchasing power of Berkshire Hathaway's equity was multiplied by the availability of insurance reserves several times as great. (Buffett also built up the company's investment portfolio by investing the "float" represented by funds earmarked for future redemption of Blue Chip trading stamps.)

John Train summarizes Buffett's method as follows:

> When one reads that "Warren Buffett" has bought, [for example], an interest in General Foods, it usually means that an insurance subsidiary of Berkshire Hathaway—using its reserves built up against future claims—has made the investment, which can cost more than Berkshire Hathaway, the parent company, could readily afford. . . . The same maneuver, using insurance companies, is performed by such operators as Henry Singleton, Larry Tisch, Carl Lindner and Saul Steinberg, among others.[63]

$\sim$

Lest readers infer that Buffett has treated his insurance companies as nothing more than vehicles for industrial acquisitions, it is important to note that he has masterminded a canny strategy in the property and casualty business. In reinsurance, which consists of insuring the exposure of other insurance companies, competition periodically drives pricing to unattractively low levels. At such points in the cycle, Berkshire Hathaway allows its premiums to shrink dramatically, rather than write unprofitable policies. In contrast, the company's competitors tend to focus on market share. They inevitably suffer losses as a consequence of accepting unprofitable business. In their weakened state, they pull back, leaving Berkshire Hathaway vast underwriting opportunities, just as pricing becomes attractive again. Buffett, in short, has not overlooked the huge profit-making potential of an insurance business that is managed on unremittingly bottom-line principles.

Neither has he squandered the magic of insurance-company leverage on indiscriminate investments. In selecting companies to invest in or acquire, Buffett has emphasized strong, but underexploited franchises. Additionally, he has looked for the pricing power inherent in a dominant market position. By way of illustration, when Buffett acquired the *Buffalo Evening News* through Blue Chip Stamps in 1977, it boasted the highest household penetration rate of any big-city daily in the United States.

The newspaper's upside potential lay in the fact that it was one of only a handful of major metropolitan dailies that published no Sunday edition. The rival *Courier-Express,* which ran a distant second to the *Evening News* from Monday to Saturday, had long had Buffalo's Sunday circulation and advertising revenues all to itself. Once in the Buffett fold, however, the *Evening News* announced that it would begin publishing seven days a week.

At first, Buffett's frontal assault on the *Courier-Express* appeared to be a costly mistake. The *Courier-Express* parried his Sunday thrust by initiating an antitrust action. According to the suit, Buffett intended to operate the *Evening News*'s Sunday edition at a loss. His alleged plan was to drive the *Courier-Express* out of business, leaving him free to monopolize the Buffalo market. The judge bought the story, up to a point, and granted an injunction limiting Buffett's ability to market the Sunday edition. Hamstrung by the court and vilified as a predatory competitor, the Sunday *Evening News* managed to attract only one-fourth the advertising space of its *Courier-Express* counterpart.

As the red ink flowed, the *Evening News*'s delivery truck drivers went on strike, figuring that Buffett's precarious position would force him to meet their demands. The newspaper's other unions initially crossed the picket lines, but when they finally yielded to the teamsters, the presses stopped. Buffett quickly calculated that he could remain shut down for six days and still start up the operation again. He laid it on the line: If the strikers stayed out for more than six days, he would close the paper permanently and their jobs would be lost.[64] Convinced that Buffett was not bluffing, the teamsters caved in. The strike ended and hostilities resumed in the great Buffalo newspaper war.

Next on the list of the *Evening News*'s ordeals was a devastating recession. Buffett's sole consolation was that the competition, too, was hemorrhaging from the combination of a circulation battle and an economic downturn. Luckily, the *Courier-Express* proved to be the combatant less capable of surviving the war of attrition. It folded in 1982, leaving Buffett in command of the city's sole daily newspaper.

In short order, the renamed *Buffalo News*'s Sunday circulation zoomed from a little over 200,000 to over 360,000. By the late 1980s, the paper that Buffett had bought for $32.5 million was earning $40 million (pretax) annually. It was a testament not only to Warren Buffett's skill in identifying hidden value, but also his determination to bring that value out of hiding.

By introducing the Sunday edition and facing down the teamsters, Buffett played a key strategic role in transforming the *Evening News* into a lucrative business. Consistent with his preferred practice, however, he did not immerse himself in day-to-day operations. By and large, Buffett relies on strong managers who share his passion for return on investment.

As a reflection of his search for extraordinary managers, Buffett lore is rich with characters such as Rose Blumkin. Barely literate in English, the Russian-born immigrant parlayed a $500 investment into Nebraska Furniture Mart, the nation's largest furniture store, with an astounding two-thirds of the total market in Omaha. Well into her nineties, Blumkin worked 10- or 12-hour days, seven days a week, and listed her hobby as driving around to spy on competitors. If she ran out of stock, she would sell furniture out of her own home.[65] At the age of 95, unhappy that her grandsons were cutting her out of key decisions, Blumkin retired. Just three months later, she launched a competing store, Mrs. B's Clearance and Factory Outlet, directly across the street from the Nebraska Furniture Mart. Within two years, the new venture had become Omaha's third largest carpet outlet. Buffett bought Mrs. B's the following year and joked that he would never repeat the mistake of letting Rose Blumkin retire without signing a noncompete agreement.[66] Under Buffett's hands-off policy, such highly motivated managers generally produced excellent results.

Ironically, one of Berkshire Hathaway's few unsuccessful businesses was its original textile operation. The manufacturer of suit linings lacked the distinctive franchise that became the hallmark of successful Buffett investments in companies such as Coca-Cola and General Foods. As Buffett later recalled:

> We went into a terrible business because it was cheap. It's what I refer to as the "used cigar butt" approach to investing. You see this cigar butt down there, it's soggy and terrible, but there's one puff left, and it's free. That's what Berkshire was when we bought it—it was selling below working capital—but it was a terrible, terrible mistake.[67]

Buffett finally liquidated the textile mills after a long, unsuccessful effort to boost their rate of return to an acceptable level. Thereafter, he followed the precept that a bad business usually prevails over a good management.

Beyond Graham and Dodd

By poking fun at the "used cigar butt" approach to investing, Buffett refutes those who persist in pigeonholing him as a value investor in the mode of his mentor, Benjamin Graham. As a student of Graham's at Columbia, Buffett earned the only A+ ever given out by the "Father of Security Analysis." He similarly distinguished himself within a talented group of security analysts at the money management firm of Graham-Newman during 1954–1956. Since that time, however, Buffett has had only a few scattered opportunities to "buy low" according to the strict formulas devised by Graham.

After suffering devastating losses in the 1929 stock market crash, Graham geared his efforts to avoiding the mistakes of the preceding period. In the New Era of the 1920s, optimistic investors had abandoned historical standards for valuing securities. The result, in the view of Graham and many others, was that stocks became grossly overvalued. Determined never again to pay for fluff, Graham developed a rigorous investment discipline. His method emphasized such financial measures as net asset value and the price-to-earnings ratio, while casting a skeptical eye on intangibles.

As Buffett points out, there is a serious limitation to Graham's approach: It is not always possible to liquidate a company immediately and pocket the difference between its inherent value and its low stock price. While the clock ticks away, moreover, the company may be losing money (a good reason why its stock is depressed in the first place). The outcome is a long wait for a disappointing payoff, which translates into a mediocre return on the supposed bargain purchase.[68] A further problem is that although attractive "value stocks" are plentiful after a severe downturn such as U.S. stocks suffered in 1973–1974, they can be extremely hard to find in better times. In short, readers should not expect to reap billions by personally investing in stocks on the basis of Graham's statistical measures. Certainly, that is not what Warren Buffett has done, despite the impression created by the financial media.

Buffett long ago described his own approach as 85 percent Graham and 15 percent Philip Fisher.[69] Like Graham, Fisher was an investment counselor who attempted to systematize the purchase of stocks,[70] but the similarity ended there. Fisher emphasized companies' prospects for earnings growth, rather than ratios derived from their existing profits and balance sheet numbers. He preferred well-managed companies that invested aggressively in research and development to achieve superior sales growth within their industries. "Used cigar butts," often companies that satisfied Benjamin Graham's standard of cheapness precisely because they were shaky, were the antithesis of Fisher's ideal investment. Finally, Fisher advocated holding a small number of superior companies for long periods, whereas Graham advised investors to diversify broadly and take profits on winners.

On the last point, Berkshire Hathaway's portfolio strategy more closely resembles Fisher's approach. Under the influence of his longtime associate and billionaire in his own right, Charlie Munger, Buffett has leavened Graham's value-driven methods with Fisher's willingness to pay a seemingly full price for a company with superior growth prospects.[71]

Buffett's fondness for companies with unique business franchises appears to be his own addition to the formula.[72] The final element is an overlooked aspect of Graham's work that prefigured Carl Icahn's career as a corporate raider.

~

While it is clear that Buffett did not amass billions through rote application of Benjamin Graham's statistical methods, he profited greatly by emulating another of his mentor's methods. Long before publishing his 1934 masterpiece, *Securities Analysis* (coauthored by David Dodd), Graham made his mark in the field nowadays known as "shareholder activism." His most celebrated triumph involved a crude oil transporter, Northern Pipeline. As one of the 31 companies that emerged from the 1911 breakup of the Standard Oil monopoly, Northern Pipeline had continued the highly conservative financial policies favored by John D. Rockefeller Sr. Graham learned from regulatory filings that the company held a bond portfolio worth the equivalent of $90 a share, which had no relevance to its operations, while its stock was trading at $65. He urged Northern Pipeline to liquidate the securities and distribute the proceeds to shareholders. Although the company's president obstinately resisted, Graham prevailed by enlisting the support of the Rockefeller Foundation, which owned 23 percent of Northern Pipeline's shares.[73] The conflict over the disposition of Northern Pipeline's assets was echoed in subsequent decades in proxy contests and hostile takeovers. Picking up this less widely appreciated strain of Graham's work, Buffett injected himself into a number of battles for corporate control.

In corporate control struggles, Buffett was not limited to the insurgent's role, in the manner of Graham at Northern Pipeline. Thanks to Berkshire Hathaway's huge financial power, he could also enter the fray on management's side. For example, in 1984, Buffett offered to become a white knight for Time Inc. (i.e., a large, friendly shareholder who could help Time minimize the danger of a hostile takeover). Management turned down Buffett's proposal, a decision it came to regret when Time was later "put in play" as a takeover target. Capital Cities Communications, on the other hand, placed a large block of stock in Berkshire Hathaway's friendly hands following its purchase of the ABC broadcasting network in 1985. (The huge acquisition made Cap Cities itself vulnerable to a hostile bid.) Around the same time, Buffett acquired Scott & Fetzer after the company became the target of a takeover bid from risk arbitrageur Ivan Boesky.[74] In these transactions, naturally, Berkshire Hathaway extracted fair compensation for its assistance to management in repelling unwanted suitors. Put another way, Buffett negotiated terms that were unavailable to passive investors.

Buffett's skill at cutting an inside deal was epitomized in 1987, when he helped Salomon Inc. ward off a takeover bid by financier Ronald Perelman. Instead of buying the publicly traded common stock in the low 30s, Berkshire Hathaway custom-designed a convertible preferred stock with a 9 percent coupon.

> Salomon's senior managers had a heated discussion over the terms, which they thought far too sweet for Buffett. "The feeling was, it had a very small premium [the conversion price was $38] and a very high dividend. Warren had it both ways," William McIntosh, the head of Salomon's Chicago office, recalled. As a bonus, Berkshire's $63-million-a-year dividend (like all such payments received by corporations) would be mostly tax-exempt.[75]

Despite such shrewdly negotiated, one-of-a-kind investments, investors widely seek to copy Buffett's methods, as if he were simply cherry-picking the best values on the stock exchange. Robert C. Hagstrom maintains, in his book describing the "investment strategies of the world's greatest investor":

> Some critics argue that, despite his success, Warren Buffett's idiosyncrasies prevent his investment approach from being widely adopted. I disagree. . . . Whether you are financially able to purchase 10 percent of a company or merely a hundred shares, *The Warren Buffett Way* can help you achieve profitable investment returns.[76]

Possibly so, but memorizing Buffett's investment adages backward and forward will not enable passive investors to parlay their personal holdings into billions.

The Intelligence Factor

Warren Buffett has used many of the same tools as other self-made billionaires, but he enjoys a special advantage. It is summed up in a comment that John J. Byrne Jr. offered at a presentation at Salomon Brothers in the early 1980s: "Warren Buffett is smarter than the average bear."[77] (Byrne, who executed the Buffett-engineered GEICO turnaround and later headed Fireman's Fund, was not comparing Buffett to stock market short sellers, but quoting the animated cartoon character, Yogi Bear.) Buffett is renowned for his ability to retain massive amounts of financial data and calculate securities values in his head. His bridge game is close to international standard.[78] When a reporter remarked that his office contained no computers, Buffett replied, "I am a computer."[79]

Byrne has extensive firsthand exposure to the Sage of Omaha's fascination with probabilities. Once, he recalls, Buffett showed him several dice with an unusual arrangement of dots on their faces. Byrne could pick any of the set, said Buffett. He would select another and guarantee that he would win the majority of 20 rolls. Byrne hauled out a calculator, figured the odds, and picked a die. Buffett then chose one and proceeded to roll a higher number than Byrne on 14 out of 20 tries. Challenged to play again for lunch, Byrne craftily selected the die that Buffett had chosen in the first round. This time, Byrne lost 16 out of 20 rolls. What he had not figured out was that given the arrangement of the dots, each die could always be beaten by one of the others, given a sufficient number of rolls.[80]

Buffett has played this trick on many acquaintances over the years. One of the few who ever figured out how to win—that is, who insisted that Buffett choose first—was his close friend, Bill Gates.[81] The two brainy billionaires share a passion for bridge, as well as a puckish sense of humor. When Gates was in the market for a wedding ring, Buffett persuaded him to surprise his fiancée by flying her to Omaha. He met the couple at the airport and escorted them to Borsheim's, the jewelry retailer owned by Berkshire Hathaway. Buffett then recounted that when he got married, he spent 6 percent of his net worth on a ring and thought Gates should do likewise.[82] The number one and number two rankings of Gates and Buffett on the roster of wealthiest Americans in recent years demonstrate that intelligence is no impediment to making money, notwithstanding the sneers of many poor but proud intellectuals.

For his part, Buffett downplays the importance of IQ in material success, stressing instead the importance of character and drive.[83] Fair enough, but there are several different proven strategies for turning those traits into billion-dollar fortunes. Not all of them require exceptional intellectual capacity. To the extent that Buffett's success has relied on discerning superior values among stocks being scrutinized by millions of other investors, on the other hand, brainpower has been an invaluable asset. This is a fact worth considering as you try to match your own talents to a specific strategy for reaching the billion-dollar circle.

8

THRIVE ON DEALS

The big print giveth and the fine print taketh away.
—Bishop Fulton J. Sheen[1]

There are several different ways to realize value in buying and selling businesses. Negotiating favorable prices, both on the way in and on the way out, is only the most obvious. Another means of maximizing the gain on the round trip is to finance the purchase on advantageous terms. Further gains are achievable from increasing the asset's value, following its purchase, through capable management. Not to be ignored, either, is the compensation that can be extracted during the ownership/management phase.

By exploiting all these profit sources in every transaction, and by doing many transactions, it is possible to amass a sizable fortune. Identifying the opportunities requires a keen sense of where the deals are at a given time. Clues can be found in the economic environment, the state of the capital markets, and conditions in various industries. Essential to astute deal making, as well, is a grasp of complex transactions in which one side may wind up with a subtle, but ultimately decisive, edge.

This chapter focuses on three billionaires who have built their fortunes largely on skillful dickering: Kirk Kerkorian, Carl Icahn, and Phil Anschutz. Exceptionally successful deals played pivotal roles in the wealth accumulation of several billionaires profiled in other chapters, however. A prime example was H. L. Hunt's purchase of the Daisy Bradford #3 well from "Dad" Joiner, allegedly plying the seller with liquor and women until the terms turned in his favor. Similarly, Bill Gates's purchase of the rights to the DOS operating system for $50,000 was instrumental in turning Microsoft into a multibillion-dollar company. Ross Perot added substantially to his already vast fortune by extracting a large premium for his General Motors stock. Taking a page from Kerkorian and Icahn's book, he agreed to sell his shares back to the company in exchange for agreeing to cease being a director and gadfly.

Studying the titans' deal-making methods can be immensely valuable to you in striving to make your own billion. Tenacity, willingness to risk a huge loss, and creativity in forging agreements are recurring themes. At the same time, the billionaires' negotiating styles reflect the wide diversity of their talents and personalities. You will have to pick the pieces that feel most natural to you.

A critical capability to develop is a manner that reassures all participants in the transaction. When Laurence Tisch was negotiating to buy the Traymore Hotel in Atlantic City, he studied the property thoroughly, as usual. In fact, he was so thorough that the seller, Frank Gravatt, feared Tisch knew its value better than he did and was getting the better of the deal. Frozen with indecision as the transaction was about to close, he decided to make up his mind by flipping a coin. Tisch grabbed Gravatt's arm, later explaining, "I just couldn't let him toss that coin. Once he did, we had only a 50–50 chance."[2] Reckoning that the odds were better if he reasoned calmly with Gravatt, Tisch eventually got the signature on the contract.

John D. Rockefeller Sr., a veteran of many negotiations in the course of creating Standard Oil Company, threw his counterparts off guard by speaking as little as necessary. He made it easier for independent refiners to sell out by not always driving for the lowest possible price, but he generally bargained from a position of strength. They knew that if they did not sell, Standard Oil could use its power with crude oil producers and the railroads to prevent them from making a profit.

Rockefeller also exploited his facility with numbers to gain an edge in negotiations. On one occasion, he deliberately kept the seller talking for half an hour so that he could calculate in his head the costs of several alternative methods of paying interest on the transaction. By the end of the discussion, Rockefeller had won the other party's consent to terms that saved him $30,000 in interest.[3]

Aside from his mental acuity, Rockefeller relied on the same sort of imperturbability for which Kirk Kerkorian is known nowadays. He liked to tell how an angry contractor once burst into his office and furiously denounced him. Rockefeller sat quietly at his desk without looking up until the man was exhausted from his tirade. He then spun around in his swivel chair and said, "I didn't catch what you were saying. Would you mind repeating yourself?"[4]

Another industry consolidation that provided plenty of instruction in deal making was Wayne Huizenga's creation of Waste Management. In acquiring independent waste haulers, he minimized the haggling over price by beginning at a level within 5 or 10 percent of the maximum that he would pay. Then, he would focus the discussion on such issues as the tax benefits of taking Waste Management stock in payment and the seller's ongoing relationship as an operator.

Sometimes, the owner would insist that Huizenga's proposed price was too low and that the business was about to experience a profit surge. Instead of arguing the point and potentially antagonizing the owner, Huizenga would plan to call again to see if the two parties could get together on price. In some instances, he would point out that if the owner delayed in selling, Waste Management might meanwhile acquire a competitor in the region and therefore have less interest in buying.

Stamina and patience were additional keys to Huizenga's success in acquiring waste-hauling operations. One negotiation took place at the owner's office above a transfer station, where garbage was dumped and reloaded for further shipping. The weather was hot and humid, making the stench nearly unbearable. After a full day of negotiating, Waste Management's corporate attorney was nauseated, but Huizenga ignored the distracting smell and closed the deal.[5]

Later, as chairman of Blockbuster, Huizenga applied the lessons of the Waste Management consolidation to buying up video chains. He employed a "good cop–bad cop" approach, using his personable style to work out the broad terms of the transaction, then relying on lawyers to take the heat inherent in hammering out the details. Behind the low-key approach was a hardheaded business proposition not unlike Standard Oil's in Rockefeller's day: If the chain's owner did not sell out, Block-buster might open additional stores in the region and become a greater threat. According to the company's general counsel at the time, "Wayne was famous for 'do the deal now for $100, do it tomorrow for $90.' He was very good at that."[6]

Both at Waste Management and at Blockbuster, Huizenga sought to get deals completed quickly. His team would begin negotiating on Monday morning and work 18 hours a day, seven days a week, until the transaction closed. He stuck rigorously to two rules:

Wayne Huizenga's Cardinal Rules for Closing Deals

1. Don't lose a deal by failing to pay attention to it.
2. Never talk about a deal until it is signed.[7]

Deal making on the scale that produces billionaires requires nerves of steel. At one time or another, the three superb negotiators profiled in this chapter have all been in tight spots, facing potential bankruptcy. If they did not enjoy the rush of adrenaline that accompanies a successful

---

THE BILLIONAIRE HOW-TO

Fundamental Strategies

- Thrive on Deals
- Take Monumental Risks
- Buy Low

Key Principles

- Rules Are Breakable
- Keep the Back Door Open
- Keep on Growing
- Develop a Thick Skin

deal, they could not have pursued the deal maker's route to massive wealth accumulation. To replicate their success, you too will have to learn to love the deals for their own sake.

Kirk Kerkorian

There was a time when I was aiming at $100,000. Then I thought I'd have it made if I got a million dollars. Now it isn't the money.[8]

On May 6, 1998, Kirk Kerkorian made $660 million. That sum represented the one-day rise in the value of his Chrysler Corporation shares when the automaker announced that it would merge with Daimler-Benz. All told, he had more than tripled his investment of $1.4 billion to nearly $5 billion since beginning to accumulate the stock in 1990. Along the way, he also collected $500 million in dividends. As the *New York Times* aptly observed, the 81-year-old multibillionaire was showing little sign of slowing down. A month before his big Chrysler payday, he became a father for the third time.[9]

Six and a half decades into his remarkable career, Kirk (born Kekor) Kerkorian was still hard at work, but getting paid much better for his efforts than in his early days. After dropping out of high school, he held a succession of jobs, none of them very remunerative. Concealing his age, he signed up with the New Deal's Civilian Conservation Corps, building roads and felling trees in Sequoia National Park for $30 a month. Kerkorian earned only 40 cents an hour as a laborer at Metro-Goldwyn-Mayer (MGM), although in his later involvement with the motion picture studio he dealt in much bigger numbers. A stint as a furnace installer paid him 45 cents an hour.

The big payday continued to elude Kerkorian after he set his sights on a prizefighting career. He told a friend that his powerful right hand would earn him a million dollars, but the prize money in amateur bouts was modest. In one fight, "Rifle Right" Kerkorian won four dollars in prize money for knocking out a badly mismatched opponent with a single punch. Trained by his older brother Nishon, a/k/a "the Armenian Assassin," Kirk boxed his way to the Pacific amateur championship. Trainers dissuaded him from turning professional, however, judging him too slight at 140 pounds on a 5-foot, 11-inch frame.

While working as an engine cleaner for used-car dealers, Kerkorian started a business and began to develop his deal-making skills. His technique was to buy four or five jalopies from the dealers for $100, repair them, and sell the refurbished vehicles for a profit of $5 or $10 apiece. He gained additional small-scale business experience by running a two-pump gasoline station and a car-wash stand.

At long last, Kerkorian discovered the route that led to the big money when he fell in love with flying after a single recreational flight with a fellow furnace installer. Even then, his financial fortunes did not improve immediately. First, he had to pay for flying lessons by milking cows and shoveling manure at his instructor's ranch.

To clear the next hurdle to his success, Kerkorian employed a core billionaires' technique of sidestepping petty regulations. He induced a Los Angeles school system employee to fake a letter indicating that he had completed high school. That credential enabled him to obtain a pilot's license and led to a couple of years of work as a flight instructor.

Kerkorian Takes Off

With World War II on the way, Kerkorian became a civilian pilot for the British Royal Air Force, ferrying bombers from Canada to England and Scotland. At long last he was earning good pay for his efforts, to the tune of $1,000 a month (about $10,000 in 1999 dollars), tax-free. In the process, he set a new speed record for the North Atlantic run from Labrador.

Out of his wartime earnings and poker winnings, Kerkorian managed to save $12,000. Combining that grubstake with a $5,000 investment by his sister, he went into the business of buying and selling surplus military planes. Initially, the operation consisted of purchasing DC-3s in Hawaii, flying them to the mainland, and converting the planes into commercial aircraft. Conceptually, the business was not much different from his earlier one of repairing and selling used cars, but the money was considerably better. Planes that cost him only $7,000 to $10,000 fetched as much as $60,000.

In one of his biggest scores, the future billionaire constructed a viable airliner from the still-usable parts of two Lockheed Constellation

transport planes that had crashed. Between the cost of the wrecks and re-
pair work, Kerkorian sank $480,000 into the project. He recouped
$350,000 by leasing the plane for a couple of years, then sold it for
$600,000.

As a side venture, Kerkorian began flying charter groups and honeymoon couples to Las Vegas. The charter business, which he incorporated as the Los Angeles Air Service, complemented his airplane
trading. By keeping a plane in service, rather than in mothballs, he
dispelled any doubt about its airworthiness, thereby making it far easier
to sell.

After launching his charter service with a single plane, Kerkorian
doubled his fleet by shelling out $98,000 for a used DC-4 in 1950. When
the Korean War broke out, aircraft prices soared in response to the military's increased airlift needs. The following year, to the dismay of his associates, Kerkorian sold the recently acquired DC-4 for $345,000. Within
months, the market vindicated his decision to part with the scarce asset.
The price of DC-4s plummeted to $100,000, earning Kerkorian a repu-
tation for possessing a sixth sense about airplane trading. He disclaimed
any unique timing ability, however, saying that it was simply a matter of
not holding out for the peak price. "It's just that I don't try to get all the
meat off the bone," Kerkorian explained. "When I get a good figure, I just
move something."[10]

Another key to Kerkorian's success in trading aircraft was a technique he called "keeping the back door open."[11] If he could not resell a
new plane at a profit, he might be able to use it in his charter fleet. Failing that, he would sell it back to the manufacturer at a previously
agreed-upon price. This strategy of maintaining several different options was evident in Kerkorian's later dealings such as the Chrysler
affair. It was reminiscent, too, of Laurence Tisch's hedged approach
of leasing the Laurel-in-the-Pines hotel before committing himself to
buying it.

To some observers, Kerkorian's unorthodox approach "often
seemed the work of a confused man."[12] A shrewder assessment, however,
came from Alan (Ace) Greenberg, chairman of Bear, Stearns & Co. Told
by a vice chairman of the investment bank that Kerkorian wanted to buy
10 percent of Chrysler without undertaking a detailed study of the corporation, he replied, "Don't ever tell Babe Ruth how to hold his bat."[13]

Kerkorian acquired another charter airline in 1947. He named the company TransInternational Airlines and, in 1962, made it the first charter carrier to buy a jet. That move doubled Kerkorian's military business, but his dreams for further expansion exceeded his capital. He resolved the problem by selling the airline to Studebaker Corporation, while retaining operating control. By capitalizing on the larger company's vastly superior financial resources, he reckoned, he could build TransInternational into a regional powerhouse.

The sale price consisted of an initial payment of $1 million in stock plus a share of future profits. Kerkorian quickly and successfully put his plan into action, collecting an additional $1.7 million of Studebaker shares in the process. After just two years, Studebaker rethought the wisdom of being in the airline business and sold the operation back to Kerkorian and his associates for $2.5 million.

By 1965, charter airlines were in a phase of rapid growth. Capitalizing on the boom, Kerkorian took TransInternational public. At the initial offering price, his shares were worth roughly $7 million. The huge gain in a year's time, however, was just a hint of what was to come. In 1968, Kerkorian sold TransInternational to Transamerica Corporation for stock. The sale price for the entire company, of which Kerkorian held 58 percent, was $148.3 million. The following year, Kerkorian liquidated the last of his Transamerica stock, realizing $104 million, all told.[14]

∼

By now, the pace of Kerkorian's deal making was accelerating and the numbers were escalating. In 1955, correctly foreseeing the coming prosperity of Las Vegas, he invested $50,000 in a hotel in that city. His timing was off, however. Hotel expansion had temporarily gotten ahead of growth in gambling and Kerkorian lost his investment. He resolved not to invest thereafter in a business he did not run, but remained convinced of the city's bright future. In 1962, he paid $960,000 for 40 vacant acres across the Las Vegas Strip from the Flamingo hotel and casino.[15] The investment paid off in spades when the property became the site of Caesars Palace in 1996. Kerkorian collected $4 million per annum in rent for two years, then sold the property to the hotel-casino's owners for $5 million.

In the meantime, Kerkorian had acquired another piece of Las Vegas real estate for $5 million. He launched a new company, International Leisure, to construct the world's largest casino on the site. Financed through a public offering of 17 percent of International Leisure's shares, the International was an immediate success. Along the way, Kerkorian bought the Flamingo in order to acquire experienced staff, hired a skilled manager who turned it into a highly profitable investment, and decided to keep the casino. By late 1969, Kerkorian was sitting on International Leisure stock worth $180 million, the fruit of an investment of just $16.6 million. Adding in his Western Air Lines and MGM holdings, plus other assorted assets, *Fortune* estimated his total net worth at more than $260 million.[16]

Entering the ranks of the superrich seemed only to whet Kerkorian's appetite for bigger deals. Following the International Leisure sale, he was asked what continued to drive him. "What would you want me to do, he replied, "sit with a mint julep in my hand?"[17]

Stepping up the pace, Kerkorian bought 28 percent of Western Air Lines over the fierce opposition of the company's president. Unfazed by the chilly reception, Kerkorian launched a proxy battle, meanwhile parrying management's attempt to thwart him through regulatory hearings. Ultimately, he struck a deal that awarded him 9 out of 21 board seats, a position strong enough to allow him to dominate the company's direction. Under his guidance, Western reduced its costs and significantly boosted its revenues. In 1976, fearful that Kerkorian would sell out to a competitor, Western's management bought back his shares for $30.3 million, which represented an 18 percent premium to the prevailing market price.

Without pausing long to savor his financial coups in airlines and casinos, Kerkorian moved on to motion pictures. He began buying shares of Metro-Goldwyn-Mayer in 1969, once again braving intense management opposition. By 1974 he had acquired a 50.1 percent controlling interest in the studio. The only problem was that Kerkorian had borrowed heavily to purchase the MGM stock, planning to repay the loans through a public sale of International Leisure shares. That plan backfired when the Securities and Exchange Commission blocked the offering. In the end, Kerkorian was compelled to raise cash by selling International Leisure to Hilton Hotels in 1971.

More timid souls might have turned cautious after a brush with financial disaster. Kerkorian, on the contrary, proceeded to make a hostile bid for Columbia Pictures in 1978. After initially agreeing to limit his stake to 25.5 percent, he moved to increase his holdings, claiming that management had failed to live up to its obligation to consult him on business strategy.

Fending off an antitrust suit arising from his control of MGM, Kerkorian ultimately sold his Columbia shares back to the company at a 50 percent premium to the market value. In the process, he ran a $43 million investment up to $134 million. According to Fay Vincent, then Columbia's chief executive officer and later commissioner of baseball, "He was very destabilizing and we had to get rid of him."[18] By extracting a payment to cease being a thorn in management's side, Kerkorian was perfecting a technique that Carl Icahn would also employ with considerable success.

The senior management of Columbia Pictures may have been weary of Kerkorian, but the indefatigable deal maker was merely getting started in Hollywood. He followed up with an unsuccessful bid for the 20th Century–Fox studio in 1981. In the same year, he bought United Artists for $380 million and combined it with MGM. Over the next few years, a dizzying sequence of transactions followed. First, the newly consolidated enterprise split into two separate public companies. The first, MGM/UA Entertainment, focused on movie and television production, while the second, MGM Grand Hotels, operated hotels, casinos, cruise ships, and an airline. In 1983, Kerkorian proposed, then abandoned, a plan to take the whole enterprise private. He sold MGM/UA to Turner Broadcasting Systems in 1986, then bought back the MGM logo and all of United Artists in 1987, netting an estimated $500 million profit when all the dust settled.

Kerkorian sold MGM/UA again in 1990, but before long the studio ran into severe financial difficulties under the aegis of its acquirer, Pathé Communications. Accused of fraud in the sale, Kerkorian settled the case out of court. In 1996, he led an investment group that bought MGM/UA one more time.[19]

Not one to let up the frenetic pace, Kerkorian kept busy by selling MGM Grand Hotels properties to Bally Manufacturing in 1986, meanwhile renewing his interest in the airline business. Thwarted by regulators in an effort to start a London route for MGM Grand Air, a first-class-only transcontinental carrier, he tried to acquire Pan Am Corporation. When his offer for the troubled airline was rejected, Kerkorian went after Trans World Airlines, but was rebuffed again when regulators approved the purchase of TWA's London routes by American Airlines. He then sold MGM Grand Air in 1995, meanwhile opening the MGM Grand Hotel and Theme Park in Las Vegas in 1993.

Amidst all this activity, Kerkorian became involved in Chrysler, the deal with which this profile began. As in the earlier Western Air Lines and Columbia Pictures transactions, he encountered vehement opposition from management. Predictably, too, critics grumbled that he had no particular experience in the automobile business, aside from his early involvement in reconditioning cars for profit.

Kerkorian knew quite a bit about realizing a gain on his investment, however, and pursued several tracks to that end. He pressed Chrysler to reduce its huge cash reserves, which produced little return to shareholders. Management steadfastly maintained that the cash represented a necessary cushion in a highly cyclical business. Unable to bring Chrysler around to his point of view, he teamed up with the automaker's former chairman, Lee Iacocca, in an attempted leveraged buyout of the company in 1995. The widely derided transaction failed to obtain financing, but Kerkorian was not finished with his attempt to squeeze more value out of his investment. In 1996, his persistent pressure on management resulted in a pact that granted him board representation. Through his representative, he continued to promote his ideas for enhancing Chrysler's value until his $660 million payday arrived with the Daimler-Benz merger agreement.

The Chrysler episode highlighted one of Kirk Kerkorian's most fascinating characteristics, namely, the sharp divergence of opinion about his character and methods. An early *Fortune* profile described him as an enigma. "To many people," the magazine commented, "he appears to be a western wheeler-dealer who treats companies like commodities—or chips on the gaming table."[20] Kerkorian rejected that characterization, however, arguing that his seemingly disparate businesses all revolved around the leisure industry.

Kerkorian's friends invariably emphasize his politeness. "For a billionaire, he's almost meek," observes former Secretary of State Alexander

M. Haig Jr. "I've never heard him raise his voice. It seems like he would just as soon have his actions speak for him."[21] Noting his "modest reticence,"[22] *Fortune* pointed out that when he was chairman and majority shareholder of TransInternational Airlines, he declined to preside over the annual meeting. He merely introduced himself, then quickly turned over the proceedings to the company's president. When he controlled MGM, he stood in line at the theater to see the studio's releases instead of attending special screenings or premieres.

Noting Kerkorian's aversion to publicity, Fried, Frank, Harris, Shriver & Jacobson senior partner Stephen Fraidin observed, "What Kirk's privacy hides is what a decent and generous person he is."[23] Actor Cary Grant described Kerkorian as "the most honest, straightforward, and considerate person" he knew.[24] Even Hollywood executive Jerry Weintraub, whom Kerkorian fired as chairman of United Artists, calls him "a terrific guy."[25]

A generally favorable *Forbes* 1997 article contended that Kerkorian had never preyed on companies, in the customary sense of "pressing every advantage, picking every bone clean."[26] The author further argued that he had not taken advantage of minority shareholders. According to an unnamed executive, who was otherwise critical of Kerkorian's management of MGM, "If you invested with Kirk, you had every advantage he did."[27]

When Kerkorian took his run at Western Air Lines, the Bank of America agreed to lend him $73 million on an unsecured basis. Being able to borrow such a large amount on the strength of his signature was critical to the deal. If the bank had made a secured loan, Federal Reserve Board rules would have required Kerkorian to post collateral of five times the principal, which would have exceeded his resources. According to the Bank of America's vice chairman, Kerkorian deserved such special treatment because in 20 years of dealing with the bank, he had proven himself "a man of his word, a man of integrity."[28] Motion pictures executive Alan Ladd Jr. commented, "He's a very tough man to do business with, but that's all part of his personality—I can't say he was ever dishonest when I was around him."[29]

Fay Vincent, who recalled Kerkorian's switch regarding the size of the stake he planned to take in Columbia Pictures, had a very different opinion. "He seems to view a written contract as the beginning of a negotiation," complained the former baseball czar.[30] (Kerkorian justified his decision to go above the 25.5 percent holding he had agreed to in a standstill agreement by asserting that Columbia's directors had violated the pact.) Financial columnist Christopher Byron, in sizing up a planned initial public offering by MGM in 1997, disputed *Forbes*'s view of Kerkorian's benign treatment of fellow shareholders. What did Kerkorian intend to do with the studio following the deal? asked Byron. "Suck the blood from it, what else?"[31] According to the columnist, sharp financial practices explained why Kerkorian was "one of the best-known sharks prowling Wall Street—but they also help explain why he's a billionaire and his backers are not."[32] Financier Felix Rohatyn took an equally dim view of Kerkorian's battle with Chrysler:

> I think what Kerkorian is doing at Chrysler is totally destructive and totally against what American industry needs. It is a very short-term attempt to destabilize a company at the expense of its long-term interests.[33]

Money manager Seth Glickenhaus stated the anti-Kerkorian case even more bluntly, calling him "the most self-serving guy to ever happen on the scene." In the Chrysler affair, Glickenhaus claimed, Kerkorian was "looking to take out a lot of cash in a hurry."[34]

These widely divergent perceptions of Kerkorian are largely explained by the adage that what you see depends on where you sit. From the opposite side of the negotiating table, you see a man determined to win. "Rifle Right" Kerkorian did not stop looking for the knockout when he abandoned the ring. If the kayo requires him to mix it up with a company's incumbent managers, he is willing to face their inevitable attempts to discredit him. Outside of the business sphere, however, Kerkorian is a genial and self-effacing man. He has maintained a low profile even in his substantial philanthropic activities.

"Let's Start Working on It"

Ultimately, the impetus behind Kirk Kerkorian's success has been his restlessness. The wide variety of businesses he has engaged in supports his claim that he started out with no specific ambition. "I just tend to get dissatisfied easily and want to do something else," he once explained.[35] Day-to-day operations hold little appeal for him, but buying and selling companies clearly does, even when incumbent management fights him tooth and nail. "I don't think he enjoyed being part of MGM or UA," said Alan Ladd Jr. "What he liked was owning a movie studio that was for sale. And we were always for sale."[36]

Thriving in the high-stakes environment he relishes requires a strong stomach for fluctuations in fortune. In his first go-around with MGM alone, Kerkorian came close to being wiped out on three separate occasions.[37] Between 1969 and mid-1970, the paper loss on his securities amounted to nearly $400 million. "Many people will gamble in the stock market, gamble in business, or just gamble on cards," commented a friend, "and if they got into the kind of situation Kirk got into they'd blow their brains out or just fall to pieces. Kirk goes right back in there and says, 'Well, what can we do here? Let's start working on it.' "[38]

Kerkorian has partaken more fully of the perquisites of wealth than his fellow billionaires Ross Perot and Warren Buffett. Long before becoming a billionaire, he bought a 147-foot ocean-going yacht and became one of the first private owners of a DC-9 jet (worth about $18 million in 1999 dollars). He hung out with movie stars Cary Grant and George Raft and dated actresses Priscilla Presley and Yvette Mimieux.

Like his more abstemious colleagues, however, Kerkorian has continued amassing wealth at an age when most of his contemporaries have long since kicked back and relaxed. Many years ago, he wagered legendarily huge sums at the craps tables in Las Vegas. That game ultimately lost its appeal to him, but he has never tired of the game of making deals.

Carl Icahn

It's exciting when you're playing for high stakes and you feel you have an edge.[39]

Carl Icahn is renowned for his tenacity in negotiations. He wears down his opponents by dickering long into the night, rambling on about unrelated topics. Then, when his adversaries have lost their train of thought, he picks up right where the bargaining left off, pounding on a point he hopes to carry. According to James Freund, a partner in the law firm of

Skadden, Arps, Slate, Meager & Flom, he refuses to concede the smallest point, never offering to split the difference. Freund calls Icahn's strategy "confrontational negotiating," characterized by continuous threatening, analogous in some ways to Bill Gates's "confrontational style" of management. An investor who has faced him across the bargaining table claims that by yelling and screaming, Icahn makes it worthwhile to pay him something just to go away. "He nudges you to death," comments an investment banker.[40]

To Icahn, life is a continuous negotiation. "If the price is right, we are going to sell," Icahn told the judge in a 1984 proceeding. "I think that's true of everything you have, except maybe your kids and possibly your wife."[41] As a matter of fact, when his 18-year marriage broke up, Icahn dragged on the divorce proceedings much as he prolonged business negotiations to extract maximum advantage. His wife's attorney, who had previously represented a number of celebrity clients, commented, "In my twenty-seven years of matrimonial law, I have never met a more worthy opponent."[42]

Case Study: Trans World Airlines

During his 1985 takeover battle with Trans World Airlines, Icahn showed up at 11 P.M. for a bargaining session scheduled to begin at 9 P.M. While the other parties had been tiring themselves out in negotiations, he had gone home, taken a nap, and showered. He walked in looking fresh and invigorated, while the TWA team was already fatigued. The pilots union's representative carped that it was impossible to deal with Icahn. Every time he thought he had reached an agreement, Icahn would come back to the negotiating table with a new wrinkle or a revised number that altered the terms radically in his favor. He delighted in extracting one wage concession after another from the unions by threatening to abandon his bid and sell out to Frank Lorenzo of Texas Air, a buyer that the pilots and machinists found even more unpalatable than Icahn.

At one point in the TWA struggle, attorney Freund confronted Icahn with his habit of shifting ground. Icahn had said that if a better bid than his emerged, he would not act as a spoiler. Freund charged that his negotiating stance at that juncture made him no more than 50 percent a man of his word. Icahn retorted by reeling off numerous instances in which he had kept his word during the bargaining. As Freund recalled the incident, he conceded that Icahn was 75 percent a man of his word. "Come on," Icahn replied. "Give me 80 percent. I'm at least an 80 percent man of my word."[43] To an inveterate deal maker, everything is subject to negotiation.

Even after gaining control of TWA, Icahn was far from through negotiating. The airline's advertising agency, Young & Rubicam, resigned the account, claiming that it could not make money on the revised fee structure that he proposed. According to one Young & Rubicam executive, Icahn was "an impossibly demanding client"[44] who would make an insultingly low offer just to see what would happen. If the agency protested that it could not cut its fees by $3 million, Icahn would come back and propose a $2 million cut.

Icahn's game plan after taking TWA private in a highly leveraged transaction was to get his money out by merging the carrier with another airline. His selling price, however, always turned out to be higher than potential buyers were willing to pay. In 1988, TWA's president, Joe Corr, lined up financing for a $425 million offer, but Icahn demanded $450 million. According to Corr, Icahn then took the financing plan and tried to get his friends to outbid him.[45] Angered, Corr eventually left TWA, but Icahn bargained on.

In 1992, weighed down by the debt of Icahn's buyout and losing money, TWA filed for reorganization in bankruptcy. Now Icahn had a new party to negotiate with, namely, the Pension Benefit Guaranty Corporation (PBGC). The agency was determined that if the airline were ultimately liquidated, it would not be stuck with the carrier's estimated $1.2 billion of unfunded pension liabilities.

As holder of more than 80 percent of TWA's stock, personally and through an investment group, he was legally deemed a "control group." By virtue of having put himself in this position, which observers generally viewed as a tactical error, Icahn was liable for the pension obligation and the liability extended to his other businesses. In fact, Congress had enacted special "get Icahn" legislation to ensure that if his ownership fell below the 80 percent threshold as a result of a reorganization, he would still be on the hook. (Missouri Senator John Danforth, who pressed for the legislation with particular vigor, had once said, "There are some people who shouldn't be allowed to run airlines, and I don't want to name names, but his initials are Carl Icahn.")[46] With TWA's viability in question, Icahn was faced with the loss of his entire business empire.

Diane Burkley, PBGC's deputy director, had acquired a reputation as an astute negotiator, but Icahn drew on his full repertoire of wily tactics. Burkley proposed that Icahn settle the pension liability by lending TWA $200 million and signing a note worth $350 million, payable to the PBGC. Icahn countered with a steeply lower offer involving a secured loan to the airline and a pledge of TWA assets to the PBGC. He strove to baffle Burkley by putting several different proposals on the table at the same time, while she tried to proceed in straightforward quid pro quo fashion. Finally, he presented an ultimatum, saying he would make the requested $200 million loan, but only if his pension liability were restricted to approximately $100 million. Icahn ran the risk that the PBGC might obtain a loan for part of the pension liability from another source, then terminate the TWA pension plans and sue Icahn for the balance of the estimated $1.2 billion liability. He accepted the gamble, however, knowing that he could litigate for years and ultimately wind up paying little or nothing.

In the end, Icahn made a $200 million loan and agreed, in the event of termination of the pension plans, to make eight annual payments of $30 million each. The $240 million total was a far cry from the $1.2 billion that the PBGC initially claimed. As part of the deal, Icahn also consented to make up shortfalls in the annual funding of the pension liabilities. Under the terms of the agreement, however, his obligation was substantially reduced by gains on TWA stock that the PBGC received in the bankruptcy reorganization. He also negotiated the right to manage $1.4 billion of the pension fund's assets, earning additional credit against his liability to the extent that he achieved superior investment returns.

As a closing touch, Icahn showed that when necessary he could use creativity, rather than bluffing and bluster, to achieve his objective in a negotiation. When his $200 million loan came due in 1995, TWA lacked the cash to repay him, having by then gone bankrupt a second time. Icahn found a solution by agreeing to accept repayment in airline tickets, issued to him at a discount, which he could then sell to third parties. The arrangement enabled the airline to work down its loan balance, although a new dispute arose when TWA's management began to perceive the deeply discounted fares of "Air Icahn" as a threat to its own revenues.

TWA turned out to be anything but a home run for Carl Icahn. Some observers, including competing bidder Frank Lorenzo of Texas Air, assumed that he had no intention of actually taking over TWA, but merely hoped to make a quick profit on his shares. Had he not been willing to buy the airline if push came to shove, however, he would have been negotiating from a substantially weaker position. Similarly, he would never have made it to the billionaire category if he had quivered at the sort of risk represented by the heavy debt load he assumed to acquire TWA.

Rewards of a Tough Bargaining Stance

By taking huge risks in a string of takeover battles, Icahn has parlayed a $100-a-week position as a broker trainee at Dreyfus & Co. into a billion-dollar fortune. From the base of a tiny brokerage firm that he founded, he has gained ownership of railcar manufacturer ACF Industries and grabbed headlines with struggles for the likes of Marvel Entertainment, Pan Am, RJR Nabisco, Texaco, and USX. Although certainly not a passive investor, Icahn has utilized the securities markets perhaps more directly than anyone else in his ascent of the Billionaires' Olympus. Many other brilliant stock operators have tried and failed to do the same; but then, few individuals negotiate as tenaciously as Carl Icahn.

Phil Anschutz

I am a student of strategic timing and cycles.[47]

"I might be a seller, I might be a buyer. It depends on who looks like a good dance partner."[48] That is how Phil Anschutz sized up his options as a key player in the railroad industry in 1992. To most of the rest of the world, his options looked considerably less rosy.

Rio Grande Industries, which Anschutz had acquired in 1984, bought the Southern Pacific Railroad in 1988. The highly leveraged deal combined the Southern Pacific with the Denver & Rio Grande Western Railroad to form Southern Pacific Transportation Company. Anschutz expected to pay off the deal's massive borrowings by liquidating nonrail land, but a real estate slump delayed the intended sales. Southern Pacific was left with a huge interest burden, which together with its required capital expenditures measured roughly double the cash that the business was generating. Additional pressure emerged in the form of demands for profits from the partners that Anschutz had brought in to create Southern Pacific Transportation.

The fundamental problem was underinvestment in the rail business by Southern Pacific's previous management. Most of the company's profits had come from nonrail operations, which were not included in the assets sold to Anschutz. After years of neglect, the "Struggling Pacific" could not match the service of rival railroads, which had adopted more advanced technology. Southern Pacific's traditional traffic, including lumber, food, and auto parts, had been declining for 20 years. Stiff competition from truckers compounded the revenue problem. Even after Anschutz managed to get the land sales back on track, the company ran heavy losses and had to renegotiate its loans to remain solvent.

Skepticism mounted as Anschutz began acting increasingly like The Little Engine That Could. His bankers pleaded with him to break up the Southern Pacific and sell the pieces.[49] Why, asked *Forbes*, did Anschutz not extricate himself by obtaining regulatory approval to merge the Southern Pacific with another carrier? All he had to do was persuade the Interstate Commerce Commission that the Southern Pacific was no longer viable on a stand-alone basis. The only explanations that *Forbes* could offer were a large ego and perhaps a touch of masochism, combined with plain old stubbornness.[50]

Unwilling to accept defeat, Anschutz vowed to boost the quality of Southern Pacific's service. His locomotives might have been run-down, but he invested heavily in keeping his tracks in good condition. Sooner or later, Anschutz insisted, the Southern Pacific's extensive connections to Mexican lines would prove invaluable. "We look at what some of the other railroads are doing, and it's great," he commented. "But we can't afford and we don't need all the bells and whistles. One thing I've stressed: This railroad is going to do more for less—and we're going to learn to like it that way."[51]

Anschutz's tenacity paid off, defying his critics. In 1993, he landed a new chief executive, Ed Moyers, who had won fame by turning around the Illinois Central. Moyers immediately began cutting jobs and improving service, two strategies that often went hand in hand. When a transportation officer admitted he did not know the whereabouts of a customer's overdue shipment, Moyers snarled, "Well, you'd better know tomorrow or you won't have a job." Soon after arriving at Southern Pacific, Moyers called together 27 vice presidents and told them that within two months many of them would be gone. The meeting was over.

Inevitably, the strong-headed Moyers experienced some run-ins with the equally strong-headed Anschutz. The two squabbled over compensation and various operating decisions. At one senior staff meeting, Anschutz interrupted his chief executive's presentation by tugging on his jacket to indicate that he ought to sit down.[52]

Despite the friction, Moyers brought the railroad vital credibility. In August 1993, Southern Pacific was able to shore up its finances by going public at $13.50 a share. Within a year of the initial public offering, the railroad floated two secondary offerings at prices of $21 and $19.75. Anschutz retained a 32 percent stake valued at $1 billion.[53]

The real payday, however, came on August 6, 1996. On that date, regulators gave the green light to Anschutz's exit strategy—a merger between the Southern Pacific and Union Pacific railroads. Combining the two lines had been considered a shrewd business idea for about a hundred years. Nevertheless, no less formidable a railroad magnate than E. H. Harriman had failed to bring it about, ultimately meeting rejection at the United States Supreme Court.[54]

Anschutz's merger proposal united the United States Agriculture, Justice, and Transportation departments, as well as the Texas Railroad Commission, in opposition. Even so, heavy lobbying by the Southern Pacific and Union Pacific secured the approval of the newly created Surface Transportation Board. Anschutz's original equity investment in the Denver & Rio Grande Western, which he leveraged into ownership of the Southern Pacific without putting in any new money, amounted to just $90 million. His stake in Southern Pacific Transportation, which had been reduced to 26 percent by the time of the Union Pacific deal, was worth $1.4 billion in the merger.[55] One commentator called Anschutz's coup "probably the biggest single profit ever made in the history of U.S. railroading."[56] The transaction created the nation's largest railroad and left Phil Anschutz as its largest shareholder. Now it was time for him to go into high gear by applying the billionaires' principle "Keep on Growing."

An ordinary entrepreneur might have simply declared victory after parlaying $90 million into $1.4 billion, but not Anschutz. While cashing in his railroad investment, he held on to a fiber-optics operation he had constructed along the Southern Pacific's rights-of-way. The company, Qwest Communications International, went public less than a year after the Union Pacific–Southern Pacific merger cleared its last regulatory hurdle. Within six months, the stock had risen by about 175 percent. The 85 percent stake that Anschutz retained was valued at $3.5 billion; his initial investment in the venture amounted to only $55 million.[57]

The Qwest venture corroborated the judgment of one of Anschutz's business associates:

> Phil is very astute in analyzing what it is that is going to be the next most important business or marketplace. He takes advantage of his assets in ways most other people don't.[58]

Between 1993 and 1997, Anschutz's astuteness helped to raise his estimated net worth from $1.9 billion to $6.2 billion.[59]

Anschutz's triumphs in railroads, real estate, and telecommunications do not exhaust the range of his activities. His other ventures have included uranium and coal mining in Colorado and tungsten and antimony mining in South America. In addition, Anschutz has acquired professional franchises in hockey and soccer. The stock market has been another productive field of activity for Anschutz, who cleared close to $100 million on sallies into ITT and Pennwalt. At one point he invested $60 million in cement producer Ideal Basic, clearing a $30 million profit on a deal that looked extremely iffy.[60] All in all, it is easy to forget that Phil Anschutz made his first billion in oil.

The Kansas native and Denver resident got his start in the oil-rig operations of his father, Fred, a colorful wildcatter. When Fred's health declined, Phil left his law studies and took charge of the business in 1962.

He ultimately sold the drilling operations and plowed the proceeds into Wyoming and Utah ranch land. As it turned out, the Utah property sat on top of one of the 50 largest gas reserves ever discovered in the United States. Following the discovery in 1978, Anschutz expanded his exploration program, acquiring leases on 10 million acres. He soon emerged as a key figure in the Overthrust Belt, a vast zone of oil and gas deposits spread over several western states.

In 1984, at a market peak in energy prices, Anschutz sold half of the ranch-land mineral rights for $500 million, $90 million of which became his cash investment in the Denver & Rio Grande Western.[61] He also made a sizable investment in independent producer Forest Oil. By pumping in substantial sums he helped to revive its moribund exploration program and effect a turnaround in profits.

Anschutz's deal-making skills became legendary. When oil producers scrambled to get a piece of the Overthrust, he shrewdly sold properties at advantageous prices while retaining interests in subsequent discoveries. He demonstrated his hard-nosed bargaining style even when the state of Utah offered him $700,000 for Antelope Island, a Mormon historical site. Anschutz rejected the offer and sued to block the state's effort to condemn the island. After a seven-year struggle, the tenacious negotiator extracted a price of $3.9 million, while retaining certain mineral rights.[62]

～

Like most successful deal makers, Anschutz showed a keen eye for value from his earliest days. He was only 27 when he learned of a collection of western art in the basement of the Atchison, Topeka & Santa Fe Railway's Chicago headquarters. The railroad had originally commissioned the paintings as models for travel posters. Managing to gain an interview with the company's chairman, Anschutz offered to catalog the largely forgotten works in exchange for the right to purchase a few. The 85 paintings that he bought for a song a few days later were eventually valued at several million dollars.[63]

～

Along with his ability to spot a bargain, Anschutz's negotiating success relies on a high tolerance for risk. He appears to have inherited this trait from his father, whose fortunes swung widely in the turbulent oil market of the 1950s. At times, Fred Anschutz's family was unsure of making the next mortgage payment.[64] His son has managed to avoid such narrow scrapes, but has certainly experienced his ups and downs. At a low point in energy prices in 1987, he was forced to lay off more than half of his employees. He even cut out free snacks and soft drinks.[65]

The younger Anschutz made his first major strike in 1968, while contract-drilling for Chevron. Aiming to make the most of the discovery, he borrowed heavily to buy up surrounding leases. Then disaster struck as a spark from a truck set the entire field ablaze. Faced with possible bankruptcy, Anschutz nevertheless bought another driller's interests in exchange for assuming all his liabilities. It so happened that Universal Studios was filming *Hellfighters*, starring John Wayne as the oil-field firefighter "Red" Adair. For $100,000, Anschutz agreed to let Universal's camera crew take real-life footage of his burning well. That sum was enough to bring in the real Adair to put out the fire, ultimately enabling Anschutz to realize a healthy profit.

"It's important to have your back to the wall," Phil Anschutz commented, recollecting the oil-field fire. "It teaches you how to think outside the box."[66] Sheer determination has been a consistent theme of the marathon runner's long-run success in amassing wealth. As one associate observed, "He lays down his stipulations and then won't budge. He's a smart guy out to make a buck. The amount he's already made doesn't matter."[67]

9

OUTMANAGE
THE COMPETITION

Luck is the residue of design.
—Branch Rickey

Superior management skills have played a critical role in the foundation of many great fortunes. By and large, however, it would be inac-
curate to characterize the subjects of *How to Be a Billionaire* as hands-on
managers. Getting bogged down in operational details would have di-
verted their attention from the more essential task of amassing personal
wealth. Instead, they have focused on three essential aspects of management: organization, recruitment, and motivation.

Organization

The very word "organization" is anathema to many rugged individual-
ists who hope to become billionaires. To them, much of the attraction
of becoming independently wealthy is the freedom for self-expression
that it affords. Richard Branson can defy convention, just as H. L.
Hunt could publish controversial political opinions, without greatly

215

worrying about public opinion. Thanks in large part to William H. Whyte's 1956 book, *The Organization Man*, business organizations have become associated with quite the opposite sort of person—namely, a faceless conformist.

Fear not. Sacrificing your individuality is by no means a prerequisite for amassing extraordinary wealth. In fact, most the self-made billionaires are mavericks, at least in their approach to business, if not invariably in their social, theological, or political views. Group-thinkers have not cracked the Forbes 400 in significant numbers for one simple reason: Doing the same thing in the same way as everyone else is decidedly not the way to overcome the leveling effects of competition.

Outorganizing the competition, in contrast, is one proven method of breaking away from the pack. The opportunity arises precisely because of certain maladies that give the word "organization" a negative connotation. Companies that exhibit the following sorts of behavior become sitting ducks for rivals that can respond quickly and effectively to an evolving competitive environment:

- Long lines of communication keep senior management unaware of changes in the marketplace.
- Fear of rocking the boat discourages employees from coming forward with worthwhile ideas.
- Primary focus on avoiding mistakes deters managers from taking risks.
- Obsession with defending turf diverts managers from capitalizing on business opportunities.

The leaders of organizations that run circles around procedure-bound companies are not people who emphasize protocol over results. If a creative idea must undergo endless rounds of formal review, it will not be implemented soon enough to provide a competitive advantage. Innovations turn into action much more swiftly in organizations run by individuals who feel as frustrated as Ross Perot did by the slow response to events of General Motors. What makes the self-made billionaires' knack for building effective companies distinctive has little to do with the formal elements, such as organizational charts and performance measurement. It is more a matter of giving their organizations the stamp of their invariably strong personalities.

Sam Walton created a successful organization by ceaselessly gathering information from the front lines. Both he and his regional vice presidents made endless rounds of visits to Wal-Mart stores, collecting ideas from employees at all levels. Walton further avoided the pitfall of insularity by constantly checking out competitors' stores. Throughout the week, Walton and his top managers gleaned up-to-the-minute intelligence, unfiltered by multiple layers of corporate functionaries. Each Saturday, they met to set merchandising decisions for the next few weeks. By the end of the same day, the plans were communicated all the way down to the store level.

The final word on organization should go to John D. Rockefeller Sr. He would have been rightly regarded as an organizational genius if he had done nothing more than introduce the trust structure in 1882. Previous cartels had never managed to keep their loosely linked members from cheating (i.e., cutting prices). Standard Oil achieved centralized control, despite severe legal impediments to conducting business across state lines, and successfully enforced uniform pricing throughout a company that controlled 90 percent of the American refining business. In addition to putting into action the soon to be widely imitated trust form of organization, Rockefeller pioneered the modern, large-scale, global corporation.

He achieved all of this, with no previous model to copy, while never owning more than one-third of Standard Oil's stock. Cohesiveness also arose from his widely noticed aversion to using the pronoun "I" when discussing the company's business. Rockefeller exhorted his associates to say "we" to emphasize that they were partners acting in the interest of the entire enterprise.

In his personal relations, Rockefeller was cordial, rather than warmly outgoing in the manner of Walton or Huizenga. His hold over Standard Oil's executives derived rather from an awe-inspiring quality much like Bill Gates's. Like Gates, he preferred smart, strong-willed associates and encouraged vigorous debate over policies, yet remained a level above the throng. "Rockefeller always sees a little further than the rest of us," said one leader of the Standard Oil crowd, "and then he sees around the corner."[1]

To make a complex collection of separately state-incorporated companies work together smoothly, Rockefeller devised a highly effective committee system. At the top stood an executive committee, which exerted control through its authority to approve all major expenditures. Other committees focused on areas such as purchasing, exports, and pipelines. Each company within the trust adapted the innovations developed by these specialized committees. At the same time, the committee system enabled the overall enterprise to rationalize its operations by such means as closing inefficient plants and consolidating production into three huge refineries. In addition, Rockefeller's organizational plan facilitated competition among the subsidiaries through the awarding of prizes. This spur to good performance was critically important for managers who were operating, from an external standpoint, as monopolies.[2]

A century later, John D. Rockefeller Sr.'s organizational principles remain sound models, notwithstanding the difference that today's companies face bona fide competition. He gave managers considerable autonomy, sitting in on committee meetings without speaking much, but after due deliberation offering well-conceived solutions to problems. Bill Gates interacts with Microsoft's small teams in similarly productive fashion, albeit with a more confrontational style. In the future, corporate structures will no doubt adapt further to changes in the economy, but Rockefeller's basic principles of effective organization will remain timeless.

Recruitment

Most business enterprises that are vast enough to create billion-dollar fortunes are too complex to be run effectively by a single presiding genius. Therefore, recruitment of capable managers has been an essential ingredient to most of the great fortunes. Far from finding it difficult to delegate authority over day-to-day operations, most self-made billionaires have preferred to focus on more lucrative activities. By swinging more deals and overcoming the leveling effect of competition, they have become far wealthier than managers who were much more adept at handling the details.

John D. Rockefeller Sr. hired talented people whenever he found them, rather than according to need, confident that Standard Oil's growth would create many spots to fill. He recognized talent even in opponents, recruiting as his eventual successor a refiner who initially denounced Rockefeller's monopoly as "the great anaconda." (John D. Archbold's fellow resisters in Oil Creek, Pennsylvania, were even more scathing, calling Rockefeller "the Monster" and labeling his associates "the Forty Thieves.")[3] In choosing lieutenants, Rockefeller looked above all for individuals who had the knack of dealing with people. This ability, he said, was a commodity as purchasable as sugar or coffee.[4]

Skillful recruitment was vital to Ross Perot's success in building Electronic Data Systems. He began by raiding his former employer, IBM. From the Dallas office alone, Perot hired the senior technical person, several engineers, and some sales trainees. He then moved on to pick off ace programmers from an IBM unit in Houston devoted to the National Aeronautic and Space Administration. From there, he proceeded to strip other major Dallas companies of their best and brightest. After a Naval Academy classmate proved successful despite a total lack of background in computers, Perot devised a special training program for technological novices.

As EDS grew, it became imperative to recruit a special type of internally motivated individual who was willing to leave home for months at a time and work 14-hour days to get the job done. Recruitment therefore became the company's first formal department, imbued with the same spirit that characterized the company's salespeople and project managers. Recruiters would call a computer outfit and vaguely ask to speak to "John." In the process of straightening out their request by getting several different employees on the line, they would find five or six prospects. They would then interview the most promising prospect, from whom they would obtain the names of other likely candidates.

Perot put extraordinary effort into evaluating new hires. He devised a 20-page application that asked candidates, among other questions, what they considered the greatest accomplishments of their lives. He met with the wives of the candidates, exploring whether they would tolerate the demands that EDS would put on their husbands. In the early days, a candidate did not get hired before interviewing with every single existing EDS employee. Eventually, the screening group was streamlined to the candidate's prospective manager, an experienced EDS employee, and a recent recruit. All were asked whether they would hire the candidate, and whether they would work with and for that person.

Microsoft uses a similarly intensive process to identify top-caliber employees. Bill Gates's company subjects candidates to intensive interviews by the teams to which they will be assigned if hired, putting great emphasis on the team members' evaluations. Steve Ballmer, the architect of the software producer's recruitment strategy, follows a policy similar to John D. Rockefeller's method of hiring according to talent, rather than need. There is no point in fooling around with head-count budgets, he explains, when an interviewer discovers the sort of candidate who comes around only once in a lifetime.

During its early days, Microsoft tried raiding competitors for proven talent, but could not find individuals who fit its desired profile. Recruitment efforts therefore shifted to a select group of colleges that regularly produced smart, highly motivated candidates. Executive Scott McGregor described the interviewing process that evolved:

> We would rip people to pieces. We would ask them very difficult technical questions, hand them a piece of paper and pen and say solve this problem. We probably lost some people but the people we did hire were good at solving very difficult problems under pressure.[5]

In past years, interviewees were given such problems as estimating the volume of water discharged by the Mississippi River or explaining how to represent numbers in base negative one.[6] Over time, Microsoft has had to generate new interview questions as unsuccessful candidates have circulated its established ones on campus.

One way or another, the senior managers and organizations recruited by the self-made billionaires have reflected their own personalities. While Microsoft has attracted aggressively intellectual types characterized as clones of Bill Gates, Sam Walton's top aides were typically ambitious small-town men like himself. Wayne Huizenga's senior managers have tended to be former football players with middle-class, Midwestern backgrounds. Ross Perot created EDS in his own image by hiring hard chargers with military backgrounds.

In recruiting people who shared their views of the world, however, the billionaires did not seek yes-men. Confident enough not to feel threatened by strong subordinates, they generally valued aides who were willing to defend opposing points of view. In addition, they brought in senior managers who complemented their own talents, typically individuals better equipped than themselves to handle operational details. Instead of hiring underlings whom they could easily dominate, they built exceptional teams and became exceptionally rich.

Motivation

The motivator par excellence, Sam Walton, relied far more heavily on praise than on criticism. By all accounts, his interest in listening to employees' ideas was sincere. Considering also Wal-Mart's broad profit-sharing plan, which induced workers to identify strongly with the company's success, Walton's practices read like a case study in effective human relations.

Bill Gates employs a contrasting approach, to put it mildly. "That's the stupidest thing I ever heard" is the defining phrase of his famed "confrontational style."[7] According to one source, a more precise quotation runs, "That's the stupidest [expletive deleted] thing I've ever heard!"[8] To motivate a programmer who is having difficulty completing a project, Gates might say, "This stuff isn't hard! I could do this stuff in a weekend!"[9] As a hint that an employee's initial solution to a problem has fallen short of Microsoft's lofty standards, the chairman may comment, "That's brain-damaged!"[10] If the recipient of the reproof fails to grasp his point, Gates will probably follow up by saying the same thing again, but louder. Breaking the news that a new employee really is not Microsoft material after all might be phrased, "Where the [expletive deleted] did we hire you from?"[11]

Unconventional though it may be, Gates's motivational style gets results. Microsoft hires bright, aggressive individuals much like its chairman. They rise to the challenge implicit in Gates's claim that he could do the task better and more quickly himself. Being the target of the "stupidest thing" phrase confers as much status as receiving an e-mail from Gates in the middle of the night.[12] Microsoft employees attest that they distinguish between the alleged stupidity of their ideas and what Gates does not imply, namely, that they themselves are stupid. By standing their ground in the face of the chief's invective, they gain his respect and win esteem within the organization. Employees have been known to defend their positions by standing on a table in a conference room and yelling at Gates. Such exchanges typically conclude with Gates murmuring, "Okay."[13]

Significantly, too, Gates reserves his "stupidest thing" line for the times when it can serve a purpose. A story that has assumed legendary proportions at Microsoft involves a bug discovered in the company's Multiplan software product after 20,000 copies had already been sold. The estimated cost of shipping corrective updates to every buyer was $200,000. When Gates took the news philosophically, he demonstrated to the Multiplan development team that he respected their abilities. He also showed that he understood the limited utility of his outbursts. A sharply worded challenge might spur product developers to extraordinary efforts, but could accomplish nothing worthwhile after the product was shipped.[14]

The chief executive's motivational techniques are not the only unconventional aspects of Microsoft's organizational style. Visitors to the company's Redmond, Washington, headquarters comment on how few telephones ring. Employees communicate continuously by e-mail, with the chairman himself spending at least two hours a day reading and composing electronic messages.

Gates estimates that he devotes 70 percent of his time to review meetings with small product development teams. Unlike Sam Walton, he does not lavish praise on employees, but he does listen intently. The discussion may, however, veer into topics as wide-ranging as quantum physics and genetic engineering.

Somehow, an effective organization has emerged from employees hired on the basis of their "intellectual bandwith" and led by the individual acknowledged to be the brainiest of the bunch. One result of Microsoft's informal, confrontational culture is adaptability. In an impressively short time, for example, the company radically and successfully shifted its strategy for the Microsoft Network after initially being left behind by the introduction of the Internet.[15] Companies that avoid honest communication in the name of politeness cannot compete effectively against Gates's minions.

Along with Gates's personal touch, a heavy emphasis on stock options accounts for much of Microsoft's esprit de corps. Widespread equity participation is a formula that has proven effective since the early days of Standard Oil Company. John D. Rockefeller Sr. encouraged employees at all levels to own stock, thereby increasing their loyalty to the company. Every man, woman, and child ought to be a capitalist, he said, saving their earnings and becoming owners of American industry.

To be sure, Rockefeller relied on more than the motivational power of stock ownership. When he toured Standard Oil plants, he quizzed the superintendents as diligently as Walton pumped Wal-Mart employees for useful information. Rockefeller wrote down suggestions for improvements in a small red notebook that he carried with him. He zealously followed up on the ideas, noting gleefully that pulling out the notebook sometimes caused sweat to break out on managers' foreheads.[16]

Like Gates and Rockefeller, Ross Perot believes strongly in the power of giving employees a piece of the action. The main reason for taking Perot Systems public in 1999, he says, was to motivate employees. "I want them to know what their work has produced in the way of value. Nothing motivates a team like having them have stock."[17]

At Electronic Data Systems, Perot used stock as part of his effort to bring his managers' spouses into the fold. About a year after founding the company, he mysteriously disappeared from the office for several hours. When he returned, he ducked questions about where he had been, but that evening the company's managers learned the answer. Perot had visited each of their homes, thanked their wives for putting up with the demands of their husbands' jobs, and presented them with 100 shares apiece of EDS stock. Twenty-five years later, those shares were worth $400,000.[18]

Aside from financial incentives, Perot won the allegiance of his EDS lieutenants by creating a company that was the antithesis of the ineffective organization described in bullet points earlier in this chapter. He gave them big challenges and wide latitude to figure out how to meet them, always displaying confidence that they would succeed. Additionally, he showed genuine concern for his people. When one executive's son was born in New York with a congenital heart defect, Perot enlisted a heart surgeon he knew in Dallas to advise on the emergency. Corrective surgery saved the infant's life. A retired EDS executive living in southern Texas summarized the personal loyalty that Perot commanded by taking a direct interest in his employees' lives:

> If Ross asked me to drive to Alaska but he couldn't tell me why until I got there, I would be in my car an hour later. Not only that, my wife would be packing my suitcases before I hung up the phone.[19]

Wayne Huizenga has utilized strikingly similar strategies. At Waste Management, he built an effective organization on a foundation of equity participation by the owner-managers whose operations he acquired. At Blockbuster, he offered stock options lucrative enough to induce some managers to take pay cuts as large as 60 percent to join the company.[20] The options program extended well down into the employee ranks.

In addition to emphasizing equity participation, Huizenga applied his boundless energy to instilling pride and building morale within the organization. Like Perot, he made a special effort to show appreciation for the sacrifices made by the spouses of his fanatically hardworking managers. At gatherings of Waste Management managers, he demanded slavish attention to detail. If too little food were ordered for a reception, he said, the last guests to arrive would talk about nothing but the host's stinginess.[21] Much like Walton, Huizenga stayed informed on operations by making time to talk to people at all levels, from managers to truck drivers to office workers.

The Common Substance beneath Contrasting Styles

The preceding discussion demonstrates that superior management is not a one-size-fits-all affair. Sam Walton's warm-and-fuzzy approach would not suit Bill Gates's personality, yet both created phenomenally successful organizations. If you are not folksy by nature, attempting to remake yourself in Walton's image will only succeed in making you sound insincere. That will cost you the trust of your people, which is essential regardless of your particular management style.

Looking beneath the differences in the self-made billionaires' styles, several common factors emerge that represent the substance of effective management. To replicate their success, you must develop an approach that is compatible with your personality and achieves the following objectives:

- Attract managers with enough self-confidence to challenge your own judgment on matters.
- Delegate authority to detail-oriented executives who can free you to concentrate on billion-dollar ideas.
- Stay close enough to operations to be aware of problems and opportunities, making sure that your lieutenants follow up on suggestions for improvement.
- Constantly reinforce a focus on controlling costs.
- Use equity incentives to provide your managers and other key employees a realistic chance to become millionaires.
- Show genuine, personal concern for people within your organization.
- Promote morale by maintaining a sense of fun along with seriousness of purpose.

While these common principles of management are observable in the careers of many self-made billionaires, each has applied them in a distinctive fashion. This statement is truer of Richard Branson than of any other individual profiled in *How to Be a Billionaire*. Britain's most celebrated entrepreneur violates almost every convention of the business world except making money.

THE BILLIONAIRE HOW-TO

Fundamental Strategies

- Outmanage the Competition
- Take Monumental Risks
- Do Business in a New Way
- Thrive on Deals

Key Principles

- Rules Are Breakable
- Pursue the Money in Ideas

Richard Branson

Back in 1970, I couldn't decide whether to call the company Virgin or Slipped Disc Records. I guess I chose Virgin because it reflected an inexperience in business—among other things—and also a freshness and a slight outrageousness.[22]

Beginning with a magazine that he published as a 15-year-old student, Richard Branson has entered more than 100 different businesses through a process he calls "organic expansion." His activities encompass record retailer Virgin Megastores, Virgin Atlantic Airways, and Virgin Hotels Group, as well as publishing, television, radio, ballooning operations, soft drinks, bridal wear, and a modeling agency. In April 1999, he registered Virgin Galactic Airways as a company aiming to provide spaceflights to tourists by 2007.

In 1998, the *Economist* counted 200-odd firms owned by Branson, plus joint ventures accounting for a similar volume of sales. The complex structure included family trusts based in the Channel Islands, as well as holding companies in the British Virgin Islands and sub–holding companies in the United Kingdom. Branson acknowledged that the setup was "indirectly" designed to reduce taxes, while the company's finance director said that the original purpose of locating companies in the British Virgin Islands was to keep information away from British Airways during a commercial dispute.[23]

Branson rejects the notion of making his sprawling business empire more efficient by consolidating its operations. In service businesses, he argues, the key is to have happy and well-motivated employees. Accordingly, he perceives greater value in keeping his companies small-scale, with no more than 50 or 60 people in one building, than in saving money by putting everybody under one roof. Once a company becomes so large that people no longer know one another, says Branson, it is time to break it up.

The unconventionality reflected in Branson's managerial style is a personality trait that has made him a highly successful innovator throughout his career. Initially dismissed as a "hippie businessman,"[24] he showed up the British record retailing industry by launching the country's first discount record mail-order business, Virgin Records. When that business was endangered by a seven-week postal strike, he moved his inventory to an empty floor in the back of a shoe store and opened Britain's first discount record store. Meanwhile, he bought a recording studio and produced a smash hit with his first album, Mike Oldfield's *Tubular Bells*, which sold more than seven million copies worldwide. Unconstrained by conventional thinking, Branson scored again with the Sex Pistols, a controversial punk rock group that other record producers were afraid to touch. Androgynous recording sensation Boy George was another of Branson's highly profitable discoveries.

Conventional wisdom held that Branson's next major venture, Virgin Atlantic Airways, was doomed to failure. To begin with, Branson had no experience in the notoriously tough airline business, which has bruised even such savvy billionaires as Warren Buffett and Carl Icahn. Other low-fare carriers, including Freddie Laker's Skytrain, had already failed to compete head-to-head against British Airways, the world's most highly traveled international airline. Branson's own advisers warned him against trying. Financial experts said that the Virgin empire was becoming overextended. All of these factors contributed to a broad consensus that "the airline that Boy George built" would go bust quickly. Branson himself remarked at one point that the best way to become a millionaire was to start with a billion and buy an airline.[25]

In the opinion of British Airways' chairman, Branson was "too old to rock and roll and too young to fly."[26] What he overlooked was his upstart competitor's compulsion to disprove anyone who said that a thing could not be done. Branson had a completely different take on the airline business than the established carriers. In his view, flying was all about entertainment.

Beginning with a single daily round-trip between London's Gatwick Airport and Newark International Airport, Virgin Atlantic transformed the transatlantic passenger's experience by providing extra legroom and seat-back video screens. As the carrier grew, its Upper Class service added lounges, free neck massages, manicures, and gourmet meals, as well as kazoo instructors and face painters to entertain the children. Passengers received these amenities while paying about half as much as British Airways charged for first class. Virgin's economy passengers paid fares that roughly matched the competition's, but they received service comparable to that which other carriers offered in business class.

Similarly innovative thinking got Branson around the problem of an advertising budget much smaller than the major international carriers' outlays. Breaking out of his past pattern of resolutely keeping his personal life private, he began staging stunts that attracted widespread media coverage. He began by announcing the creation of Virgin Atlantic dressed as a World War I aviator. Next, he attempted to break the record for crossing the Atlantic in a small powerboat. That 1985 attempt failed when his vessel sank 150 miles short of its destination, but he tried again the following year and succeeded in setting a new record. Additional millions of dollars worth of free publicity followed in 1987, when he and Swedish aeronaut Per Lindstrand made the first successful crossing of the Atlantic in a hot-air balloon.

By now, Branson's image as an "adventure capitalist" has become a living public relations vehicle for the Virgin Group. His celebrated antics include throwing fully clothed people into swimming pools, a practice he has defended on the grounds that the boss should set the tone at a party by having lots of fun. For similar reasons, he enjoys practical jokes such as festooning a hot-air balloon with blinking lights to make it look like a UFO, manning it with a costumed midget, and landing it at dawn in a field near London, to the astonishment of incoming commuters. At his wedding, Branson arrived at the altar hanging from the landing struts of a helicopter.

To launch Virgin Cola, he dispatched a Sherman tank to New York's Times Square. For the Virgin Bride bridal wear store's opening, he appeared in a $10,000 silk lace bridal gown, complete with a veil and train. During Virgin Atlantic flights, Branson used to walk the aisles in an air-hostess skirt until he wore out the joke. When the airline publicized the opening of its London–Los Angeles route, aides had to talk him out of going out on the catwalk in a bikini.

Both wealth and acclaim have proceeded from Branson's eccentric ways. In 1998, *Forbes* estimated his net worth at $1.9 billion.[27] In one most-admired poll of young Britons, he ranked second only to Mother Teresa.[28] Another placed him third behind the Pope and the Prince of Wales.[29]

While Branson is sui generis from a personality standpoint, many of his business tactics parallel those of his billionaire peers. For example, when he started Virgin Atlantic Airways, he mimicked Sam Walton's technique of learning from competitors' mistakes by closely quizzing managers of other low-fare carriers that had been driven under by British Airways. Branson also precisely replicated Kirk Kerkorian's policy of "keeping the back door open" in acquiring aircraft. The deal for the airline's first Boeing 747 allowed him to sell the plane back to the manufacturer at nearly the original price if Virgin failed.

∼

Branson motivates employees to excel by putting them into slightly higher positions than they expect. Like Kirk Kerkorian, Branson has no difficulty delegating day-to-day operations, much preferring to spend his time on new ventures. As long as a business is doing well, he does not bother to meet with management, while making himself available for crises. Virgin Atlantic Airways is the one business in which he maintains a tight grip on operations.

Constantly on the lookout for new businesses to spin out of existing ones, Branson sees employees as a source of ideas. In 1996, a Virgin Atlantic flight attendant told Branson that she had just gotten married and found it extremely difficult and time-consuming to make the arrangements. She proposed opening a store in which a bride could buy her wedding dress, have her hair done and receive a manicure, obtain help in planning the reception, and then use Virgin's travel service to arrange the honeymoon. Branson made her dream come true by opening Virgin Bride in London and immediately began thinking about adding Virgin Babies and Virgin Dating to the product line.[30]

Many of Virgin Group's top executives have become millionaires and Branson has found other ways of spreading the wealth, as well. When he won damages of nearly $1 million in a lawsuit against British Airways, he distributed part of the proceeds to employees. Receiving $400 from the company's archrival was not only pleasant, but a great morale booster, he observed.[31]

In another unusual move that reinforced employee loyalty, Branson asked employees for suggestions when a recession necessitated a 400-person staff reduction. Six hundred volunteered to take off three to six months as a sort of sabbatical. When they returned, according to Branson, they felt rested and inspired. He claims that a similar approach would work in most companies, provided employees were assured that volunteering for temporary down time would not affect their jobs. Fifteen to 20 percent of employees, he estimates, could afford periodic sabbaticals and would view the program as a benefit.[32]

~

For Richard Branson, risk taking is not confined to business ventures. After successfully traversing the Atlantic, he and his balloonist partner Per Lindstrand attempted to cross the Pacific. Flying in the jet stream, they encountered no difficulties for the first 1,000 miles, but then their capsule lurched 30 degrees and lost half its fuel. Gales were whipping through the Pacific, precluding a landing at sea by making it impossible for a rescue ship to reach them. Their only choice was to fly where the jet stream carried them, swept along by 240-mile-an-hour winds. Previously, balloonists had rarely flown in winds of more than 100 miles per hour.

Branson and Lindstrand finally succeeded in getting across the ocean, but missed their California destination by 1,800 miles. Instead, they landed on a frozen lake in the Canadian Arctic. "I popped out of the capsule like a banana out of its skin and crawled across the ice and Per followed," Branson subsequently recounted. "There was nobody to see us, except an otter who came waddling across with an inquisitive expression on its face."[33]

A rescue helicopter would have been more helpful. None showed up until six hours later, by which time the intrepid pair might have frozen to death. Branson nevertheless considered the experience lovely, noting that he never would have seen the Arctic if he had not inadvertently landed there.

Branson has shown equal willingness to take chances in the business sphere, as evidenced by the close calls and failures that inevitably arise from frequent risk taking. For example, Virgin Records suffered severe cash flow problems during a recording industry downturn in 1980. *Event*, an entertainment magazine that he launched the same year, folded within 12 months. Other ventures that flopped included a film company and a chain of clothing stores. Branson also failed in an attempt to take over British independent television network ITV in conjunction with entertainer David Frost. During the late 1980s, moreover, most of Branson's operations began to lose money, necessitating the sale of his music recording business in 1992.

A more recent venture into the railroad business certainly must be deemed audacious. In undertaking to turn Britain's publicly owned, money-losing rail lines into a profitable private enterprise, Branson committed himself to huge expenditures for new trains. To be sure, he could point to Virgin Atlantic Airways as a previous success in a transportation business despite formidable odds. As the *Economist* pointed out, however, Virgin Atlantic was a start-up in an overregulated market, rather than a turnaround effort in a bad business.[34]

Although not averse to risk, Branson seeks the same big-upside/low-downside mix that other self-made billionaires have sought. Conscious of the value of the Virgin brand name, he licenses it on advantageous terms. In November 1996, for example, he reentered the music recording business with a new label, V2, selling a 30 percent stake for $100 million while making no financial commitment on Virgin's part.[35]

Rule breaking was an element of Branson's style from the time that, at age 15, he launched his magazine, *Student*. To sound credible to potential advertisers, he had to disguise the fact that he was soliciting their business from a pay phone. Claiming that he had lost his money in the phone, he persuaded the operators to connect him directly with his party, thereby avoiding a telltale pay phone signal. "Then, I put on one voice for Mr. Branson's secretary, and another from Mr. Branson," he later recalled.[36]

Somehow, Branson persuaded literary luminaries such as Jean-Paul Sartre and John Le Carré to contribute articles to *Student*. After obtaining an interview with James Baldwin, he bluffed his way into the American author's hotel room and mistakenly began interviewing his bodyguard.[37] After clearing up the confusion, he interviewed Baldwin without benefit of having read any of his books. In fact, Branson may not have ever read a complete book in his life, having too short an attention span.[38] As he has explained, his parents raised him to *do* things, not to observe or listen to what others were doing.

In the discount record mail-order business, Branson cut a few corners to overcome frequent shortages of funds. A favorite ploy was to put postage on the top three packages in a bundle and hope the postal worker would not notice that the 500 packages beneath them had no stamps. When caught in the act, he would go to a different post office.

At one point, Branson got rather carried away with breaking the rules. Authorities nabbed him selling tax-exempt export records domestically. He spent one night in jail before his parents bailed him out by mortgaging their home. After pleading guilty, Branson paid $85,000 in fines. Thereafter, he said, he played strictly by the book. He actually recommended the experience of spending a night in jail in order to learn that sleeping well is all that really matters.[39]

Informality is another rule-breaking feature of the Branson style. For many years, he oversaw his immense businesses from a houseboat. Investment bankers were especially intrigued, he noted, and he never had difficulty persuading people to come meet him. Later, Branson transferred Virgin's headquarters to a building that doubled as his residence until he moved his family to another nearby house.

Unconventional offices go back to the origins of Branson's business empire. He ran his magazine, *Student,* from a basement apartment where the staff slept at night on mattresses that they leaned against the wall during the day. After being evicted from those quarters, Branson shifted his base to the crypt of a church, launching Virgin's mail-order business from a room above two coffins.

One concession to convention in Branson's office is the presence of a computer, although he does not use it. He relies instead on black ledger notebooks, taking meticulous notes much as John D. Rockefeller Sr. did in his small red notebook a century earlier. Whenever he flies on Virgin Atlantic, Branson makes lengthy lists of things he wants improved, from improperly reclining seats to excessively long waits for assistance by wheelchair-bound passengers. Like Rockefeller and Walton before him, he delegates the resolution of such matters in order to stay focused on strategic issues, yet pushes relentlessly to improve operations. By 1999, Branson had accumulated 122 black ledger notebooks. That figure is net of nine that he lost during a failed attempt to circle the earth in a hot-air balloon.

∼

Before revolutionizing the airline business, Branson transformed British record retailing. Virgin's competitors were stuffy shops that displayed easy-listening Andy Williams records right alongside Frank Zappa's iconoclastic rock records. Branson's customers could sit on pillows while listening to music on headphones and buy bootleg recordings that other retailers refused to carry.

Virgin Megastore broke every known rule of the music retailing business when it opened in Paris in 1988. The store defied industry practice by remaining open until midnight every day, including Sunday, and until 1:00 A.M. on Friday and Saturday nights. Differentiating itself from more tradition-bound French record merchants, Branson's outlet became an entertainment experience, complete with a café. It offered plentiful headphones and screens to allow shoppers to listen to compact discs, watch videos, and play computer games. The Megastore even featured a condom vending machine emblazoned with the slogan *"l'amour sans 'stress' "* ("love without stress"). By providing a friendly environment, the store generated the largest annual sales of any record shop in the world and attracted more visitors each year than the Louvre or Eiffel Tower.

~

When businesspeople encountered long-haired Richard Branson in his early twenties, many refused to take him seriously. A few years later, Bob Last, manager of the Human League rock band, was far less deprecating. He described Branson as an "intransigent" deal maker. Branson, said Last, "knows what game he's playing and is very rarely outwitted. He's only interested in the chase of the deal—at the point he feels he has it locked up, he loses interest in the details."[40] Associates of consummate deal maker Wayne Huizenga describe him in similar terms.

In 1992, Branson defied pundits by getting his asking price of $1 billion for Virgin Records in a sale to entertainment conglomerate Thorn EMI. Profit margins were thin at the time and he was under pressure to sell as a result of losses in his other businesses. Conventional wisdom held that no sale of an independent record producer would top the $540 million price that MCA paid for Geffen Records in 1990. Sticking to his selling price became even more of a challenge for Branson when the field of potential buyers narrowed to one. At the end of the day, however, a senior member of Branson's negotiating team was able to crow, "The numbers are the same as the Geffen deal. Only substitute a pound for the dollar sign."[41] Yet another group had learned what a record executive who used to make licensing deals with Branson had discovered years earlier: "He's fun, but *brutal*. I mean, he gets what he wants."[42]

Branson's extraordinarily diverse empire is testimony to his knack for turning ideas into dollars, even when he enters an entirely unfamiliar business. The foundation of his fortune, the original Virgin recording business, succeeded despite his lack of interest in as passive an activity as listening to music. "He doesn't actually know much about music," remarked a noted editor, "but he's a very good businessman."[43]

Fearless Competitors

Beneath Richard Branson's flamboyant exterior is an effective, if unconventional, manager, a formidable negotiator, and above all, a fierce competitor. Oddly enough, the stunts for which he is best known arose from a business need, namely, to stretch an advertising budget far smaller than his competitors'. In order to reach the billionaires' ranks, Branson had to overcome an innate aversion to the limelight. Often, amassing extraordinary wealth requires doing what comes unnaturally.

A fascinating footnote to Branson's management involves his 1992–1995 collaboration with Wayne Huizenga in the United States music retailing market. Blockbuster Entertainment had begun to expand into music retailing from its core business of video rentals by acquiring the Sound Warehouse and Music Plus chains. On a European trip, Blockbuster's chief executive officer, Steve Berrard, visited the Paris Virgin Megastore and told Huizenga that he had found the perfect approach to the music business. Branson, who was preparing to open his first test store in the United States, knew that other British retailers had found the American market extremely difficult to crack. In short order, the two self-made billionaires struck a deal in which Blockbuster became an equal partner in Virgin's 15 European stores and 75 percent owner of as many stores as Virgin could open in the United States.[44] Virgin kept management control, while gaining strategically vital financial backing for its American expansion.

Inevitably, the ambitions of the two strong-willed entrepreneurs clashed. Huizenga envisioned Virgin-Blockbuster megastores that would capitalize on his company's brand name and large base of cardholders. He was therefore dismayed to find in early 1993 that a Los Angeles–area store about to open did not display the Blockbuster logo anywhere. The owner of the shopping center explained that he thought Blockbuster's wholesome, unhip image was incompatible with a store that dispensed free condoms, but Huizenga was not mollified. Meanwhile, Blockbuster proceeded with its original plan to acquire music retailing chains consisting of small, neighborhood stores that would not compete directly with the Blockbuster-Virgin jointly owned megastores in major shopping centers. Following the billionaires' principle "Copying Pays Better Than Innovating," the Blockbuster Music Plus stores installed a large number of listening posts and used rack designs that resembled Virgin's. When the two chains began to find themselves competing for store sites, they ended their collaboration on the megastores.

Conflict arose between Richard Branson and Wayne Huizenga as much as a result of the similarities as the differences in their management styles. On the face of it, they operate quite differently, with Branson generally starting companies from scratch and Huizenga usually consolidating existing businesses. Ian Duffell, who dealt with the two billionaires as head of Virgin Retail Group in the Americas and Asia, describes both as fearless. For the Briton as well as the American, says Duffell, "The challenge is more important than the actual process of the deal."[45] He adds that Branson and Huizenga are both unshakable once they make up their minds to do something, a shared trait that is bound to create friction.

Finding Your Management Style

Several biographical sketches in this book demonstrate that creating an exceptionally effective organization is not a prerequisite to making a billion dollars. Warren Buffett has prospered as a hands-off chief of Berkshire Hathaway, delegating authority for its diverse operating companies while closely monitoring his carefully chosen managers. Carl Icahn and Kirk Kerkorian have amassed huge fortunes primarily through their financial savvy and deal-making skills. Their stewardships of Trans World Airlines and Metro-Goldwyn-Mayer, respectively, have drawn more criticism than praise.

Honest self-assessment will tell which model is best for you to follow. Either way, though, you will have to supplement your native talent with acquired skills. To become an outstanding builder of organizations, Wayne Huizenga had to correct an early tendency to be curt toward people who did not grasp points he considered self-evident. Intimidated by this reaction, employees would sometimes fail to pass along important information. Ross Perot and Sam Walton had to revise their original inclination to reward only senior managers generously, which caused lower-level employees to feel like second-class citizens. This sort of adaptability is one of the most important traits that you should strive to stamp on your organization.

10

INVEST IN
POLITICAL INFLUENCE

No one ever asked me for anything more than an unfair advantage.
—J. Cordell Moore, Assistant Secretary of
the Interior under Lyndon Johnson

Unlike many developing countries, the Western industrialized nations are not places where billionaires arise through political influence alone. Even where the corruption rate is fairly low, however, local, state, and federal governments routinely dispense substantial economic benefits. These range from simple zoning variances to contracts for government work, tariff protection, and special tax incentives. Officeholders are also in a position to forestall the imposition of huge costs on business enterprises. They can decide not to pursue antitrust cases, not to expand existing environmental protection provisions, and not to eliminate favorable tax provisions.

Lobbying legislative and regulatory bodies is one lawful and effective way for a company to influence government's impact on its profits. A more indirect approach is to contribute to the election campaigns of candidates for strategically important offices. Candidates cannot, in principle, trade their stances on issues for cash infusions to their campaign coffers. They are disposed to look kindly on the policy recommendations of major contributors, however.

For someone already rich enough to have a fair shot at becoming a billionaire, becoming a major contributor is far from an impossible dream. Despite all the talk about the high cost of seeking office, the scale of political campaigns is modest in the business world's terms. For example, Republican Michael Huffington stirred up a hullabaloo by spending the supposedly outrageous sum of $29 million in an unsuccessful 1994 race for the United States Senate. The American Association of Political Consultants pointed out that Sony Music spent $30 million to promote a Michael Jackson compact disc.[1] Furthermore, the median outlay in that year for a Senate seat was only $3.5 million, while the median candidate for the House of Representatives shelled out just under $350,000.[2] In 1998, Speaker Newt Gingrich's $6 million war chest was the largest among candidates for the House.[3]

From the perspective of someone with a 10-figure net worth, the dollars expended on elections for highly influential positions are hardly astronomical. By way of illustration, political fund-raising consultant Stan Huckaby estimated in 1999 that the Democratic and Republican presidential nominees for 2000 would have to raise $32.1 million apiece. Approximately one-third of the total would probably come from small donations, leaving only $20 million or so to be raised from major contributors.[4] In one year, a billionaire could earn more than enough to foot that entire bill by doing nothing riskier with his or her fortune than depositing it in a savings account.

One could, that is, if it were not for legislated ceilings on campaign contributions. By forcing candidates to raise more modest sums from many different contributors, the ceilings make it feasible for a budding billionaire to become a major player for considerably less cash. Moreover, instead of writing one huge check to the campaign of a candidate who might lose, wealthy individuals can hedge their bets by backing candidates for several key positions. The result is that comparatively paltry sums can gain a sympathetic hearing for proposals with colossal economic impact.

As an example, during the 1996 elections, tobacco companies donated more than $10 million to political candidates, mostly Republicans.

The following year, the industry received a $50 billion tax break from Congress.[5] Paybacks of 5,000 to 1 are rare in conventional business ventures, making it a shame that there are not more political races in which to participate financially.

The attraction of investing in political influence, in short, is that the numbers work. Some of the time, at least, the ethical ramifications are palatable to most aspiring billionaires as well. This is an area, however, in which you will have to look deeply into your soul to determine what you personally consider acceptable. Some practices that fall within the letter of the law may not pass your own moral litmus test.

Working the System

Competing in certain businesses is impossible without becoming enmeshed in politics. For example, Wayne Huizenga's success in obtaining municipal contracts to haul garbage in the 1960s depended on appearing regularly at meetings of city and county commissions. According to one of his associates:

> When you have a city contract you have to work with the whole city structure, starting at public works and working your way up to the city manager . . . or the mayor, and then work with all the commissioners. You're constantly getting calls from them, that there's a complaint here or this or that. Then you're working to tweak that contract all the time and to maintain the contract.[6]

In response to a request by the Securities and Exchange Commission, Huizenga's Waste Management found in an internal survey that one of its landfill operations had made $40,000 of off-the-books cash contributions to Florida politicians over three years. The payments were not illegal, although the use of a cash account raised eyebrows. On advice of counsel, Huizenga invoked his Fifth Amendment right to avoid self-incrimination in a deposition involving political contributions and his acquaintance with certain politicians and public officials. (Note that the investigation produced no finding of wrongdoing on Huizenga's part.)

A spokeswoman for John Kluge claims that the billionaire has never donated to politicians' campaigns "out of a sense of crossing palms to get a favorable vote." She elaborates, "He contributes to a list of politicians as long as your arm. He truly believes it's part of the process."

Be that as it may, in 1996 Kluge lent his New York apartment to the New Republican Majority Fund for a fund-raiser. The political action committee, headed by Senate Majority Leader Trent Lott, took in tens of thousands of dollars at the event from associates of Kluge. A short while earlier, Lott had overseen the passage of an amendment to a telecommunications bill granting competitive advantages to LDDS WorldCom. At the time, the Jackson, Mississippi, long-distance company's chairman was John Kluge.[7]

In his adopted state of Virginia, Kluge's generosity to political candidates has not been universally perceived as disinterested. Pointing out, in 1989, that the state set no ceiling on campaign contributions by individuals, University of Virginia political scientist Larry Sabato said of megadonors such as Kluge, "They're making an investment. I've yet to find a person who believes the line they're doing it for good government."[8]

At the time, Kluge was in the spotlight for fund-raising and direct contributions to then lieutenant governor Douglas Wilder's gubernatorial campaign. Although Wilder's aides said he would be offended by any suggestion of a promised quid pro quo, the *Washington Post* noted that Kluge had a financial stake in a state government decision to be made during the upcoming governor's term. He was among 15 investors in the Virginia Sporting Association, which was seeking approval to construct a horse racing track. Observed Sabato, "It's clear that when John Kluge gives to politicians it's not because of a party or ideology, because he gives to Republicans and Democrats. It seems possible that [his giving] may have to do with his private interests."[9]

A Simpler Time

In bygone days, there was considerably less ambiguity surrounding the leveraging of political influence. Many who would be billionaires in present-day terms freely engaged in practices that few would risk today. Regardless of whether the stratagems were illegal at the time, they carried a strong moral taint and were grist for crusading journalists.

During his epic 1867 battle with Cornelius Vanderbilt for control of the Erie Railroad, Jay Gould simply courted the New York state legislature with food, drinks, and a suitcase full of $1,000 bills. Vanderbilt's men set up shop on another floor of the same hotel and bid competitively for the public servants' votes.[10] Despite the similarity of their tactics, "the Commodore" (Vanderbilt) held the "Mephistopheles of Wall Street" (Gould) in low regard. Asked what he thought of Gould, Vanderbilt replied, "Never kick a skunk."

John D. Rockefeller Sr. conformed to prevailing practice by paying off politicians in the course of building his oil empire. For example, bribery thwarted reform-minded state legislators' efforts to introduce competition into the oil pipeline business. (Similarly effective was an ersatz grassroots movement of lawyers hired to pose as farmers and landowners, supposedly outraged by proposals to break Standard Oil's monopoly.) In its quest for the Detroit municipal natural gas franchise, the financially innovative Standard Oil organization offered local politicians a combination of cash and stock.[11] One historian remarked that Standard Oil did everything that could be done to the Pennsylvania legislature except refine it.[12]

Rather than resorting to bribery, John Jacob Astor gained political influence by lending generously to the United States government during the War of 1812. Once peace was restored, he cashed in his favors by inducing Congress to ban noncitizens from competing in the fur trade. Astor quickly pushed out British and Canadian operators and obtained a near monopoly.[13]

Another strategy no longer readily available in America, although still prevalent in many other countries, is profiting directly from political office. As a result of serving in Congress, Russell Sage learned that the mighty New York Central hoped to expand its operations by gaining control of the Troy & Schenectady railroad. Sage also sat on the board of the small line, which was owned by the city of Troy. From that position, he persuaded the city fathers to sell the Troy & Schenectady to a dummy corporation for $200,000, a small fraction of its true value. Sage then resold the line to the New York Central for a quick $700,000 profit. Political connections also came in handy in 1869, when Sage was arrested for loan-sharking. With several Congressmen among his clients, the usurer escaped a jail sentence.[14]

Leland Stanford used the governorship of California to great advantage when he and his partners built the Central Pacific Railroad. The line was the west-to-east leg of the first transcontinental rail line, joined in 1869 by the celebrated Golden Spike. Responding to lobbying (accompanied by cash) by one of Stanford's partners, Collis Potter Huntington, Congress passed the Pacific Railway Act in 1862. The legislation granted Stanford and Huntington, along with Mark Hopkins and Charles Crocker, the right to build a rail line eastward from Sacramento to meet the Union Pacific, which was building westward from Omaha. Merchants all, the principals of the Central Pacific had almost no experience in railroads. Nevertheless, Congress authorized payments to the Central Pacific of $16,000 for each mile of track laid across flat land and $48,000 for every mile laid across mountains. To extract maximum benefit from the mountainous-land premium, Stanford instructed California's official geologist to widen the Sierra Nevada mountain range by 24 miles on state maps. The venture proved so profitable that Congress later demanded an accounting. An "accidental" fire destroyed the company's financial records in the nick of time.

Stanford further exploited the governorship to push through a bond issue to finance part of the Central Pacific's construction, in addition to obtaining land grants for the line. Impervious to any notion of conflicts of interest, Stanford continued serving as president of the Central Pacific when he moved on to the United States Senate. Joining a group of senators known as the "Millionaire's Club," he concentrated on opposing governmental regulation of business.[15]

Political influence was instrumental in the creation of vast fortunes not only in the railroads, but also in the urban streetcar, or traction, business. Peter A. Widener, who became Philadelphia's wealthiest citizen, began his career as a butcher. Joining the newly formed Republican Party, he used his political connections to land a lucrative contract to supply meat to Union troops stationed near Philadelphia during the Civil War. Widener invested part of his profits in street railways and, again with the help of political contacts, achieved a near monopoly in the city's transit system. He also collaborated in ventures with New York transit mogul Thomas Fortune Ryan, who had close ties to the local Democratic Party chiefs. One journalist wrote that Ryan had become powerful enough to make Tammany Hall "a dog for his running." In 1883, Ryan and partner

William Collins Whitney tried to obtain city approval to construct new lines, but a rival, Jacob Sharp, handed out larger bribes. They promptly exposed Sharp's corrupt practices, ruining him, and bought the Broadway line from him for a 20th of what he had paid.[16]

The Modern (Lawful) Approach

Railroaders' pursuit of a helping hand from government did not end in the nineteenth century. In 1991, while Phil Anschutz was trying to turn around the ailing Southern Pacific railroad, a presidential emergency board recommended a 10 percent wage increase for the industry. Congress reaffirmed the recommendation and the Southern Pacific's fellow railroad operators deemed the increase fair. Anschutz, however, contended that his line could not afford the wage hike. A longstanding friendship with Senate Majority Leader (and later Republican presidential nominee) Bob Dole proved highly beneficial. Anchutz, who was born in Dole's hometown of Russell, Kansas, obtained an exemption allowing him to negotiate a separate labor accord. The Southern Pacific also received special consideration in negotiations involving crew size.[17]

Dole's friendship previously had come in handy in 1984, when Anschutz successfully lobbied the Interstate Commerce Commission to block the Santa Fe railroad's attempt to buy the Southern Pacific. Foiling that deal enabled Anschutz's Denver & Rio Grande Western line to snatch the prize. Then, in 1996, when the debate turned to Anschutz's highly profitable exit strategy of combining the Southern Pacific with the Union Pacific, Dole was obliged to recuse himself. The proposed merger was a controversial issue in Kansas, but the chairmen of the two railroads, Phil Anschutz and Drew Lewis, respectively, were among his largest campaign contributors.[18]

When the railroads initially submitted their merger proposal, it fell into the Interstate Commerce Commission's bailiwick. The new Republican majority in Congress, however, was intent on abolishing the agency. With the ICC out of the picture, authority over the Southern Pacific/Union Pacific combination plan would pass to the Justice Department's Antitrust Division, which was thought likely to oppose it. In addition, routine rail regulation would become a state matter, which might present additional obstructions. For example, Colorado's constitution specifically forbade the sort of mergers that the Southern Pacific and the Union Pacific proposed. Accordingly, the two railroads successfully lobbied for the creation of a new regulatory body to oversee rail mergers, the Surface Transportation Board, which ultimately approved their amalgamation.

At least one journalist attempted to link these maneuverings to $363,250 of hard and soft money contributed to various 1996 election campaigns by "people, companies, and foundations named Anschutz."[19] That may have been stretching a point, but Anschutz has pursued his interests through political channels with the same zeal he has shown for cutting deals, collecting art, and running marathons. For example, in the late 1980s he conceived the idea of exploiting Southern Pacific rights of way by constructing a 132-mile oil pipeline from California's Kern County to Los Angeles–area refineries. Environmentalists opposed the project, whereupon the pipeline company spent $394,000 in an advocacy effort soon dubbed "the full-employment act for lobbyists." To Anschutz's credit, his willingness to agree to provide various services to communities affected by the pipeline was instrumental in securing approval of the project from the Los Angeles County Board of Supervisors.[20]

Additional Gambits

Howard Hughes developed close relationships in Washington through his role as a defense contractor. Hughes Aircraft received its initial entrée to government work with the aid of Jesse Jones, a friend of Hughes's father who was head of the Reconstruction Finance Corporation under Franklin Roosevelt.[21] The president's son, Colonel Elliott Roosevelt, also provided enthusiastic support for Hughes Aircraft's efforts to win contracts during World War II.

John W. Meyer, a Hughes publicist, was instrumental in enlisting that support. He introduced the younger Roosevelt to actress Faye Emerson, who shortly thereafter became his wife.[22] Another politician's relative, Richard Nixon's brother Donald, was not a bad connection for Hughes to have when he set up a medical research institute.

The background involved a 1953 oil industry boom that produced big profits for drill bit producer Hughes Tool Company, but also a whopping income tax liability. To lessen the tax hit, Howard Hughes and Hughes Tool undertook a series of complex transactions that included the creation of the Howard Hughes Medical Institute. In brief, the research institute received all the stock of Hughes Aircraft and purchased certain inventories and accounts receivable in exchange for assuming certain liabilities. The charitable institute also signed a three-year promissory note, at an interest rate of 4 percent, for the $18 million difference between the acquired assets and the assumed liabilities. Finally, Howard Hughes Medical Institute leased real estate from Hughes Tool and subleased it to Hughes Aircraft. When all the dust settled, Hughes Tool, solely owned by Howard Hughes, was enjoying a tax deduction on the new lease payments and collecting interest on the $18 million note. Those benefits were on top of an immediate $2 million tax deduction arising from the creation of the institute.

There was, however, one snag in Hughes's sweet deal. The Internal Revenue Service had to approve the research institute's application for federal tax exemption. In 1955, the IRS denied the request, concluding that Hughes's charity was in reality "merely a device for siphoning off otherwise taxable income to an exempt organization, and accumulating that income."[23]

Perhaps it was merely coincidental, but a month after Richard Nixon won reelection as Vice President in 1956, Hughes Tool Company lent $205,000 to Donald Nixon's troubled business, Nixon's Inc. The business, consisting of a supermarket and three restaurants specializing in Nixonburgers, might have seemed an odd investment for a manufacturer of oil drilling equipment. Odd, too, was the collateral—a vacant lot worth approximately $52,000, just a quarter of the loan amount.[24] By the end of 1957, the IRS had granted tax-exempt status to the Howard Hughes Medical Institute, reversing its previous ruling, and Donald Nixon's doomed enterprise had collapsed. Hughes Tool never collected on its loan to Nixon's, Inc. Observers inclined to view matters in a sinister light might infer that Hughes made an uneconomic loan to a relative of the Vice President and received a tax benefit as a quid pro quo. Be that as it may, the IRS subsequently went to great lengths to prevent details of its deliberations from becoming public.[25]

Like Howard Hughes, Sam Walton emphasized a targeted approach in his politically related investments. Scattershot outlays did not appeal to the famously frugal retailer. Senator Dale Bumpers of Arkansas, where Wal-Mart is headquartered, once observed that waiting for campaign contributions from the Walton family was akin to leaving the lights on for Amelia Earhart.[26]

On the other hand, in 1987 Walton willingly coughed up $80,000 in a lobbying effort to repeal an Oklahoma statute requiring retailers to mark up merchandise by at least 6.75 percent. (The state had passed the law, which prohibited retailers from selling goods below cost as "loss leaders" to create store traffic, in 1941.) Walton and his allies enlisted the Oklahoma House majority leader to author the repeal bill, which was quickly dubbed the "Wal-Mart" bill. The leading opponent denounced it as the "plywood bill." He explained, "Should this piece of legislation pass, we'll be putting plywood on the windows and doors of businesses up and down Main Street, Oklahoma."[27] Firing back, Wal-Mart's beloved store greeters collected 200,000 names on petitions supporting the repeal campaign. The company ran pro-repeal advertisements in rural newspapers. Walton personally entered the fray, writing to newspapers, public officials, and his shareholders in defense of free enterprise. All the same, the repeal bill failed.[28]

Walton was more successful at the local level, where at least until the early 1970s, the tiny Southern towns that he targeted welcomed Wal-Mart stores as symbols of their progressiveness. With small towns actually writing or sending delegations to Wal-Mart headquarters, asking to be considered as possible sites for new stores, Walton cannily capitalized on the petitioners' civic pride. Insisting to the municipal leaders that any of several other sites would serve just as well (even when he was in fact eager to open a Wal-Mart in their town), he demanded concessions on property taxes, use of tax-exempt financing, infrastructure subsidies, and zoning changes. He generally succeeded in extracting significant benefits, even persuading towns to extend their boundaries so that his stores could receive municipal services on the outskirts of town.[29]

Back home, Walton enjoyed a cordial relationship with Arkansas Governor Bill Clinton. He also recruited Hillary Rodham Clinton to Wal-Mart's board of directors. There has been no suggestion, however, that Walton sought improper political influence through the latter connection.

Aside from the experience she could draw on from her law practice, the state's first lady contributed a female perspective to a corporation that had been criticized for slowness in promoting women to senior management roles.

Congressmen and Computers

Prior to running for President in 1992 and 1996, Ross Perot frequently disavowed any interest in seeking office. His grasp of power politics was apparent at a tender age, however. As a 17-year-old freshman, he persuaded the board of Texarkana Junior College to reject a proposed site for expansion. The vacant block under consideration was conveniently located across the street from the school's existing facility. Perot's fellow students complained, however, that the existing physical plant was inadequate and would remain so under the planned expansion. As an alternative, Perot argued for purchasing acreage outside of town, to provide room for growth.

After a lengthy debate, the board adopted his suggestion, which turned out to be an excellent decision. As the center of Texarkana shifted toward the new campus, the college became an important economic resource. Not until years later did Perot publicly allege what he believed at the time, namely, that the owner of the originally proposed site was a friend of some of the board members. "I never surfaced that," he said, "but I knew it and they knew it and they knew I knew it." In years to come, reliance on damaging information to achieve an objective became a Perot trademark.[30]

Notwithstanding candidate Perot's denunciation of lobbyists in alligator shoes, businessman Perot was no stranger to working the political system. As a major contributor of both cash and his subordinates' time to Richard Nixon's 1968 Presidential campaign, he obtained significant access to the White House. Secretary of Health, Education and Welfare Robert Finch intervened on Perot's behalf (unavailingly, as it turned out) when Perot's Electronic Data Systems lost part of its California Blue Shield contract for processing Medicare claims. Nixon's assistant for domestic affairs, John Ehrlichman, was more successful in persuading the Army Corps of Engineers to reverse a decision to deny renewal of Perot's lease on 36 acres near public land at the Grapevine Reservoir in Denton County, Texas. An Army investigation found that Perot, "under the guise of a grazing lease, [attempted] to create a private area bordering the reservoir for his personal use." Despite the Army's conclusion that Perot's actions violated important policies dealing with public use of government lands, the White House's intervention resulted in a renewal of the lease.[31]

In 1974, Perot ranked as the largest individual contributor to Congressional candidates, doling out more than $90,000. Twelve members of the House Ways and Means Committee were among the beneficiaries. Ten of them voted for a 1975 federal tax bill amendment that was custom-tailored to enable Perot to recoup some of the personal losses he incurred in the failure of the du Pont Walston brokerage house. (To be sure, many other taxpayers also would have benefited from the special carryback of capital gains taxes, which was drafted by one of Perot's lawyers.)[32] Perot stood to save $15 million, representing possibly the largest tax break ever granted to a single taxpayer up to that time.[33] The Representative who introduced the amendment, a recipient of $1,000 of Perot campaign funds in 1974, claimed he had no idea that his donor would benefit. Be that as it may, once the situation came to light, the House Ways and Means Committee's chairman promised a swift death to the proposed loophole. Commenting on the situation, Perot said that he saw nothing hypocritical about playing by the rules, although he believed the rules ought to be changed.

In 1980, Perot launched a vigorous, and ultimately successful, campaign to reverse a Texas agency's decision to replace EDS as processor of its Medicaid claims. Among other tactics, EDS put together a large dossier of negative information about the rival company, Bradford National, and Perot referred to an official who had recommended dumping EDS as "a disturbed individual." During his 1992 campaign for the White House, Perot was confronted with tough questions about how he had persuaded government officials to grant $200 million of cash and tax benefits for a cargo airport located on property near Fort Worth owned by Perot family members. There were no allegations of illegality, but the incident undercut Perot's effort to differentiate himself from the political insiders nominated by the major parties.[34]

Onetime Eagle Scout Ross Perot's political dealings did not exactly conjure up the phrase "Boy Scout" as it is sometimes used to imply an almost comically naive hewing to the straight and narrow. Another former Scout, Bill Gates, made it well past the billion-dollar mark before he gave much thought to pursuing political influence. Unlike the heads of many corporations, who go to the nation's capital several times a year to cultivate legislators, his practice was to make a once-a-year, one-day tour of Washington along with his counterparts from several high technology companies.

Microsoft did not open a Washington lobbying office until two decades after its founding. When the company finally took the plunge, it housed the effort in a Microsoft sales office several miles from downtown and initially staffed it with just one lawyer and no secretary. As for campaign contributions, Microsoft's outlay of $61,000 (from its political action committee and other sources) was negligible, relative to its size. Gates's modest personal involvement in politics hardly helped his cause with the era's Republican majority in Congress. His modest contributions to special interest groups in Washington State supported liberal causes that were anathema to many Republicans, including gun control and opposition to tax ceilings.[35]

The indifference that Gates long showed toward political affairs at first seems surprising. After all, it was through a family connection with Representative (later Senator) Brock Adams that he landed a position as a Congressional summer page in 1972. The previous year, he had served as a page in the Washington state capital. During that stint, he stayed at the official residence of Governor Daniel Evans, another family friend. Culturally, though, Gates belonged to a group that tended to be somewhat dismissive of politicians. As one high-tech person put it, Washington, D.C., was "dynamically anticlueful" about cyberspace.[36] The general attitude was to desire nothing from the government except to be left alone.

Gates's interest in goings-on in the nation's capital picked up in the late 1990s, as momentum built for a federal antitrust suit against Microsoft. Among the instigators of the government's investigations were several of Microsoft's competitors, who had already become fairly sophisticated about investing in political influence. More broadly, high technology companies were adopting an increasingly activist stance toward government affairs. The American Electronics Association's head noted, "The traditional passivity is changing from, 'Keep those bastards off our backs' to 'If we don't get involved, those bastards will screw us.' "[37] Gates wondered aloud whether it was a mistake to concentrate on developing good products instead of paying attention to Washington.

At long last, Gates beefed up Microsoft's lobbying effort to a staff of three, while also putting three outside lobbying firms and a public relations outfit on retainer.[38] Among the lobbyists pleading Microsoft's case were two Republican and two Democratic former members of Congress, as well as former aides to the House and Senate majority leaders. Additionally, the company retained former Republican Party chairman Haley Barbour to present its position to Republican governors.[39]

The state-level effort focused on arguing against the antitrust litigation. At the national level, one possible strategy was to encourage Congress to override whatever resolution of the antitrust case the courts might impose. Another route available to Microsoft was to persuade Congress to prohibit the Justice Department from using any funds to enforce the court decree.[40] As a further objective, Gates apparently hoped to mute criticism that the company had neglected its political self-interest. "And now that we've done tiny things in that direction," he sighed, "the headlines are: 'Microsoft Buying Influence.' You're damned if you get involved and damned if you don't."[41]

True, Microsoft's effort remained small in comparison to other corporations of its size. Its growth rate was high, however. During the first six months of 1998, the company's lobbying expenditures doubled to $1.28 million from year-earlier levels. For the full year, total campaign contributions (political action committee gifts, plus "soft money" given directly to political parties, plus gifts by individual employees) more than tripled to almost $1 million. About 63 percent went to Republicans, despite Gates's vaguely Democratic leanings, according to the nonprofit Center for Responsive Politics. Jennifer Shecter, who studied Microsoft's political contributions for that nonprofit organization, commented that the company was "clearly building an arsenal and preparing for war." She added that the company's political action committee was now "in the major leagues" among special-interest lobbies.[42]

As a neophyte in the political wars, Microsoft was not consistently successful in its efforts to counter the government's antitrust offensive. In 1998, the company tried to persuade newly elected state attorneys general to withdraw their states' support for the federal antitrust case. In New York, the transition coordinator for the incoming attorney general labeled

Microsoft's effort "crude, obvious, and unsuccessful." Bill Gates personally campaigned for the reelection of Senator Trent Faircloth, a critic of the federal antitrust action, but the North Carolina Republican was defeated. Meanwhile, in South Carolina, Microsoft contributed $20,000 to the state Republican Party. That state's Republican attorney general, Charlie Condon, later dropped his support for the federal suit, citing new competition from America Online. (Microsoft commented that its dollars were not used in support of Condon's campaign and that its contribution and the attorney general's decision were merely coincidental.)[43]

The Great Depletion Allowance

Perhaps the most instructive political case history of all is the saga of the oil depletion allowance. The tax deduction contributed heavily to the fortunes of oilmen such as J. Paul Getty and H. L. Hunt. Not surprisingly, preservation of the depletion allowance and related tax benefits became a central focus of politically minded billionaires. For example, some observers cited Lyndon Johnson's unwavering support for the allowance during his Senate career in explaining Hunt's endorsement of Johnson's bid for the 1960 Democratic Presidential nomination. Hunt, although a registered Democrat, usually backed more conservative candidates, heading a movement to secure the 1952 Republican nomination for General Douglas MacArthur and favoring Barry Goldwater over Johnson in 1964.[44]

The oil depletion allowance came into existence, along with the federal income tax itself, in the Revenue Act of 1913. To enable taxpayers to recover capital invested in "wasting assets," Congress authorized a deduction of up to 5 percent annually of the gross value of a mine or oil well. The Revenue Act of 1916 replaced the 5 percent cap with a "reasonable allowance" for the reduction of oil flow over time, requiring only that the deduction not exceed the original costs of discovery of the well.

Increased demand for oil during World War I led to further liberalization of the depletion allowance, with the intention of stimulating exploration. Under the Revenue Act of 1918, depletion for newly discovered wells ceased to be limited to the costs of discovery. Instead, owners could base the deduction on the fair market value of the well on the discovery date, which was usually greater than the cost of discovery. Finally, the Revenue Act of 1926 allowed taxpayers to deduct 27.5 percent of gross income for depletion, not to exceed 50 percent of net income. (The arbitrary-sounding 27.5 percent rate was a compromise between the Senate's proposal, 30 percent, and the House's proposal of 25 percent.)

When all was said and done, oil producers enjoyed a huge tax benefit. Unlike ordinary depreciation deductions available to all industries employing plant and equipment, the depletion allowance was not limited by the amount of capital invested. To be sure, mining companies (including producers of sand, gravel, and even clamshells) also benefited from depletion allowances. They could not deduct as much as 27.5 percent of gross income from their taxes, however. Depletion rates for nonoil minerals were as low as 5 percent. Moreover, the oil companies' comparatively generous depletion allowance was enhanced by United States Supreme Court and Treasury Department rulings that expanded the industry's range of deductible expenses. Particularly valuable was a provision allowing immediate deduction of intangible costs associated with successful wells.[45]

The oilmen's conspicuously favorable tax treatment survived for many decades, despite growing controversy. As early as 1933, Secretary of the Treasury Henry Morgenthau Jr. urged elimination of the oil depletion allowance, calling it "a pure subsidy to a special class of taxpayers."[46] Until 1969, however, all attempts to reduce the 27.5 percent depletion rate failed. In that year, Congress cut the allowance to 22 percent despite strong industry opposition. The Tax Reduction Act of 1975 repealed the depletion allowance for the "major" integrated oil companies (those involved in refining and retail distribution, as well as production) and phased it out over five years for all but the smallest independent producers.

To some extent, the oil depletion allowance owed its long life to public acceptance of economic arguments presented by the industry. Special tax incentives for exploration were required, according to the oil companies, to avoid shortages during national emergencies. Furthermore, without a subsidy for the highly risky undertaking of exploring for oil, said the beneficiaries of the subsidy, new discoveries would not keep pace with consumption of known reserves. Oil would therefore become scarce and prices to consumers would rise.

Aside from research sponsored by the oil companies, however, there was little empirical support for the notion that the depletion allowance furthered the public interest. On balance, the evidence showed that the level of exploration activity varied according to the price of oil, rather than in response to tax incentives. Economists found that the depletion allowance did not embolden companies to bear the risks of wildcat exploration in new areas not already known to be oil-producing. Instead, the subsidy encouraged "developmental" drilling in established oil regions, an activity less likely to generate huge additions to available reserves.[47]

In short, oil producers received a huge tax benefit for behaving just as they would without the benefit. Other taxpayers gained nothing in exchange for shouldering a larger portion of the tax bill than they otherwise would have. The allowance ultimately amounted to a transfer of wealth to Getty, Hunt, and other oilmen. Furthermore, as income tax rates rose during President Franklin Roosevelt's administration (1933–1945), the dollar value of the 27.5 percent deduction increased. Even though technological advances were making oil exploration less risky, the supposed subsidy for risk taking was increasing!

For anyone who hopes to exploit the political process in the future, the key question is how the oil industry successfully defended a private benefit in the guise of a boon to the public interest. There may never again be as great an opportunity available as the oil depletion allowance. Its lessons, however, are potentially applicable to a wide range of wealth enhancements available through political action. Those lessons can be summarized in a three-step program:

1. Cultivate an underdog image.
2. Find a friend in government.
3. Devise a complex benefit.

Cultivate an Underdog Image

Historian Robert Caro gives much of the credit for the oil producers' favored tax treatment to Sam Rayburn, Speaker of the House of Representatives between 1940 and 1961. The long-serving Democrat's district adjoined Dallas, where many successful wildcatters lived. Rayburn had befriended them in their early days of "poor-boying"—that is, drilling on credit and frequently halting operations until they could raise a little more cash.

According to Caro, Rayburn never fully appreciated the significance of the great East Texas pool discovery in 1930. The same men Rayburn had known when they were hand-to-mouth operators wound up with immensely valuable stakes in a field that by 1935 produced more oil annually than any entire nation previously had. In Rayburn's mind, these new giants remained little people battling the massive, integrated oil companies of the East for control of the Texas fields.

If Rayburn's friends in the oil business told him that special tax incentives were essential to their struggle, he was willing to block the efforts of Treasury Secretary Morgenthau and President Roosevelt to repeal them. Meanwhile, Rayburn's protégé, Representative Lyndon Johnson, set about gathering campaign contributions for Democratic candidates from the newly rich independent producers. By ensuring a Democratic majority, the beneficiaries of the oil depletion allowance could keep their friend Rayburn in place as Speaker.[48]

Find a Friend in Government

Gaining a sympathetic ear in the halls of power is paramount and not as difficult as it might seem. Making friends in politics is easy, just as it is in philanthropic circles. Political fund-raisers, like the development offices of educational and cultural institutions, prospect for donors as assiduously as the sales organizations of well-organized businesses prospect for customers.

You can make it easy for seekers of campaign contributions to find you by throwing a few dollars into the coffers without waiting for them to prod you. It will surprise you how quickly the political operatives will learn to like you and how eager the officeholders will be to meet you. As a Yiddish proverb says, "With money in your pocket, you are wise, and you are handsome, and you sing well, too."[49]

Best of all, politicians are surprisingly casual about ideological consistency. As governor of Arkansas, Bill Clinton did not seem to hold Bill Walton's Republican sympathies against him. Richard Branson was one of Conservative Prime Minister Margaret Thatcher's favorite business-men, but was not spurned when he showed enthusiasm for Tony Blair's new-style Labour policies.

Even in today's highly regulated market for political influence, it remains possible to build valuable personal ties. In recent years, for example, contributors have gotten around limitations on campaign contributions by agreeing to buy large numbers of books containing a politician's collected speeches. That gambit has acquired an unsavory image, but dollars can still be deployed to win the goodwill of pivotal officeholders. A method that has recently gained popularity is to donate sizable sums to academic centers named for prominent elected officials, a type of honor formerly reserved mainly for the dead. "This has increasingly become standard operating procedure in the world of politics," says telecommunications lawyer Brian Moir. "If you can't contribute directly, you contribute to activities that members of Congress hold dear."[50]

Devise a Complex Benefit

A benefit that is complex, with costs that are spread wide and thin throughout the population, tends to minimize the incentive for potential opponents to become well informed.

In a lengthy study of the oil depletion allowance, political scientist Jon Roy Bond concludes that it was enacted in 1913 with little opposition because of a "rational ignorance" phenomenon. Briefly, most individuals invest little time in informing themselves about issues that they expect to have little impact on themselves. That was a reasonable judgment in light of the original income tax rate of just 1 percent. Whatever amount an individual taxpayer may have been transferring to oil producers was trivial. On the other hand, the benefit to a concentrated group of oil producers was substantial. It was well worth their time to master the complexities of the tax code and exert their influence with key members of Congress.

After 1913, the oil depletion allowance was sustained by the disparity between individual taxpayers and oil companies in the cost and benefit of being informed. By the 1960s, however, resentment was mounting against the tax burden imposed by a greatly expanded federal government. The oil depletion allowance became a symbol of tax loopholes and consequently came under increased scrutiny. For the first time, the public became widely aware of the magnitude of the oil industry's tax benefit and Congress cut it back severely.[51]

A Closing Thought

The pursuit of profit through political influence validates the cliché "It takes money to make money." More precisely, it takes a lot of money to make a proverbial pile, because the audibility of campaign contributors' voices is proportional to the size of their contributions. Instead of wasting cash in a shoestring effort to acquire clout, it is best to regard political influence as a technique for speeding your transition from millionaire to billionaire.

11

RESIST THE UNIONS

In all labor there is profit.
—Proverbs 14:21

Nobody has made a billion dollars purely by defeating labor unions in organizing votes. For several of the billionaires in this book, unionization has played no material role and seems unlikely to in many high technology industries that will likely spawn future billionaires. In Warren Buffett's negotiations with organized labor at the *Buffalo Evening News* and Carl Icahn's dealings at Trans World Airlines, unions were already well entrenched and there was no issue of trying to decertify them. Neither are the financial implications of successfully resisting unionization efforts invariably clear-cut. On a straight wage comparison, the savings available to a nonunionized company can be immaterial, because management may pay workers high wages specifically to reduce their incentive to organize.

Notwithstanding all of the above, a number of billionaires past and present devoted significant time and energy to keeping unions out of companies that they controlled. Evidently, they considered the disadvantages of organized labor material enough to warrant their attention. Therefore, the techniques they employed represent a potentially useful tool, albeit one that you must use according to your own ethical principles.

The Gilded Age: Goons with Guns

The tactics employed during the 1800s, to be sure, have limited relevance today. For one thing, it is considered passé to arm goons with machine guns. In addition, organized labor wields sufficient political influence to make Presidents of the United States think very hard before calling out the troops to intervene in a strike. Still, a brief review of the nineteenth century's momentous confrontations between capital and labor puts today's more carefully nuanced management approaches in useful perspective.

Henry Clay Frick was credited with setting back unionization of the steel industry 40 years by his firm stand in the 1892 Homestead Strike in Pennsylvania. Frick was general manager of the Carnegie Steel Company when a proposed wage reduction prompted a strike by the Amalgamated Association of Iron and Steel Workers. Determined to break the union, he brought in Pinkerton detectives. An armed battle ensued in which several men were killed or wounded, leading the governor to call out the state militia.

The plant reopened and the strikers eventually conceded defeat, but Frick became the target of an assassination attempt. Anarchist Alexander Berkman sneaked into the Pittsburgh office of the "Coke King of Pennsylvania" and shot him in the ear and the neck. For good measure, the assailant then stabbed his victim several times before Frick's associates arrived on the scene. Keeping his wits about him, Frick cried out that his rescuers should check the assassin's mouth. It turned out to contain a capsule with explosives sufficient to blow up the office. Unfazed by the incident, Frick bandaged his wounds and put in a full day's work, declining anesthesia when a doctor extracted the bullet from his neck.[1]

John D. Rockefeller Sr. did not try to fatten the profits of Standard Oil by exploiting workers. At times, he willingly paid his employees more than the going wage. His stated objection to labor unions was that he viewed them as frauds engineered by irresponsible workers:

> It's all beautiful at the beginning; they give their organization a fine name and they declare a set of righteous principles. But soon the real object of their organizing shows itself—to do as little as possible for the greatest possible pay.[2]

Rockefeller, in short, resisted unionization out of concern that he might not get full value for the wages he laid out. The same worry gnawed at him in his retirement. If he spied idle workers on his estate, he would stop his automobile and wait to see whether the men would recommence their labors.[3]

In 1903, Standard Oil of New Jersey broke a strike by workers at its Bayonne refinery seeking union recognition. At his Pocantico, New York, estate, Rockefeller refused to allow his employees to take off Labor Day and fired a group that attempted to form a union. At one point, the great philanthropist had to be talked out of denying contributions to YMCA construction projects that relied on closed-shop (union-only) labor.

Rockefeller's uncompromising resistance to unions contributed to the impasse that resulted in the "Ludlow Massacre" in 1914. In 1902 he had plowed some of the vast profits from his sale of the Mesabi iron ore fields into a controlling interest in a steel company, Colorado Fuel and Iron (CFI). To supply coke to its mills, the company mined coal, an activity notorious at the time for dangerous working conditions and harsh supervisors.

Rockefeller soon discovered that he had made a poor investment. After five years of unsatisfactory profits, he installed an uncle who had no previous coal-mining experience as CFI's manager. His son, John D. Rockefeller Jr., served as liaison between the Colorado mines and the controlling shareholder in New York. While the elder Rockefeller had no direct management role, he backed his surrogates' hard antiunion line, all the more so because the mines had proven unprofitable. When the United Mine Workers of America threatened a strike to organize the miners, CFI, along with the state's other leading coal producers, brought in gun-toting detectives.

With both sides accumulating arsenals, violence inevitably broke out in October. The management forces inflicted several fatalities with an armored car nicknamed the "Death Special," which rained machine-gun fire on a tent colony that the strikers had erected on company grounds. Another skirmish followed in November. A fire swept through the tent colony, allegedly set by national guardsmen who had been dispatched to maintain order. Two women and 11 children died from smoke inhalation.

In the ensuing uproar, Rockefeller had to summon the fire department to his estate to discharge water cannons on demonstrators. (Among the protestors was Alexander Berkman, Henry Clay Frick's unsuccessful assassin of 20 years earlier.) Due to the crush of newspaper reporters and photographers who were intent on recording the incident, Rockefeller was forced to interrupt his daily golf game. In the end, President Woodrow Wilson sent in federal troops to Colorado to quell the strife.[4]

Violence also marred the labor relations of an early railroader who would qualify as a billionaire in today's dollars. John W. Garrett was no stranger to armed conflict. He made his fortune during the Civil War through control of the Baltimore & Ohio, which snaked back and forth across the Union and Confederate lines. Workers rebelled when the B&O twice cut wages and began running "double-headers," trains that measured twice the standard length but were manned by standard-sized crews. The 1877 walkout at the B&O was the first major railroad strike. It turned violent as it spread to the Pennsylvania Railroad and halted rail traffic all along the East Coast. President Rutherford Hayes finally sent in federal troops to protect strikebreakers and the strike dissolved.

Railcar manufacturer George Pullman, another of the wealthiest Americans ever, precipitated the next landmark railroad strike. In the wake of the Panic of 1893, he slashed wages at his plant near Chicago, but granted no corresponding reduction in rents in his company town. Enraged local members of the American Railway Union struck in May 1894. In sympathy, other locals refused to work on trains containing Pullman cars, resulting in a nationwide rail tie-up. Following a riot that destroyed several million dollars of railroad property in Chicago, President Grover Cleveland dispatched federal troops. The soldiers put down the Pullman strike by storming the company town with machine guns.

In the aftermath of the Pullman Strike, union leader Eugene Debs was convicted of interfering with interstate commerce. The case established that the Sherman Antitrust Act, originally designed to control business monopolies, could also be invoked to thwart union efforts. Equally important, the affair demonstrated that union efforts could be defeated through federal injunctions. While railroad owners at large benefited from these developments, the strike was not an unqualified victory for Pullman. The battle significantly reduced his net worth and left him fearful of reprisals by the workers. To prevent his grave from being desecrated, Pullman left instructions to lay his casket on an 18-inch concrete slab and cover it with steel rails and another layer of concrete.[5]

Modern Times: Outfoxing the Organizers

The National Labor Relations Act (1935) substantially altered the landscape for responding to unionization efforts. Employers could no longer lawfully fire workers for organizing or joining unions. The legislation also established a National Labor Relations Board and empowered it to order elections in which workers could choose to be represented by a union. Companies could not refuse to negotiate with unions that triumphed in these elections and thereby gained certification by the Board. Latter-day billionaires, in short, have operated under very different ground rules than their nineteenth-century predecessors.

Ross Perot had little reason to be concerned about labor relations in the early days of Electronic Data Systems. The company had few hourly employees, focusing as it did on sales and engineering of computer systems. Perot gave his people operating independence and generous stock options in lieu of extensive pension benefits. As long as they did not mind his corporate ban on facial hair and infidelity, they thrived in the highly entrepreneurial environment he created.

In 1969, however, EDS landed a contract to take over the computer room of California Physicians Service, the state Medicaid processing agent. At this major customer's insistence, Perot agreed to put a large number of keypunch operators onto the payroll. The traditional EDS formula of self-directed work did not mesh with the routinized task of data entry. Workers were more interested in bread-and-butter issues such as breaks and sick days. EDS's plans for running a tight ship in keypunch operations encountered another snag when management learned that under California law, the company could not summarily fire workers who were caught sleeping on the job. Such dismissals were illegal if a clear policy against napping was not already in place.

Capitalizing on the friction between workers' expectations and the EDS ethos, the Teamsters attempted to organize two of the company's

California keypunch sites. EDS responded icily. "I'm all for unions," said Perot, "but we don't need them."[6] At one shop, the ex-Marine in charge ejected a union organizer from his office. Then, for good measure, he ejected the National Labor Relations Board official who followed. The manager avoided being jailed only because EDS agreed to post bail.

In the end, the unionization vote produced a split decision. The keypunch operators at one facility, most of whom were wives of white-collar employees, rejected the Teamsters' organization plan. At the other shop, however, most of the workers were married to longshoremen or autoworkers. Generally sympathetic to organized labor, they voted in favor of the union. In response, Perot closed the newly organized facility and transferred its work to nonunion employees elsewhere. Thereafter, EDS made it a policy to locate data entry operations in white-collar suburbs, where wives would likely be more inclined to side with management. At the same time, Perot assigned one of his more affable lieutenants to deal with employee dissatisfaction. EDS never lost another organizing vote.[7] (Note as well that when Perot served as a director of the highly unionized General Motors, workers on the factory floor regarded him as a friend. Evidently, the hourly employees assumed that management was to blame for the company's problems, a belief that Perot reinforced by publicly criticizing GM's top brass.)[8]

Much like Perot, Sam Walton's initial strategy was to build his organization by offering heavy cash and stock incentives to managers, while keeping a tight rein on hourly workers' compensation. In fact, in the 1950s he paid employees less than the federal minimum wage requirement, claiming that his multistore operation qualified for an exemption granted to small businesses. When the Labor Department instructed Wal-Mart to begin paying the minimum wage, the company fought the order in federal court, but lost the case. Years later, Walton conceded that he had been "chintzy" in his early days, paying workers as little as possible.

Walton's tightfisted ways started to change in 1970. The Retail Clerks Union, seeing Wal-Mart as a threat to the survival of stores with higher-paid, unionized workers, began trying to organize the discount retailer's employees. The initial organizing effort, in the town of Mexico,

Missouri, commenced when a Wal-Mart worker was fired after her husband convened a meeting to discuss the merits of forming a union. (The National Labor Relations Board later ruled that she had been unfairly dismissed.)

To meet the unfamiliar challenge presented by the union, Walton brought in John E. Tate, a lawyer who specialized in fighting organizing efforts. Tate was adamantly opposed to unions, but he was no advocate of strong-arm methods. From experience, he had concluded that companies could best resist unionization by improving their communication with workers. In the Mexico affair, Tate formulated a two-pronged strategy. While he personally concentrated on persuading the workers of the disadvantages of unionizing, Walton replaced an unpopular manager, who appeared to be the source of much of the workers' dissatisfaction. Wal-Mart's nonconfrontational approach successfully defused the unionization effort.

A short while later, Walton called Tate in again. The Retail Clerks Union had resolved to organize a store that Walton was building in Clinton, Missouri. In addition, the union demanded Wal-Mart use union workers to install the store's fixtures.

The managers of the new store adopted a strategy that Tate had previously employed in a similar situation. Covering the windows with brown paper to conceal their activities, they worked all night to set up the fixtures for opening day. The union, they knew, would retaliate by setting up a picket line, so they posted signs proclaiming a "Strike Sale." Lured by absurdly low prices, shoppers stampeded their way through the pickets.

Notwithstanding the victories in Mexico and Clinton, Walton was all ears when labor lawyer Tate proposed a way out of endless battles with union organizers. His plan was to win the workers over by demonstrating that management genuinely cared about them. Tate's concept called for including hourly employees in profit sharing and sincerely listening to their complaints and suggestions. As the program evolved, Wal-Mart created bonuses for raising sales and reducing shrinkage (loss of merchandise to theft or damage). Other elements included a monthly employee magazine, filled with praise for stores and workers, and an annual picnic at Walton's home. Union organizing initiatives slackened considerably after Wal-Mart adopted the new strategy.[9]

The basic strategies employed by Perot and Walton still have application, but tactics for certification votes continue to evolve. For many future billionaires, the matter will be moot, given that organized labor is less of a force in today's postindustrial economy than it was formerly. Many industries remain heavily unionized, however, and labor contract negotiations can still influence the value of companies bought and sold by deal makers. To gain fullest advantage in bargaining with union representatives, you are well advised to review the general negotiating methods of masters such as Wayne Huizenga and Carl Icahn.

PART THREE

PUTTING IT ALL TOGETHER

12

YOUR TURN

---

*Happiness lies not in the mere possession of money; it lies in the joy of
achievement, in the thrill of creative effort.*

—Franklin D. Roosevelt

The self-made billionaires whose methods you have examined in this
book are gold medalists in their chosen field of accumulating wealth.
Their supremacy is doubly impressive when you consider that many more
people in the world are striving to get rich than are attempting to become
Olympic champions. The creators of the world's greatest fortunes prevailed over far more numerous competitors than any concert pianist or
chess grandmaster ever faced. How did the billionaires do it? To begin
with, an analysis of the great fortunes founded since the nineteenth century showed you that they greatly improved their chances by focusing
their energies in high-growth industries. You then studied the nine fundamental strategies that the self-made billionaires pursued:

- Take Monumental Risks
- Do Business in a New Way
- Dominate Your Market
- Consolidate an Industry
- Buy Low
- Thrive on Deals
- Outmanage the Competition

267

- Invest in Political Influence
- Resist the Unions

As you delved into these fundamental strategies, you found that they were not all as simple as they at first appeared. For example, the self-made billionaires willingly incurred major risks, but they did not hesitate to take some money off the table rather than gamble for the last dollar. Those who did business in a new way did not typically originate the approaches that made them rich. Instead of inventing better mousetraps, they recognized the potential of ideas that were in the air and executed the concepts more effectively than their competitors. The titans of wealth who dominated their markets did not simply exploit their power by charging exorbitant prices. When appropriate, they sacrificed profit margins to avoid inviting new competition. Successful industry consolidations were not based solely on the operating efficiencies they could achieve, but also on astute financial techniques. The billionaires who ostensibly prospered by buying low were, in reality, adept at adding value to the assets they acquired. Finally, the great deal makers thrived not only through their skill in structuring transactions, but also by exhausting their opponents' patience. Some of the most lucrative deals hinged on possession of pivotal information that the other party lacked.

In addition, the billionaires' stories showed you the extraordinary power of the following key principles:

- Pursue the Money in Ideas
- Rules Are Breakable
- Copying Pays Better Than Innovating
- Keep on Growing
- Hold on to Your Equity
- Hard Work Is Essential
- Use Financial Leverage
- Keep the Back Door Open
- Make Mistakes, Then Learn from Them
- Frugality Pays
- Enjoy the Pursuit
- Develop a Thick Skin

Regardless of whether you set your target as high as a billion dollars, you will improve your chances for achieving your personal wealth objective if you employ these strategies and principles. Before you try to put them into practice, however, you need to take an even more important step. You must answer the question posed by the title of the first chapter of this book with an unequivocal yes.

Make up Your Mind to Be Superrich

Merely desiring riches is easy. The popularity of lotteries proves that millions of people want to be extremely wealthy. Only a few hundred in all the world are billionaires, however. This shows that making up your mind to be superrich is an altogether different matter. Genuinely resolving to become a billionaire means committing yourself wholeheartedly to the goal. It requires a dedication no less intense than training to swim the English Channel. Making up your mind to be superrich means subordinating other goals to an all-consuming quest for wealth. Accordingly, you should think carefully about the question of just how high a price you are willing to pay. The right answer for you may be that the sacrifices required to achieve billionaire status are too great. You may instead define "superrich" as a multimillionaire level that enables you to live extremely well without having to work for a living, if you choose not to. Regardless of the net worth figure you decide to strive for, you will face many difficult choices. Countless occasions will arise in which tending to your fortune must take precedence over family obligations, recreation, or sleep. By the same token, you will discover that an intense focus on becoming wealthy will liberate you from the levelers that thwart most aspirants to immense wealth. You will devise strategies for overcoming the wealth-equalizing effect of competition because your thoughts will never be far from business. Like J. Paul Getty, who spotted the apex of a spectacularly valuable oil-bearing formation in California where others saw flat land, you will notice profit-making opportunities wherever you go. Through heightened awareness, you will perceive when the world is changing around you, just as Sam Walton foresaw the revolutionary impact of discount retailing.

Social conventions that represent impediments to others will become stepping-stones to you. Chances to encroach on your rivals' markets will appear as they adhere to unwritten pacts designed to preserve the competitive status quo. Businesspeople more sensitive than you to public opinion will hand you opportunities by forgoing actions that would cause them to be reviled as despoilers of the traditional, small-town way of life. At the bargaining table, you will get the better of negotiators who lack your total commitment to winning. Unlike you, they will not have the brass to contest each tiny point and then, when the terms appear settled and the opposite party is emotionally committed to the deal, raise a new objection that starts the process all over again.

Equally to their own disservice, the losers in the battle to become superrich will shrink from withholding critically important information in order to cut a better deal. Few will be as determined to prevail as H. L. Hunt, who allegedly kept "Dad" Joiner in the dark about the enormous value of the Daisy Bradford #3 well, plying the aging oil driller with liquor and women until he signed away his rights for a comparative pittance. Total commitment to becoming rich will fortify you to say to your critics, "Evil to him who thinks evil of it." [1]

Living Life out Loud

In case you are worried that "total commitment" to becoming superrich means complete abandonment of every other interest in life, set your mind at ease. The individuals profiled in *How to Be a Billionaire* are anything but one-dimensional characters. Without exception, they have passionately thrown themselves into other activities with the same zeal that characterized their pursuit of wealth. Wholehearted enthusiasm, in play as well as in work, is a trait you absolutely must develop if you hope to replicate the self-made billionaires' success. Their experience indicates that you will not prosper by performing any activity in a perfunctory way, regardless of whether it has to do with making money. Far from distracting you from the goal of becoming superrich, intensely applying yourself to other aspects of your life will cultivate the habit of excelling. To Phil Anschutz, living life out loud means training for his next marathon by rising at 4:30 A.M. to run 10 miles. For Richard Branson, it consists of daredevil adventures that have repeatedly put him into the *Guinness Book of World Records*. H. L. Hunt promoted his political views by recording a daily radio broadcast that was carried by more than 300 stations and writing a utopian novel entitled *Alpaca*. Ross Perot went a step further by organizing his own political party and mounting the most successful third-party race for President of the United States since Theodore Roosevelt.

Even in retirement, John D. Rockefeller Sr. remained a veritable dynamo. After catching the golf bug at the age of 60, he constructed courses at his various estates and was soon playing four to six hours a day. When it snowed, he brought in horses and snowplows to clear the course and handed out paper vests to keep his golfing partners warm. Rockefeller also devoted himself to landscaping his grounds at Pocantico, north of New York City. Initially, he hired the firm of Frederick Law Olmsted, most famous for designing Central Park. Rockefeller then took the supervision into his own hands, even heading the work gangs personally. He took pleasure in transplanting trees as tall as 90 feet and planting as many as 10,000 saplings at a time, some of which he sold for profit.[2]

In addition to these other activities, Rockefeller devoted an hour a day to his far-ranging philanthropies.[3] In his nineties, he would wake from a nap, summon his grandson Nelson (later governor of New York and Vice President of the United States), and bombard him with questions about John D. Rockefeller Jr.'s progress in the construction of Rockefeller Center in Manhattan.[4]

J. Paul Getty collected art with fervor. Intent on amassing every available shred of information about his acquisitions, he invited art dealers and historians to his residence near London and bombarded them with questions until late at night. He spent entire afternoons at museums and dealers' shops tracking down details of the history and physical composition of works. Determined to prove that a painting he had acquired for just £200 was an authentic Raphael, Getty set out to learn why the blue used by the artist was not made of lapis lazuli, but of less expensive azurite. After several months of investigation, he triumphantly informed an authority who had doubted the work's authenticity that in 1508, when it was painted, azurite was selling at a higher price than lapis lazuli. Uncovering that fact hardly proved that Raphael was the artist (which appears doubtful), but it appeased Getty's voracious appetite for information.[5]

Bill Gates's intensity extends beyond the workplace. When he was dating Ann Winblad, another pioneer in the computer software industry, the couple chose motifs for the brief vacations they could spare the time to take. On a physics-themed vacation, for example, they read as many books on the subject as they could pack and listened to recordings of a lecture series by Richard Feynman.[6]

Intimate summer barbecues that Gates began to host quickly evolved into an annual event called Microgames. Guests split up into teams and competed in puzzle solving, singing, races, water events, and scavenger hunts. One year, participants had to communicate an assigned message to their teammates via smoke signals. Another time, Gates and his parents trucked in six tons of sand for a sandcastle-building contest.[7]

Self-made billionaires, in short, approach every activity with fervor. While some are remarkably frugal, considering their means, none leads a cramped, miserly existence. Their friends speak of their incredible energy and zest for life. If these phrases do not already describe you, then you should immediately begin developing the habit of welcoming each day as an exciting new adventure. Tenacity is another trait invariably ascribed to the great fortune builders. The individuals profiled in this book have not grown immensely wealthy through luck alone. Instead, they have persevered until the breaks came. This, too, is a habit that you can and should form. The gold medalists in wealth accumulation are people who like to set goals and perpetually seek new challenges. At some point in their lives, as early as their grade school years, they made up their minds to be rich. Few if any started with a target of a billion dollars, but as their fortunes expanded, they kept raising their sights. Somewhere along the line, a seven-figure net worth became just one more height to scale. As soon as they achieved that rarefied level of wealth, they aimed still higher. More than loving money, the self-made billionaires loved the pursuit of money. To follow in their footsteps, you must adopt their mind-set, as well as their strategies, tactics, and principles.

The Open Road

When all is said and done, are the methods identified in *How to Be a Billionaire* different from the formulas dispensed in the success manuals of former years? In one sense, no, for the inspirational writers of the past got the basics right, even if they were light on the specifics. The careers of the billionaires confirm that to create a ten-figure fortune, you must commit yourself firmly to your purpose, continually reinforce your motivation, and work tirelessly toward your objective. This formula has been summed up in three words: aspiration, inspiration, and perspiration. All three elements are essential, but together they are not sufficient. To perform like a champion, you also have to outflank thousands of competitors who are perspiring every bit as profusely as you are. To avoid being leveled out with the rest of them, you must do something different. You have to contemplate bigger risks, try unorthodox business strategies, or raise the ante in making deals. It is all right to copy someone else's idea, but you have to execute it better. Ordinary efforts and conventional approaches do not produce extraordinary wealth. Neither will you begin your journey if you wait for someone to tap you on the shoulder. Among the most valuable lessons to learn from the careers of the champion amassers of wealth is that your time is today. Tomorrow will not be more opportune; prospects will not be brighter 10 years hence. Right here and right now, it is your turn to use the billionaires' methods to be more successful than you ever dreamed possible.

NOTES

CHAPTER 1   Do You Sincerely Want to Be Superrich?

1. Napoleon Hill, *Think and Grow Rich* (New York: Fawcett Crest, 1983, copyrighted by Napoleon Hill in 1937), 36.
2. Roger Lowenstein, *Buffett: The Making of an American Capitalist* (New York: Doubleday, 1996), 16.
3. From the *Smart Set*, February 1921. Quoted in *Dictionary of Quotations*, collected and arranged by Bergen Evans (New York: Avenel Books, 1978), 83.
4. Michael Klepper and Robert Gunther, *The Wealthy 100: From Benjamin Franklin to Bill Gates—A Ranking of the Richest Americans, Past and Present* (Secaucus, New Jersey: Citadel Press, 1996).
5. Mark Stevens, *King Icahn: The Biography of a Renegade Capitalist* (New York: Dutton, 1993), 100.
6. Stevens, *King Icahn*, 179.
7. Stevens, *King Icahn*, 6.
8. Stevens, *King Icahn*, 75.
9. Stevens, *King Icahn*, 150.
10. Roger Lowenstein, *Buffett: The Making of an American Capitalist* (New York: Doubleday, 1996), 221.
11. Ron Chernow, *Titan: The Life of John D. Rockefeller, Sr.* (New York: Random House, 1998), 444, 453.
12. Chernow, *Titan*, 767.
13. Quoted in Evelyn Waugh, *Brideshead Revisited: The Sacred and Profane Memories of Captain Charles Ryder* (Middlesex: Penguin Books Ltd., 1976), 167.
14. Peter Newcomb and Dolores Lataniotis, editors. "The Forbes 400: The Richest People in America," *Forbes* (October 12, 1998): 165–428.
15. Newcomb and Lataniotis, "Forbes 400," 179.

16. Stevens, *King Icahn*, 43.

17. Jeffrey Young, "Gary Kildall: The DOS That Wasn't," *Forbes* (July 7, 1997): 336.

18. Klepper and Gunther, *The Wealthy 100*, 112–116.

19. Chernow, *Titan*, 74–76, 378.

20. Chernow, *Titan*, 382–388.

21. "Leonidas Merritt," in *Dictionary of American Biography*, ed. Dumas Malone, Vol. 6 (New York: Charles Scribner's Sons, 1933), 571–572. Rockefeller later offered the Merritts the opportunity to buy back their holdings at the price he had paid, plus interest. Leonidas's son Louis accepted the offer and subsequently became wealthy as the value of the properties increased.

22. According to *Dictionary of Quotations*, ed. Bergen Evans (New York: Avenel Books, 1978), p. 468, the mousetrap quotation is commonly attributed to Ralph Waldo Emerson, but does not appear verbatim in his works. In a similar passage, however, Emerson writes of a "broad, hard-beaten road" to the house of anyone capable of producing superior chairs, knives, crucibles, or church organs.

23. Stevens, *King Icahn*, 22.

24. Charles Fleming, "The Predator," *Vanity Fair* (February 1996): 88–94, 146–149.

25. Christopher Winans, *The King of Cash: The Inside Story of Laurence Tisch* (New York: John Wiley & Sons, Inc., 1995), 20.

26. Sam Walton with John Huey, *Sam Walton: Made in America* (New York: Doubleday, 1992), 3.

27. Fleming, "The Predator," 90–92.

28. Austin Teutsch, *The Sam Walton Story: An Inside Look at the Man and His Empire* (New York: Berkley Books, 1992), 24.

29. Saul Hansell, "Vast Riches and Rude Vagaries of Internet Trading," *New York Times* (February 4, 1999): C1.

30. "Mickey on the Web," Muriel Siebert & Co. (web site: http://www.msiebert.com).

31. Irwin Russ, "Kirk Kerkorian Doesn't Want All the Meat off the Bone," *Fortune* (November 1969): 144–186.

32. Gail DeGeorge, *The Making of a Blockbuster: How Wayne Huizenga Built a Sports and Entertainment Empire from Trash, Grit, and Videotape* (New York: John Wiley & Sons, Inc., 1996), 46.

CHAPTER 2 How Important Is Choosing an Industry?

1. Peter Newcomb and Dolores Lataniotis, editors. "The Forbes 400: The Richest People in America," *Forbes* (October 12, 1998): 165–428.
2. Newcomb and Lataniotis, "The Forbes 400," 270.
3. Michael Klepper and Robert Gunther, *The Wealthy 100: From Benjamin Franklin to Bill Gates—A Ranking of the Richest Americans, Past and Present* (Secaucus, New Jersey: Citadel Press, 1996). To compare fortunes created anywhere from the early eighteenth to the late twentieth century, the authors calculate the net worth of individuals as percentages of gross national product in their respective eras.
4. See Table 2 in Chapter 5 for an explanation of scale economies. In that example, In-Pack, Inc.'s, cost disadvantage makes it more likely than Leader Corp. to be among the companies that fall by the wayside during the industry's maturing phase.
5. Important exceptions include companies that have no earnings at present. These may be very young companies that have not yet achieved profitability or mature companies that are currently reporting losses. In both cases, multiplying current-year (negative) profits by a positive number produces a negative total market capitalization. Stocks of many such companies nevertheless trade at prices greater than zero, based on investors' expectations of profits in future years.
6. Throughout the example, the profits discussed are after taxes.
7. The abrupt drop in High Flier's earnings growth rate, from 15 percent to 10 percent in a single year, is one of many simplifying assumptions in this example. More realistically, the company's growth probably would decline gradually over several years. Among other simplifications, the analysis does not consider taxes or dividends. Share prices are not rounded off to the nearest one-sixteenth of a dollar, as they would be when the stocks traded.

CHAPTER 3 Take Monumental Risks

1. Vicki Contavespi, "Tips from Winners in the Game of Wealth," *Forbes* (October 22, 1990): 32–38.
2. Tom Buckley, "H. L. Hunt Dies in Texas at 85; Billionaire Was a Conservative," *New York Times Biographical Edition* (November 1974): 1581–1582. Quoted as a frequent saying of Hunt's.

3. Ardis Burst, *The Three Families of H. L. Hunt* (New York: Weidenfeld & Nicolson, 1988), 15–17.

4. Buckley, "H. L. Hunt," 1582.

5. *Current Biography Yearbook 1970*, edited by Charles Moritz (New York: H. W. Wilson Company, 1970, 1971), 192.

6. *Current Biography Yearbook 1970*, 191.

7. Burst, *Three Families*, 11.

8. Burst, *Three Families*, 7.

9. Burst, *Three Families*, 18–19.

10. Burst, *Three Families*, 20.

11. Buckley, "H. L. Hunt," 1581.

12. Burst, *Three Families*, 13.

13. Burst, *Three Families*, 20.

14. Buckley, "H. L. Hunt," 1581.

15. *Current Biography Yearbook 1993*, edited by Judith Graham (New York: H. W. Wilson Company, 1993), 312–315. Quotation of John Kluge's ex-wife.

16. Contavespi, "Tips from Winners," 32.

17. Diane Mermigas, "Behind the Billions: Kluge Tells How He Makes Metromedia Grow," *Electronic Media* (February 10, 1992): 1.

18. Julia Reed, "The Billionaire Who Just Won't Quit," *U.S. News & World Report* (June 27, 1988): 41–42.

19. *Current Biography Yearbook 1993*, 312–315.

20. Joe Taylor, "America's Wealthiest Mogul Shares Credit with Luck," *Chicago Tribune* (October 14, 1990): 11D.

21. Reed, "The Billionaire," 42.

22. Gretchen Morgenson, "The Lovable Rogue," *Forbes* (October 29, 1990): 80.

23. Mermigas, "Behind the Billions," 1, 25.

24. Contavespi, "Tips from Winners," 35.

25. Taylor, "America's Wealthiest Mogul," 11D.

CHAPTER 4   Do Business in a New Way

1. Often-quoted Perot saying.

2. "H. Ross Perot: Texas's Minister of Culture," *U.S. News & World Report* (February 3, 1986): 10.

3. Michael J. Kennedy, "Ross Perot—A Fighter All His Life," *Los Angeles Times* (May 11, 1986): Part 1, 1–4.

4. Steven A. Holmes, "Henry Ross Perot: Billion-Dollar Enigma," *New York Times* (August 19, 1996): A1, B9.

5. N. R. Kleinfield, "The 'Irritant' They Call Perot," *New York Times* (April 27, 1986): Section 3, 1–9.

6. Peter Newcomb and Dolores Lataniotis, editors, "The Forbes 400: The Richest People in America," *Forbes* (October 12, 1998): 165–428.

7. Kennedy, "Ross Perot," Part 1, 1.

8. Arthur M. Louis, "The Fastest Richest Texan Ever," *Fortune* (November 1968): 168–170, 228, 231.

9. Judith Graham, editor, *Current Biography Yearbook 1996* (New York: H. W. Wilson Company, 1996), 428–434.

10. During Perot's 1992 run for the White House, some journalists alleged that he had actually delivered his newspapers by bicycle, rather than on horseback. However, Gerald Posner's 1996 *Citizen Perot: His Life and Times*, which *Current Biography Yearbook 1996* judged "the most exhaustively researched and documented of the Perot biographies," concluded that he had indeed delivered papers on horseback, as well as by bicycle.

11. Ross Perot, *Ross Perot: My Life & the Principles for Success* (Arlington, Texas: Summit Publishing Group, 1996), 35.

12. Kennedy, "Ross Perot," Part 1, 3.

13. Kennedy, "Ross Perot," Part 1, 3.

14. Eric Schmitt, "Perot in the Navy: Dynamic and Popular," *New York Times* (June 8, 1992): A12.

15. Schmitt, "Perot in the Navy," A12.

16. Lawrence Wright, "The Man from Texarkana," *New York Times Magazine* (June 28, 1992): 21–46.

17. Fred Powledge, "H. Ross Perot Pays His Dues," *New York Times Magazine* (February 28, 1971): 16–28.

18. Schmitt, "Perot in the Navy," A12.

19. Todd Mason, *Perot: An Unauthorized Biography* (Homewood, Illinois: Dow Jones–Irwin, 1990), 34.

20. Wright, "Man from Texarkana," 32.

21. Mason, *Perot*, 42.

22. Mason, *Perot*, 57.
23. Mason, *Perot*, 47.
24. Wright, "Man from Texarkana," 33.
25. Kleinfield, "The 'Irritant,' " 8.
26. Louis, "Fastest Richest Texan," 169.
27. Louis, "Fastest Richest Texan," 169.
28. Wright, "Man from Texarkana," 34.
29. Louis, "Fastest Richest Texan," 168.
30. Mason, *Perot*, 88.
31. *Current Biography 1971*, edited by Charles Moritz (New York: H. W. Wilson Company, 1971, 1972), 322–324.
32. Gerald Posner, *Citizen Perot: His Life and Times* (New York: Random House, 1996), 80–81.
33. Walter Guzzardi Jr., "The U.S. Business Hall of Fame," *Fortune* (March 14, 1988): 142–147.
34. Albert Lee, "High Noon at GM," *Playboy* (May 1988): 86, 94, 148–152.
35. Lee, "High Noon," 149.
36. Doron P. Levin, "GM vs. Ross Perot: Breaking Up Is Hard to Do," *New York Times Magazine* (March 26, 1989): 36–37, 68–78.
37. Wright, "Man from Texarkana," 46.
38. Lee, "High Noon," 150.
39. Lee, "High Noon," 150.
40. Levin, "GM vs. Ross Perot," 78.
41. Lee, "High Noon," 151.
42. Todd Mason, Russell Mitchell, William J. Hampton, and Marc Frons, "Ross Perot's Crusade," *Business Week* (October 6, 1986): 60–65.
43. By the time Perot sold EDS to General Motors in 1984, his share of the equity had declined to 46 percent from 81 percent at the time of the 1968 initial public offering. A $930 million cash payment represented the bulk of his roughly $1.2 billion proportionate share of the $2.55 billion sale price in 1984. The remainder, just under $250 million, was in the form of a special class of GM stock. Perot sold the stock back to GM in 1986 for $742.8 million. In effect, Perot got cashed out early with a premium; GM had guaranteed him a price of $700 million for the special shares if he held them for 12 years.

44. Wright, "Man from Texarkana," 46.

45. Kleinfield, "The 'Irritant,' " 9.

46. Dunstan Prial, "IPO Outlook: The Perot Deal Was Rough One," *Wall Street Journal* (February 16, 1999): B15A.

47. Loren Steffey, "Perot Systems Shares Rise as Investors Bet on Internet Ties," *Bloomberg Business News* (February 18, 1999).

48. Lee, "High Noon," 94.

49. Kennedy, "Ross Perot," 2.

50. Kleinfield, "The 'Irritant,' " 9.

51. Kleinfield, "The 'Irritant,' " 8.

52. Wright, "Man from Texarkana," 46 and Lee, "High Noon," 150.

53. Louis, "Fastest Richest Texan," 168.

54. Wright, "Man from Texarkana," 34.

55. Pat Jordan, "Wayne Huizenga," *New York Times Magazine* (December 5, 1993): 54–57.

56. Gail DeGeorge, *The Making of a Blockbuster* (New York: John Wiley & Sons, Inc., 1996), 26.

57. Often-quoted Walton saying.

58. Vance H. Trimble, *Sam Walton: The Inside Story of America's Richest Man* (New York: Signet, 1991), 172–173.

59. Sam Walton with John Huey, *Sam Walton, Made in America: My Story* (New York: Doubleday, 1992), 3.

60. Sandra S. Vance and Roy V. Scott, *Wal-Mart: A History of Sam Walton's Retail Phenomenon* (New York: Twayne Publishers, 1994), 57.

61. Walton with Huey, *Sam Walton*, dust jacket.

62. Walton with Huey, *Sam Walton*, 156.

63. Walton with Huey, *Sam Walton*, dust jacket.

64. Walton with Huey, *Sam Walton*, 13–14.

65. Walton with Huey, *Sam Walton*, 36.

66. Vance and Scott, *Wal-Mart*, 39.

67. Trimble, *Sam Walton*, 119–120.

68. Vance and Scott, *Wal-Mart*, 35.

69. Vance and Scott, *Wal-Mart*, 41.

70. Walton with Huey, *Sam Walton*, 80.

71. Vance and Scott, *Wal-Mart*, 70.

72. Walton with Huey, *Sam Walton*, 23.

73. John Huey, "America's Most Successful Merchant," *Fortune* (September 23, 1991): 46–59.

74. Vance and Scott, *Wal-Mart*, 75.

75. Walton with Huey, *Sam Walton*, 127.

76. Bob Ortega, *In Sam We Trust: The Untold Story of Sam Walton and How Wal-Mart Is Devouring America* (New York: Times Business, 1998), 121–123.

77. Walton with Huey, *Sam Walton*, 119.

78. Walton with Huey, *Sam Walton*, 131–133.

79. Walton with Huey, *Sam Walton*, 67.

80. Walton with Huey, *Sam Walton*, 30.

81. Walton with Huey, *Sam Walton*, 145.

82. Walton with Huey, *Sam Walton*, 72.

83. Walton with Huey, *Sam Walton*, 116.

84. Walton with Huey, *Sam Walton*, 137.

85. Walton with Huey, *Sam Walton*, 77.

86. Walton with Huey, *Sam Walton*, 95.

87. Walton with Huey, *Sam Walton*, 80.

88. Walton with Huey, *Sam Walton*, 77.

89. Trimble, *Sam Walton*, 181.

90. Vance and Scott, *Wal-Mart*, 101.

91. Trimble, *Sam Walton*, 342–343.

92. Vance and Scott, *Wal-Mart*, 92.

93. Vance and Scott, *Wal-Mart*, 105. To be sure, this calculation does not address Walton's personal philanthropy. Rigorous free market economists question the appropriateness of funding charitable causes with the shareholders' money. Warren Buffett has adopted the policy of letting shareholders designate the beneficiaries of Berkshire Hathaway's largesse.

94. Walton with Huey, *Sam Walton*, 229–230.

95. Ortega, *In Sam We Trust*, 207.

96. Ortega, *In Sam We Trust*, 202–208. In Wal-Mart's favor, taking a hard-nosed economic approach to procurement is more defensible in free enterprise terms than favoring home-country manufacturers regardless of cost. Market-oriented economists argue that all countries benefit when manufacturing migrates to regions where goods can be produced most cheaply. Wages that are low by developed-

country standards raise the standard of living in developing countries, while cost savings help developed countries to create higher-
value-added industries to replace lost jobs.

97. Vance and Scott, *Wal-Mart*, 70.
98. Vance and Scott, *Wal-Mart*, 110.
99. Vance and Scott, *Wal-Mart*, 109.
100. Walton with Huey, *Sam Walton*, 229–230.
101. Walton with Huey, *Sam Walton*, 184.
102. Austin Teutsch, *The Sam Walton Story* (New York: Berkley Books, 1992), 13–14.
103. Teutsch, *Walton Story*, 24.
104. Trimble, *Sam Walton*, 289.

CHAPTER 5   Dominate Your Market

1. Selwyn Raab, "Costs Plummet as City Breaks Trash Cartel," *New York Times* (May 11, 1998): B1, B4.
2. Peter Collier and David Horowitz, *The Rockefellers: An American Dynasty* (New York: Holt, Rinehart & Winston, 1976), 48.
3. Michael Klepper and Robert Gunther, *The Wealthy 100: From Benjamin Franklin to Bill Gates—A Ranking of the Richest Americans, Past and Present* (Secaucus, New Jersey: Citadel Press, 1996), xi.
4. Ron Chernow, *Titan: The Life of John D. Rockefeller, Sr.* (New York: Random House, 1998), 113. Chernow's exhaustively researched biography is the main source for the discussion of Rockefeller's life and career.
5. Chernow, *Titan*, 130.
6. Chernow, *Titan*, 205.
7. Chernow, *Titan*, 147.
8. Chernow, *Titan*, 206–215.
9. Chernow, *Titan*, 402.
10. Walter Isaacson, "In Search of the Real Bill Gates," *Time* (January 13, 1997): 44–57.
11. Lawrence Ingrassia, "In the Money," *Wall Street Journal* (January 11, 1999): R4, R12.
12. Robert Kuttner, "This Is a Tax Cut Whose Time Hasn't Come," *Business Week* (March 8, 1999): 24.
13. Andy Serwer, "One Family's Finances: How Bill Gates Invests His Money," *Fortune* (March 15, 1999): 68–84.

14. Katie Hafner, "Bill Gates and His Wife Give Away $3.3 Billion," *New York Times* (February 6, 1999): A12.

15. Ron Chernow, "How to Stay a Titan," *New York Times* (April 19, 1998): Sec. 4, 17.

16. Stephen Manes and Paul Andrews, *Gates: How Microsoft's Mogul Reinvented an Industry—and Made Himself the Richest Man in America* (New York: Touchstone, 1994), 250–251.

17. Manes and Andrews, *Gates*, 101.

18. Manes and Andrews, *Gates*, 63.

19. Manes and Andrews, *Gates*, 63.

20. David Shenk, "Slamming Gates," *New Republic* (January 26, 1998): 20–23.

21. John Markoff, "Top of the World. (For Now.)," *New York Times* (October 25, 1998): Sec. 4, 4.

22. The Wealth Clock's calculation reflects not only Microsoft shares that Gates retains, but also a presumed return on investment on proceeds of shares sold since 1995.

23. John Seabrook, "E-Mail from Bill," *New Yorker* (January 10, 1994): 48–61.

24. John R. Wilke, "Microsoft Moves into Big Leagues of Political Funding," *Wall Street Journal* (January 12, 1999): A24.

25. James Wallace and Jim Erickson, *Hard Drive: Bill Gates and the Making of the Microsoft Empire* (New York: HarperBusiness, 1993), 6–7.

26. Manes and Andrews, *Gates*, 16–20.

27. Manes and Andrews, *Gates*, 41.

28. Manes and Andrews, *Gates*, 48–49.

29. Isaacson, "In Search of Gates," 48.

30. Wallace and Erickson, *Hard Drive*, 74.

31. Manes and Andrews, *Gates*, 88.

32. Charles Moritz, editor, *Current Biography Yearbook 1991* (New York: H. W. Wilson Company, 1991), 237–241.

33. Manes and Andrews, *Gates*, 78–79.

34. Wallace and Erickson, *Hard Drive*, 107.

35. Manes and Andrews, *Gates*, 139.

36. IBM had failed in an earlier attempt, during the late 1970s, to market small computers.

37. "Bit," a contraction of "binary digit," is a unit of computer memory.

38. Kildall claimed that he arrived before the end of the meeting after fulfilling other business commitments. He also said that he personally had no objection to the IBM confidentiality agreement that his wife balked at, but that IBM abruptly and inexplicably decided to deal with Microsoft instead of Digital Research to obtain an operating system. (Wallace and Erickson, *Hard Drive*, 180–181.)

39. Manes and Andrews, *Gates*, 78–79.

40. Kildall declined to take on IBM in a legal battle over the question of whether QDOS infringed on Digital Research's intellectual property rights. He settled for IBM's agreement to offer CP/M-86 as an alternative operating system on the PC. (Manes and Andrews, *Gates*, 173.)

41. Wallace and Erickson, *Hard Drive*, 184–185.

42. Wallace and Erickson, *Hard Drive*, 195.

43. Wallace and Erickson, *Hard Drive*, 203.

44. Wallace and Erickson, *Hard Drive*, 204.

45. Wallace and Erickson, *Hard Drive*, 203.

46. Manes and Andrews, *Gates*, 174–175.

47. Manes and Andrews, *Gates*, 202.

48. Manes and Andrews, *Gates*, 293.

49. Wallace and Erickson, *Hard Drive*, 314.

50. Seabrook, "E-Mail," 48–61.

51. Isaacson, "In Search of Gates," 48.

52. Manes and Andrews, *Gates*, 93.

53. Manes and Andrews, *Gates*, 305.

54. Manes and Andrews, *Gates*, 305.

55. Bro Uttal, "Inside the Deal That Made Bill Gates $350,000,000," *Fortune* (July 21, 1986): 23–33.

56. Uttal, "Inside the Deal," 27.

57. Uttal, "Inside the Deal," 23.

58. Wallace and Erickson, *Hard Drive*, 358.

59. Joel Brinkley, "More Enduring than Politics," *New York Times* (October 19, 1998): C1, 10.

60. Robert H. Bork, "What Antitrust Is All About," *New York Times* (May 4, 1998): A19.

61. Walter Mossberg, "Personal Technology: Knowing the Outline of U.S. Antitrust Case against Microsoft Corp.," *Asian Wall Street Journal* (October 31, 1997): 14.

62. James Gleick, "Justice Delayed," *New York Times Sunday Magazine* (November 23, 1997): 40–42.

63. Microsoft refused to concede the point, however, saying that the judge had not truly separated Windows and Internet Explorer, as he was demanding that Microsoft do. He had merely deleted the 3 percent of the Internet Explorer code that made it immediately accessible to the consumer, without removing its program codes. See Stephen Labaton, "A Few Clicks, and Microsoft Has a Problem," *New York Times* (December 19, 1998): A1, D4.

64. Labaton, "A Few Clicks," D4.

65. Stephen H. Wildstrom, "Why I'm Rooting for Microsoft," *Business Week* (February 23, 1998): 30.

66. Joel Brinkley, "U.S. Faults Depositions of Microsoft Executives," *New York Times* (September 2, 1998): C1, C8.

67. Joel Brinkley, "Microsoft Witness Attacked for Contradictory Opinions," *New York Times* (January 15, 1999): C2.

68. Joel Brinkley, "U.S. Attacks a Microsoft Videotape as Misleading," *New York Times* (February 3, 1999): C1, C25.

69. Brinkley, "U.S. Attacks," C25.

70. Brenton R. Schlender, "Software Hardball: Microsoft's Gates Uses Products and Pressure to Gain Power in PC's," *Wall Street Journal* (September 25, 1987): 1, 11.

71. Steve Lohr and John Markoff, "U.S. Investigating Microsoft's Role in Intel's Decisions," *New York Times* (August 26, 1998): A1, D4.

72. Isaacson, "In Search of Gates," 56.

73. Amy Cortese, "There's More than One Way to Play Monopoly," *Business Week* (January 26, 1998): 36.

74. Shenk, "Slamming," 20.

75. Jeffrey Young, "The George S. Patton of Software," *Forbes* (January 27, 1997): 86–92.

76. Holman W. Jenkins Jr., "Washington Is a Hammer and Everything Is a Nail," *Wall Street Journal* (November 26, 1997): A15.

77. Richard Evans, "Going Soft?" *Barron's* (September 15, 1997): 33–38.

78. Isaacson, "In Search of Gates," 56.

79. Kenneth N. Gilpin, "In Microsoft Case, a Lot of Not Very Much," *New York Times* (November 1, 1998): Sec. 3, 7.

80. Evans, "Going Soft?" 34–36.

81. Stan Liebowitz, "Bill Gates' Secret? Better Products," *Wall Street Journal* (October 20, 1998): A22.

82. John R. Wilke and David Bank, "Bork Calls for Sherman Antitrust Case against Microsoft, Will Advise Netscape," *Wall Street Journal* (April 21, 1998): B10.

83. Bork, "Antitrust," A19.

84. Seabrook, "E-Mail," 56.

85. Steve Hamm, with Amy Cortese and Susan B. Garland, "Micosoft's Future," *BusinessWeek* (January 19, 1998): 58–68.

86. Shenk, "Slamming," 21.

87. Schlender, "Hardball," 1.

88. Isaacson, "In Search of Gates," 56.

89. Steve Hamm, Susan B. Garland, and Andy Reinhardt, "Does Everyone Do It?" *BusinessWeek* (November 2, 1998): 30–31.

90. Wallace and Erickson, *Hard Drive*, 44.

91. Manes and Andrews, *Gates*, 296.

92. Wallace and Erickson, *Hard Drive*, 353.

93. Manes and Andrews, *Gates*, 125.

94. Manes and Andrews, *Gates*, 55–56.

95. Manes and Andrews, *Gates*, 245.

CHAPTER 6   Consolidate an Industry

1. Michael Klepper and Robert Gunther, *The Wealthy 100: From Benjamin Franklin to Bill Gates—A Ranking of the Richest Americans, Past and Present* (Secaucus, New Jersey: Citadel Press, 1996), 98–103.

2. Klepper and Gunther, *Wealthy 100*, 99–100.

3. Pat Jordan, "Wayne Huizenga," *New York Times Magazine* (December 5, 1993): 54–57.

4. Jordan, "Wayne Huizenga," 57.

5. Gail DeGeorge, *The Making of a Blockbuster: How Wayne Huizenga Built a Sports and Entertainment Empire from Trash, Grit, and Videotape* (New York: John Wiley & Sons, Inc., 1996), 3.

6. Dyan Machan, "Crime, Garbage—and Billboards," *Forbes* (November 20, 1995): 52.

7. DeGeorge, *The Making of a Blockbuster*, 195.

8. DeGeorge, *The Making of a Blockbuster*, 42.

9. Andrew E. Serwer, "Huizenga's Third Act," *Fortune* (August 5, 1996): 73.

10. Peter Newcomb and Dolores Lataniotis, editors. "The Forbes 400: The Richest People in America," *Forbes* (October 12, 1998): 165–428.

11. DeGeorge, *The Making of a Blockbuster*, 18.

12. DeGeorge, *The Making of a Blockbuster*, 22–23, 35–36.

13. Jordan, "Wayne Huizenga," 56.

14. Alex Taylor III, "Car Wars: Wayne Huizenga vs. Everybody," *Fortune* (June 9, 1997): 92–96.

15. "When Opposites Attract—and Make Big Bucks," interview, *Bloomberg* (December 1997): 100–101.

16. Serwer, "Huizenga's Third Act," 76.

17. Susan Pulliam, "Is Huizenga Losing His Magic Touch?" *Wall Street Journal* (July 10, 1997): C1–C2.

18. Pulliam, "Magic Touch," C2.

19. "When Opposites Attract," 100.

20. Taylor, "Car Wars," 93–94.

21. DeGeorge, *The Making of a Blockbuster*, 14.

22. DeGeorge, *The Making of a Blockbuster*, 20.

23. DeGeorge, *The Making of a Blockbuster*, 60.

24. DeGeorge, *The Making of a Blockbuster*, 18.

25. "When Opposites Attract," 101.

26. DeGeorge, *The Making of a Blockbuster*, 18.

27. Taylor, "Car Wars," 96.

28. Serwer, "Huizenga's Third Act," 76.

29. "When Opposites Attract," 101.

30. DeGeorge, *The Making of a Blockbuster*, 73.

31. Jordan, "Wayne Huizenga," 56.

32. DeGeorge, *The Making of a Blockbuster*, 142–143.

33. DeGeorge, *The Making of a Blockbuster*, 72–76.

34. DeGeorge, *The Making of a Blockbuster*, 48.

35. DeGeorge, *The Making of a Blockbuster*, 30.

CHAPTER 7   Buy Low

1. *A Dictionary of American Proverbs*, editor in chief, Wolfgang Mieder (New York: Oxford University Press, 1992), 242. Full

quotation: "Frugality is a fair fortune, and industry a good estate."

2. David Dreman, *Contrarian Investment Strategies: The Next Generation* (New York: Simon & Schuster, 1998), 181–182.

3. Roger Lowenstein, *Buffett: The Making of an American Capitalist* (New York: Doubleday, 1996), 354–412.

4. John Carmody, "Rerunning Away from It All toward Better Ratings," *Washington Post* (June 17, 1973): M1–2, M9.

5. *Current Biography Yearbook 1993*, edited by Judith Graham (New York: H.W. Wilson Company, 1993), 312–315.

6. Ron Chernow, *Titan: The Life of John D. Rockefeller, Sr.* (New York: Random House, 1998), 180–181.

7. Chernow, *Titan*, 505–506.

8. Chernow, *Titan*, 611.

9. Lowenstein, *Buffett*, 188.

10. Often-quoted Getty saying.

11. Russell Miller, *The House of Getty* (New York: Henry Holt & Company, 1985), 208.

12. Miller, *The House of Getty*, 218.

13. Robert Lenzner, *The Great Getty* (New York: New American Library, 1987), 78–80, 86. Also, Miller, *The House of Getty*, 132.

14. Lenzner, *The Great Getty*, 140–141.

15. Lenzner, *The Great Getty*, 163–164.

16. Lenzner, *The Great Getty*, 170–171. Also, Miller, *The House of Getty*, 245–246.

17. J. Paul Getty, *How to Be Rich* (New York: Berkley Publishing Group, 1983), 43.

18. Lenzner, *The Great Getty*, 64–66.

19. Lenzner, *The Great Getty*, 81.

20. Getty, *How to Be Rich*, 3.

21. Getty, *How to Be Rich*, 4. Also, Lenzner, *The Great Getty*, 25–26.

22. Miller, *The House of Getty*, 61–62.

23. Lenzner, *The Great Getty*, 46.

24. Miller, *The House of Getty*, 185–187.

25. Lenzner, *The Great Getty*, 129.

26. Lenzner, *The Great Getty*, 127–128.

27. Barbara Rudolph, "All in the Family Fortune: The Loews Chairman

Made Billions as a Savvy Manager and Investor," *Time* (September 22, 1986): 74–76.

28. Christopher Winans, *The King of Cash, The Inside Story of Laurence Tisch* (New York: John Wiley & Sons, Inc., 1995), 43–56.

29. Winans, *King of Cash*, 24–42.

30. Rudolph, "Family Fortune," 74.

31. Under Tisch control, the apostrophe in "Loew's Theatres" disappeared, presumably a victim of the ongoing fight to eliminate corporate fat.

32. Floyd Norris, "Market Watch: Contrarian Investing Pays Off for Loews," *New York Times* (June 21, 1997): Sec. 3, 1.

33. Debra Sparks, "Tisch: The Ultimate Bear," *Business Week* (June 8, 1998): 112–113.

34. Charles Moritz, editor, *Current Biography Yearbook 1987* (New York: H. W. Wilson Company, 1987), 574.

35. Winans, *King of Cash*, 111.

36. Moritz, *Current Biography Yearbook 1987*, 570.

37. Winans, *King of Cash*, 9.

38. Winans, *King of Cash*, 96–100.

39. Winans, *King of Cash*, 170.

40. Randall Smith, "Heard on the Street: For Tisch Empire, It Looks Like It's Back to Basics," *Wall Street Journal* (August 2, 1995): C1.

41. Smith, "Tisch Empire," C1.

42. Winans, *King of Cash*, 142.

43. Winans, *King of Cash*, 34.

44. Winans, *King of Cash*, 89–90.

45. Winans, *King of Cash*, 93.

46. Raymond L. Dirks and Leonard Gross, *The Great Wall Street Scandal* (New York: McGraw-Hill Book Company, 1974), 259–260.

47. Brent Schlender, "The Bill & Warren Show," *Fortune* (July 20, 1998): 48–64.

48. Lowenstein, *Buffett*, 118.

49. Robert G. Hagstrom, *The Warren Buffett Way: Investment Strategies of the World's Greatest Investor* (New York: John Wiley & Sons, Inc., 1994), 1.

50. "Adam Smith" (George J. W. Goodman), dust jacket blurb on John Train, *The Midas Touch: The Strategies That Have Made Warren Buffett "America's Pre-eminent Investor"* (New York: Harper & Row, Publishers, 1987).

51. Lowenstein, *Buffett*, 275.
52. Schlender, "Bill & Warren," 58.
53. Dolly Setton and Robert Lenzner, "The Berkshire Bunch," *Forbes* (October 12, 1998): 110–122.
54. William Hanley, "Buffett Scoops Value with Dairy Queen Buy," *Financial Post* (October 23,1997): Sec. 2, 34.
55. Train, *The Midas Touch*, 43.
56. Lowenstein, *Buffett*, 100–101.
57. Diversified Retailing was merged into Berkshire Hathaway in 1978.
58. Lowenstein, *Buffett*, 115.
59. Peter Newcomb and Dolores Lataniotis, editors, "The Forbes 400: The Richest People in America," *Forbes* (October 12, 1998): 165–428.
60. Train, *The Midas Touch*, 59.
61. Lowenstein, *Buffett*, 133–135.
62. A "control premium" represents the cost of acquiring a majority interest in a corporation, over and above the prevailing aggregate market value of the shares. The difference reflects the value of having the power to elect the company's board of directors and thereby determine corporate strategy.
63. Train, *The Midas Touch*, 60.
64. Dyan Machan, "A Son's Advice to His Father," *Forbes* (October 12, 1998): 132–140.
65. Lowenstein, *Buffett*, 248–251.
66. Barnaby J. Feder, "Rose Blumkin, Retail Queen, Dies at 104," *New York Times* (August 13, 1998): D19.
67. Schlender, "The Bill & Warren Show," 61.
68. Hagstrom, *The Warren Buffett Way*, 45–46.
69. "How Omaha Beats Wall Street," *Forbes* (November 1, 1969): 82–88.
70. Fisher's investment methods are summarized in *Common Stocks and Uncommon Profits* (New York: Harper & Row, 1960).
71. Hagstrom, *The Warren Buffett Way*, 38–51.
72. Train, *The Midas Touch*, 18.
73. Irving Kahn and Robert D. Milne, *Benjamin Graham: The Father of Financial Analysis* (Charlottesville, Virginia: The Financial Analysts Research Foundation, 1977): 12–14.
74. Lowenstein, *Buffett*, 257.

75. Lowenstein, *Buffett*, 299.
76. Hagstrom, *The Warren Buffett Way*, ix–x.
77. The author was in attendance.
78. Ian Katz, "An Ordinary Tycoon," *Guardian* (May 9, 1992): Section 2, 2–3.
79. L. J. Davis, "Buffett Takes Stock," *New York Times* (April 1, 1990): 16–17, 61–64.
80. Lowenstein, *Buffett*, 292–293.
81. Walter Isaacson, "In Search of the Real Bill Gates," *Time* (January 13, 1997): 44–57.
82. Katz, "An Ordinary Tycoon," Section 2, 3.
83. William Kay, "Warren Buffett: The Five Golden Rules That Made Him the World's Most Successful Investor," *Mail on Sunday* (February 4, 1996): 22.

CHAPTER 8   Thrive on Deals

1. *The Harper Book of Quotations*, Third Edition, Robert I. Fitzhenry, editor (New York: HarperCollins Publishers, 1993), 66.
2. Christopher Winans, *The King of Cash* (New York: John Wiley & Sons, Inc., 1995), 36–37.
3. Ron Chernow, *Titan: The Life of John D. Rockefeller, Sr.* (New York: Random House, 1998), 179–180.
4. Chernow, *Titan*, 174.
5. Gail DeGeorge, *The Making of a Blockbuster: How Wayne Huizenga Built a Sports and Entertainment Empire from Trash, Grit, and Videotape* (New York: John Wiley & Sons, Inc., 1996), 40.
6. DeGeorge, *The Making of a Blockbuster*, 142–143.
7. DeGeorge, *The Making of a Blockbuster,* 141.
8. Irwin Ross, "Kirk Kerkorian Doesn't Want All the Meat off the Bone," *Fortune* (November 1969): 144–186.
9. Geraldine Fabrikant, "A Big Investor Stands to Get a Huge Payoff," *New York Times* (May 7, 1998): D1–D5.
10. Ross, "Kirk Kerkorian," 147.
11. Ross, "Kirk Kerkorian," 146.
12. Charles Fleming, "The Predator," *Vanity Fair* (February 1996): 88–94, 146–149.

13. David McClintick, "Don't Ever Tell Babe Ruth How to Hold His Bat," sidebar, *Forbes* (December 15, 1997): 230–242.

14. Ross, "Kirk Kerkorian," 148.

15. David McClintick, "Third Try at the Club," *Forbes* (December 15, 1997): 218–243.

16. Ross, "Kirk Kerkorian," 186.

17. Ross, "Kirk Kerkorian," 186.

18. John Cassidy, "Kirk's Enterprise," *New Yorker* (December 11, 1995): 44–53.

19. "Kirk Kerkorian," *Current Biography Yearbook 1996*, Judith Graham, editor (New York: H. W. Wilson Company, 1996), 268–271.

20. Ross, "Kirk Kerkorian," 144.

21. Ronald Grover, "Show Him a Bargain, He'll Buy. Make Him an Offer, He'll Sell," *Business Week* (May 6, 1991): 74–75.

22. Ross, "Kirk Kerkorian," 144.

23. Cassidy, "Kirk's Enterprise," 44.

24. Charles Moritz, editor, "Kirk Kerkorian,"*Current Biography* (March 1975): 20–23.

25. Fleming, "The Predator," 90.

26. McClintick, "Third Try," 237.

27. McClintick, "Third Try," 237.

28. Ross, "Kirk Kerkorian," 148.

29. Cassidy, "Kirk's Enterprise," 46.

30. Cassidy, "Kirk's Enterprise," 46.

31. Christopher Byron, "Kerkorian's Plan: Pump up MGM, 007, Float Cheesy I.P.O.," *New York Observer* (September 29, 1997): 1, 25–26.

32. Byron, "Kerkorian's Plan," 26.

33. Cassidy, "Kirk's Enterprise," 45.

34. Fleming, "The Predator," 149.

35. Ross, "Kirk Kerkorian," 146.

36. Fleming, "The Predator," 146.

37. Moritz, "Kirk Kerkorian," 23.

38. Moritz, "Kirk Kerkorian," 22.

39. Riva Atlas, "The Lone Raider Rides Again," *Institutional Investor* (June 1997): 42–56.

40. Mark Stevens, *King Icahn: The Biography of a Renegade Capitalist* (New York: Dutton, 1993), 295.

41. Stevens, *King Icahn*, 7.
42. Atlas, "Lone Raider," 55.
43. Stevens, King Icahn, 196.
44. Stevens, King Icahn, 295.
45. Stevens, King Icahn, 297.
46. Stevens, King Icahn, 304.
47. Kathleen Morris and Steven V. Brull, "Phil Anschutz: Qwest's $7 Billion Man," *Business Week* (December 8, 1997): 70–74.
48. Phyllis Berman and Roula Khalaf, "I Might Be a Seller, I Might Be a Buyer," *Forbes* (February 3, 1992): 86–87.
49. Morris and Brull, "Phil Anschutz," 74.
50. Berman and Khalaf, "I Might Be a Seller," 87.
51. Gus Welty, "SP's Strategy for Success," *Railway Age* (May 1993): 31–38.
52. Dyan Machan, "The Man Who Won't Let Go," *Forbes* (August 1, 1994): 64.
53. "The Forbes Four Hundred: Over $1,000,000,000," *Forbes* (October 17, 1994): 124.
54. Holman W. Jenkins Jr. "Business World: You'd Think We'd Have Railroading Figured Out by Now," *Wall Street Journal* (June 18, 1996): A23.
55. Ed Quillen, "Tracking a Merger: Monopoly Derails Service, Economy," *Denver Post* (November 30, 1997): G1.
56. Allan Sloan, "For Anschutz, Working on the IPO Beats Working on the Railroad," *Washington Post* (June 8, 1993): D3.
57. David Cogan and Stacie Stukin, "The Man with the Money: The Quiet Mogul from Colorado Is Fast Becoming a Force in Los Angeles," *LA Weekly* (November 7, 1997): 18–23.
58. Cogan and Stukin, "The Man with the Money," 21.
59. Peter Newcomb and Dolores Lataniotis, editors, "The Forbes 400: The Richest People in America," *Forbes* (October 12, 1998): 180.
60. Don Knox, "Obstacles Failed to Derail Anschutz En Route to Riches," *Rocky Mountain News* (August 6, 1995): 103A.
61. Cogan and Stukin, "The Man with the Money," 21.
62. Mark Ivey and Mare Frons, "Denver's Quiet Billionaire Comes Out Fighting," *Business Week* (July 27, 1987): 70–71.

63. Morris and Brull, "Phil Anschutz," 70.
64. Morris and Brull, "Phil Anschutz," 72.
65. Ivey and Frons, "Denver's Quiet Billionaire," 70.
66. Morris and Brull, "Phil Anschutz," 74.
67. Morris and Brull, "Phil Anschutz," 74.

CHAPTER 9 Outmanage the Competition

1. Ron Chernow, *Titan: The Life of John D. Rockefeller, Sr.* (New York: Random House, 1998), 230.
2. Chernow, *Titan*, 227–230.
3. Chernow, *Titan*, 139.
4. Chernow, *Titan*, 177.
5. James Wallace and Jim Erickson, *Hard Drive: Bill Gates and the Making of the Microsoft Empire* (New York: HarperBusiness, 1992), 261.
6. Stephen Manes and Paul Andrews, *Gates: How Microsoft's Mogul Reinvented an Industry—and Made Himself the Richest Man in America* (New York: Simon & Schuster, 1994), 105. Also, Wallace and Erickson, *Hard Drive*, 258–263.
7. Manes and Andrews, *Gates*, 378.
8. John Seabrook, "E-Mail from Bill," *New Yorker* (January 10, 1994): 48–61.
9. Seabrook, "E-Mail," 52.
10. Manes and Andrews, *Gates*, 123.
11. Manes and Andrews, *Gates*, 378.
12. Walter Isaacson, "In Search of the Real Bill Gates," *Time* (January 13, 1997): 44–57.
13. Manes and Andrews, *Gates*, 379.
14. Manes and Andrews, *Gates*, 249.
15. Isaacson, "In Search of Gates," 49.
16. Chernow, *Titan*, 180.
17. Loren Steffy, "Perot Makes $1.59 Billion in Profits since Company's IPO," *Bloomberg Business News*, February 5, 1999.
18. Todd Mason, *Perot: An Unauthorized Biography* (Homewood, Illinois: Dow Jones–Irwin, 1990), 52.
19. Mason, *Perot*, 51.

20. Gail DeGeorge, *The Making of a Blockbuster: How Wayne Huizenga Built a Sports and Entertainment Empire from Trash, Grit, and Videotape* (New York: John Wiley & Sons, Inc., 1996), 122.

21. DeGeorge, *The Making of a Blockbuster*, 47.

22. Roger Cohen, "How Did I Get to Be So Rich?" *New York Times* (February 28, 1993): Style, 5.

23. "Behind Branson," *Economist* (February 21, 1998): 63–66.

24. "Richard Branson," *Current Biography Yearbook 1995*, Judith Graham, editor (New York: H. W. Wilson Company, 1995), 58–63.

25. "After Virgin, Nothing Is What It Was," *World Press Review* (November 1997): 34–35. Translated from *Der Spiegel* (August 25, 1997).

26. Cohen, "So Rich," Style, 5.

27. Kerry A. Dolan, editor, "The World's Working Rich," *Forbes* (July 6, 1998): 190–252.

28. Chris Blackhurst, "At the Court of King Richard," *Management Today* (April 1998): 38–44.

29. Fred Goodman, "The Virgin King," *Vanity Fair* (May 1992): 170–174, 209–212.

30. Claudia Dreifus, "Talking Shop," *New York Times Sunday Magazine* (April 6, 1997): 83–84.

31. Cohen, "So Rich," Style, 5.

32. David Sheff, "The Interview: Richard Branson," *Forbes* (February 24, 1997): 94–102.

33. Valerie Grove, "Peter Pan Grappling for the Skies," *Sunday Times* (February 3, 1991): 5.

34. "Behind Branson," 66.

35. Sheff, "Interview Branson," 95.

36. Keith H. Hammonds, "Head of Britain's Virgin Group," *New York Times* (June 3, 1984): Sec. 3, 8–9.

37. Marc Frons, with Mark Maremont, "All Richard Branson Wanted to Be Was a Magazine Editor," *Business Week* (June 30, 1986): 84–85.

38. Goodman, "The Virgin King," 172.

39. *Current Biography Yearbook 1995*, 60.

40. Hammonds, "Head of Virgin," 8.

41. Goodman, "The Virgin King," 172.

42. Goodman, "The Virgin King," 211.

43. Hammonds, "Head of Virgin," 8.
44. The sole exception to the 75/25 split in ownership was the Los Angeles–area store, which had as a third partner a Singaporean investor.
45. DeGeorge, *The Making of a Blockbuster*, 194–199.

CHAPTER 10   Invest in Political Influence

1. "Spin Doctors at Work: Cost of Congressional Campaigns Contrasted with Spending on Barbie Dolls," *Daily News of Los Angeles* (March 3, 1997): N12.
2. New York Times Service, "Campaign Costs Soar to a Record $2.2 Billion; Median 1996 Senate Race: $3.5 Million," *Chicago Tribune* (November 25, 1997): 6.
3. Leo Rennert, "Congressional Campaign Coffers Likely to Top $1 Billion in '98," *Sacramento Bee* (October 28, 1998): A6.
4. Phil Kuntz, "Fund-Raising Is Also Part of Presidential Contest," *Wall Street Journal* (March 11, 1999): A24.
5. David E. Rosenbaum, "Selling Favors Is Allowed. Just Follow the Rules," *New York Times* (September 14, 1997): Sec. 4:4.
6. Gail DeGeorge, *The Making of a Blockbuster: How Wayne Huizenga Built a Sports and Entertainment Empire from Trash, Grit, and Videotape* (New York: John Wiley & Sons, Inc., 1996), 21.
7. Gregg Hitt and Phil Kuntz, "The Money Trail: Who Are Those People Donating to Politicos? Secrets of a GOP PAC," *Wall Street Journal* (May 28, 1998): A1.
8. Donald M. Rothberg, "Nation's Richest Man Big Contributor in Virginia Governor's Race," *Associated Press* (October 11, 1989).
9. Kent Jenkins Jr., "Charlottesville Billionaires Planning Bash for Wilder; Kluge's Political Role Touches Off Debate," *Washington Post* (September 23, 1989): B1.
10. Maury Klein, *The Life and Legend of Jay Gould* (Baltimore: Johns Hopkins University Press, 1986), 84. Also, Michael Klepper and Robert Gunther, *The Wealthy 100: From Benjamin Franklin to Bill Gates—A Ranking of the Richest Americans, Past and Present* (Secaucus, New Jersey: Citadel Press, 1996), 42.

11. Ron Chernow, *Titan: The Life of John D. Rockefeller, Sr.* (New York: Random House, 1998), 208–209, 261.

12. Robert A. Caro, *The Years of Lyndon Johnson: The Path to Power* (New York: Vintage Books, 1983), 612.

13. Klepper and Gunther, *Wealthy 100*, 21.

14. Klepper and Gunther, *Wealthy 100*, 82–83.

15. Klepper and Gunther, *Wealthy 100*, 113–115.

16. Klepper and Gunther, *Wealthy 100*, 117–118, 170.

17. Phyllis Berman and Roula Khalaf, "I Might Be a Seller, I Might Be a Buyer," *Forbes* (February 3, 1992): 86.

18. Holman W. Jenkins Jr. "Business World: You'd Think We'd Have Railroading Figured Out by Now," *Wall Street Journal* (June 18, 1998): A23.

19. Ed Quillen, "Tracking a Merger: Monopoly Derails Service, Economy," *Denver Post* (November 30, 1997): G1.

20. David Cogan and Stacie Stukin, "The Man with the Money: The Quiet Mogul from Colorado Is Fast Becoming a Force in L.A.," *LA Weekly* (November 7, 1997): 18.

21. Donald L. Barlett and James B. Steele, *Empire: The Life, Legend, and Madness of Howard Hughes* (New York: W. W. Norton & Company, 1979), 90–92.

22. Barlett and Steele, *Empire*, 108–111.

23. Barlett and Steele, *Empire*, 192.

24. The $52,000 figure is based on the usual ratio, at the time, between the assessed value of a property in Los Angeles County and its estimated market value.

25. Barlett and Steele, *Empire*, 188–200.

26. Bob Ortega, *In Sam We Trust: The Untold Story of Sam Walton and How Wal-Mart Is Devouring America* (New York: Times Business, 1998), 201.

27. Vance H. Trimble, *Sam Walton, Founder of Wal-Mart: The Inside Story of America's Richest Man* (New York: Signet, 1991), 308–309.

28. Ortega, *In Sam We Trust*, 175.

29. Ortega, *In Sam We Trust*, 166.

30. Lawrence Wright, "The Man from Texarkana," *New York Times Magazine* (June 28, 1992): 21–45.

31. Gerald Posner, *Citizen Perot: His Life and Times* (New York: Random House, 1996), 55–56.

32. Posner, *Citizen Perot*, 86.

33. "If the Loophole Fits . . . ," *Newsweek* (November 17, 1975): 84.

34. Sam Howe Verhovek, "Perot's New Campaign Propels Unanswered Questions Back to the Surface," *New York Times* (September 16, 1996): B6.

35. Jeffrey H. Birnbaum, "Microsoft's Capital Offense," *Fortune* (February 2, 1998): 84–86.

36. John Heilemann, "Outsiders Inside," *New Yorker* (June 1, 1998): 4–5.

37. Heilemann, "Outsiders," 4.

38. Birnbaum, "Capital Offense," 86.

39. Viveca Novak, "Microsoft and the G.O.P.: Antitrust Insurance?" *Time* (March 22, 1999): 84.

40. Novak, "Microsoft and the G.O.P.," 84.

41. Steve Hamm, with Amy Cortese and Susan B. Garland, "Microsoft's Future," *Business Week* (January 19, 1998): 58–68.

42. John R. Wilke, "Microsoft Moves into Big Leagues of Political Funding," *Wall Street Journal* (January 12, 1999): A24.

43. Wilke, "Big Leagues," A24.

44. "H. L. Hunt," *Current Biography 1970*, Edited by Charles Moritz (New York: H. W. Wilson Company, 1970, 1971): 191–194.

45. Jon Roy Bond, *Oil and the Policy Process: The Causes and Effects of the Oil Depletion Allowance* (Ann Arbor, Michigan: University Microfilms International, 1978), 25–30.

46. Caro, *Years of Lyndon Johnson*, 615.

47. Bond, *Oil and Policy*, 142–188.

48. Caro, *Years of Lyndon Johnson*, 612–617.

49. *The Harper Book of Quotations*, Third Edition, Robert I. Fitzhenry, editor (New York: HarperCollins Publishers, Inc., 1993), 306.

50. Frank Bruni, "Donors Flock to University Center Linked to Senate Majority Leader," *New York Times* (May 8, 1999): A1, A13.

51. Bond, *Oil and Policy*, 193–196.

CHAPTER 11   Resist the Unions

1. Michael Klepper and Robert Gunther, *The Wealthy 100: From Benjamin Franklin to Bill Gates—A Ranking of the Richest Americans, Past and Present* (Secaucus, New Jersey: Citadel Press, 1996), 107–108.

2. Ron Chernow, *Titan: The Life of John D. Rockefeller, Sr.* (New York: Random House, 1998), 574.

3. Chernow, *Titan*, 505.

4. Chernow, *Titan*, 575–580.

5. Klepper and Gunther, *The Wealthy 100*, 195, 223–224.

6. Gerald Posner, *Citizen Perot* (New York: Random House, 1996), 43.

7. Todd Mason, *Perot: An Unauthorized Biography* (Homewood, Illinois: Dow Jones–Irwin, 1990), 81–82.

8. Lawrence Wright, "The Man from Texarkana," *New York Times Magazine* (June 28, 1992): 21–46.

9. Bob Ortega, *In Sam We Trust: The Untold Story of Sam Walton and How Wal-Mart Is Devouring America* (New York: Times Business, 1998), 86–93.

CHAPTER 12   Your Turn

1. *"Honi soit qui mal y pense,"* the motto of the Most Noble Order of the Garter.

2. Ron Chernow, *Titan: The Life of John D. Rockefeller, Sr.* (New York: Random House, 1998), 403.

3. Chernow, *Titan*, 475.

4. Chernow, *Titan*, 670.

5. Robert Lenzner, *The Great Getty* (New York: Signet, 1987), 236–259.

6. James Wallace and Jim Erickson, *Hard Drive: Bill Gates and the Making of the Microsoft Empire* (New York: HarperCollins Publishers, 1992), 338.

7. Stephen Manes and Paul Andrews, *Gates: How Microsoft's Mogul Reinvented an Industry—and Made Himself the Richest Man in America* (New York: Simon & Schuster, 1994), 339–343.

INDEX

301